UN
LOST

Gail Muller

UN
LOST

A journey of
self-discovery and
the healing power
of the wild outdoors

Thread

Published by Thread in 2021

An imprint of Storyfire Ltd.
Carmelite House
50 Victoria Embankment
London EC4Y 0DZ

www.thread-books.com

ISBN: 978-1-90977-067-6
eBook ISBN: 978-1-80019-683-4

Printed and bound in Great Britain

The FSC® label means that materials used for the product
have been responsibly sourced.

AUTHOR'S NOTE

I have described my experiences as I remember them but I have changed the names and identifying characteristics of some individuals to protect their privacy.

TABLE OF CONTENTS

PART FOUR: HOME

HIKER GLOSSARY

A Bald – A bare, treeless mountaintop, usually covered in grasses or shrubs.

A Calendar Year Triple Crown – Hiking all three US long trails within one calendar year.

A Flip-Flop Hike – Instead of starting the trail at one end or another, hikers start wherever they like and hike in whatever direction they like. When they reach the terminus, they go back to where they started and hike in the other direction. Often done to beat the weather in the north or when life events constrain traditional start windows.

A Nero – A short hiking day where 'nearly' zero miles are hiked.

A Shakedown – When fellow hikers help strip out your pack and decide with you what you don't really need to be carrying.

A Zero – A rest day on trail, when zero miles are hiked.

Appalachian Trail (AT) – A US National Scenic Trail and the longest footpath-only hike in the world, running 2,190 miles from Maine to Georgia. (Exact mileage varies slightly year on year.)

Aqua Blaze – Canoeing or kayaking a part of the AT, usually along the Shenandoah River.

AT Shelters – Simple wooden structures with three walls and an open front, built a few feet above the ground, often with a lean-to-style slanted roof. They are set along the whole AT at varying points. There are about 260 in total.

Base Weight – The total weight of all your hiking gear without the consumables: water, food and fuel.

Blowdowns – Trees that have been blown down by the wind, often over the trail.

Blue Blaze – A rectangle of blue paint showing an alternative route. This route could be a shortcut on the AT, a scenic route to a beauty spot or a detour to avoid hazardous conditions.

Bump/Bounce Box – A box you load up before your hike and mail to yourself along trail, picking it up at the various towns you post it to. You take what you need, reseal the box and post it to the next place where you will want the gear/supplies. Great, for example, if over the warmer summer season you want to offload a jacket and thermals from early on in a hike and pick them up again in fall.

Cat Hole/Cathole – A small pit or hole dug into the earth in order to bury human faeces. It must be dug following a few key rules –

away from water sources to prevent contamination, to a depth of 6–8 inches and covered well to stop animals from digging it up.

Continental Divide Trail (CDT) – A US National Scenic Trail running 3,100 miles between Chihuahua, New Mexico, to Alberta, Canada. (Exact mileage varies slightly year on year.)

Day Hike – Hikers taking a short stroll or an all-day hike. These hikes can be easy and small, or tough and long, but do not involving overnight camping or more than one day on trail.

Guthook App – A navigation app used by many hikers to show the trail and to gauge elevation, water locations and to check you are on the correct path.

Hiker Trash – A term of endearment used by hikers for other hikers and themselves to refer to their more happily 'feral' state and removal from the societal normal of behaviour in the real world.

Loaners – Clothes set aside in hostels and bunkhouses for hikers to borrow when they are washing their own hiking clothes on a town day. Often bizarre, ill-fitting and fun.

Nobo – Hiking a long trail in a northbound direction (more popular), usually beginning earlier in the year.

100 Mile Wilderness/100 Mile – A section of the Appalachian Trail in Maine that stretches from the border of Baxter State

Park (where Katahdin and the southbound start is) to Monson in Maine. It is very remote, challenging and hard to exit once you have begun. The 100 Mile Wilderness is one of the reasons that a southbound direction hike of the AT is tough.

Pacific Crest Trail (PCT) – A US National Scenic Trail spanning 2,650 miles from Mexico to Canada along the West Coast of the USA. (Exact mileage varies slightly year on year.)

Pink Blazing – When a hiker deliberately slows down or speeds up their hike so they can keep pace with a potential love interest on trail.

Privy – A toilet in a small wooden building on trail. There are different types and systems to deal with human waste along different stretches of the AT.

Purist – A purist is a hiker who completes every inch of a long-distance trail without any skipping, blue blazes or detours.

Resupply – To replenish stocks of essential food and amenities in a town or store for the next section of hiking in the woods.

Retro Blaze – Taking the route of the 'old' AT after the trail was diverted.

Safety Meeting – AT code slang for being invited to smoke weed. 'Hey, would you like to head over here for a safety meeting?'

Shakedown Hike – A short hike before the main hike, to figure out what gear works for you and what doesn't.

Silk Blaze – Hiking first thing in the morning and clearing all the cobwebs that spiders have made.

Slack-pack/Slack Packing – Giving your pack and most of your items to a person off trail so that you can hike faster and farther with less weight, picking up your belongings at the end of the day.

Sobo – Hiking a long trail in a southbound direction (less popular), usually beginning later in the year.

Switchbacks – When trails zigzag back and forth up steep mountainsides or hills, making it easier to hike up and down and helping to prevent erosion by keeping the trail at a steady gradient.

The Triple Crown – The Triple Crown of hiking refers to a successful completion of the three US long trails: the AT, the PCT and the CDT.

Thru Hike – A distance hike along an established long-distance trail, moving from end to end.

Thru Hikers – Hikers that backpack along an established long-distance trail, from end to end.

To 'Yogi' – (From Yogi Bear.) To elicit kindness, rides and food/treats from day hikers or Trail Angels when you present yourself as a tired and hungry thru hiker, but absolutely *not* by asking directly. Not begging.

Trail Name – Names that get given to hikers on trail, or sometimes before, based on something silly or funny about them or their time on trail. People usually wait to be given one at random but they can choose their own if they like. No trail name that is given has to be accepted.

Ultra-Lite Hiking – Carrying the lightest and most simple gear possible whilst still being safe on trail, with a base weight often being around or below 10lb.

Vitamin I – Ibuprofen. Used by many hikers to get through trail, especially towards the end!

Water Carries – When you are entering a dry stretch of trail and have to load up with a lot of heavy water in bladders and bottles to see you safely through.

White Blaze – A rectangle of white paint 2 inches wide and 6 inches high that marks the AT for hikers in both northbound (Nobo) and southbound (Sobo) directions. It is most likely found on trees but sometimes appears on rocks and bridges, etc. Double white blazes in the same spot indicate a route change or obscure turn.

Yellow Blazing – Yellow alludes to the yellow painted dashes down a highway and refers to a hiker 'cheating' by getting a ride in a car and skipping a section of trail.

PROLOGUE

1998 – On the Train

Falmouth, Cornwall, to Warwick University

We made eye contact, the fox and me.

Or was it my imagination? There was distance between us, and a thick glass wall, yet still I knew he saw me, and I him.

Speed, the sun's reflection and the thunderous vibration of the train's engine pulling me along hadn't been enough to deter him from stopping to seek my eyes out from his field. A frozen moment passed between us: him wondering why I was trapped inside, and me wondering what adventure I had interrupted him on. Then he turned and, without warning, darted into the hedgerow. I was pulled reluctantly past, towards the city, neck craning and cheek pressed on the smudged, dirty glass to see if I could follow where he went.

I turned back to my book. A travel adventure memoir by Bill Bryson that someone had given me because it had a good mix of history, nature and adventure. It had also made them laugh and they knew I loved to laugh. I was enjoying it – in fact, *more* than enjoying it. I was taking my time reading and rereading passages because it was doing something strange to me, to my understanding of the world. It was making new things feel... possible.

Trite as it sounds, I had a pretty sheltered life. Brought up in Cornwall by the sea and amongst wild fields and countryside, these train journeys up to university and the big, smoky cities 'up the line' were my biggest adventures yet. I loved taking the train more than the car for these trips to and from my home. It gave me a feeling of being close to what I was passing through – the terrain, villages, rivers and paths – and the pace meant I could focus on and absorb what I saw. I would gaze out of the grime-streaked window and glimpse small roads and tracks, wondering where they went; see stately homes and castles from angles not accessible from the usual motorways; catch animals mid-jaunt that were not expecting any disturbance so far from traffic and people. Deer, badgers, hares and foxes (like the one I'd just seen) were all there if you looked hard enough; if you stepped outside of your hustle from one place to the next.

On the page I had been reading, Bill was walking. Even slower than a train. He didn't have to crane his neck to see what had whizzed by. He just stood and watched it go past *him*. He could stand still and *absorb* the wilderness. No cars, no traffic and no bustling noise to contend with. He was on the Appalachian Trail, a route I'd never previously heard of. In fact, what he was doing, fairly ineptly by his own admission, was something I had never even conceived could be done in my sheltered world; he was walking down the right-hand side of America and *camping* on the way. He was carrying ALL the things he needed in his backpack. He didn't have to go home every night, or to the boot of his car to collect extra stuff. He wasn't having to get to the next town to the hotel he'd planned to stay in and booked in advance. He was beholden to nothing and no one. He was free. I couldn't quite get my head around it and felt fascinated by the notion. It seemed like in America you could just… walk.

I couldn't imagine a big enough wood to walk in for so long that you stayed in it for nearly 2,000 miles. I looked back out of the window and saw fields, not woods. The woods that I had seen in my life were in clumps – copses or forested *areas* that you could walk around, or just in and out of, on a stroll.

America must be HUGE, I thought and began to wonder who let people walk around big woods for all those months. Who was in charge? Were you honestly just… free?

Maybe I could do it.

No. I couldn't. That was crazy thinking. I probably wouldn't be allowed. I didn't have the training. And anyway, that kind of thing was for men. And adventurers. And most adventurers were men. And brave people. I didn't feel that brave.

But maybe I would do it anyway. Once university was over. Once I had a job and had saved some money. Maybe once I'd started a career and got established a bit. Maybe someone would then tell me how I could step onto a winding dirt ribbon through forests and mountains and survive on my own for over 2,000 miles.

Or maybe I'd just work it out for myself.

PART ONE

Lost

CHAPTER ONE

Nearly Lift-Off

I hate packing. What a shitshow it always turns out to be. You'd think after travelling the world I'd be one of those excellent travel-blogger types who roll items in other fecking items and have a capsule wardrobe that slips inside an empty toilet roll that they then tuck inside their handbag. Nope. I'm the one who knows they don't need to pack much, feels very organised and smug, puts off packing to the last minute because it's horrible, then stuffs everything haphazardly into a bag. Sounds OK, right? But then in a flash I think of all the other things that *could* happen on the trip: cold snap, heatwave, rainstorm, need to swim, maybe gym, what if I need to journal? What if I need my previous journal to get ideas from? Heels? What if I unexpectedly need to be formal? Aaaand before you know it I have a lifetime's worth of possessions squished under me as I press the suitcase sides together and heave the zips closed. Ten pairs of pants for 4 days? *Check.* Unbelievable, but somehow *so* irresponsible to leave without them. So it's a familiar scene when the taxi driver tries to help me lift the bag into a car with a raised eyebrow and a 'Christ, love! What you got in there?' Yes, yes. Whatever.

*

It was late Spring 2019 and I was sitting on the floor of the living room at my parents' house, surrounded by enough stuff for three people to hike the Appalachian Trail. I was totally flummoxed. How had I done this? How had an attempt at an adventure around minimalism turned into more hoarding of *things*. I was beginning to realise that the things I'd been buying from the internet were an attempt to feel safer about what I was about to do. It wasn't even about being safer on the actual trail – Christ knows, I wouldn't be able to outrun a porcupine with this shit on my back – but more about pulling a cloak of stuff around me so that I'd feel less, I don't know, *naked* about the whole thing.

I had been reading endless blogs and reviews for gear. That's really great and all, but not when you're not sure you need those things in the first place. Some say you do, some say you don't, so I ordered everything just to be sure. It didn't help my initial planning that I had been deep in a rabbit hole of the wrong trail blog; off the path (which didn't bode well for the trail itself) and hadn't realised that different hiking trails needed different preparation and kit.

I hadn't needed to worry too much so far. I'd enlisted the help of an old friend, a man who had a litany of experience in mountains and the outdoors. He was a doctor and trained emergency medic. What better? He and I had planned to hike the first and most intimidating section together – the 100 Mile Wilderness – and both my family and I were deeply reassured by this. He had a habit of serving himself first but knew how important this was to me and he'd promised to be there. So, after he triple confirmed, I changed my original flights and schedule back a week to suit his busy diary, and now all there was left to do was for him to give me a pack shakedown and check I hadn't packed or not packed anything dumb.

I shoved extra items, with my rucksack, into an old suitcase and decided to worry about it at my sister's, or maybe at Heathrow after that, or in Boston, or the night before the trail. At some point anyway before I had to climb mountains with it. I knew that I was still carrying my 'teacher' mentality with me – the one responsible for others. If I didn't have supplies to offer to people – food, first aid or an extra sweater – then I'd be letting them down or endangering them. I shoulder too much responsibility really. I love to feel needed. Yes, that was it, because overthinking, along with overpacking, was my superpower.

*

The start of my trip loomed ever closer, yet time seemed to be dragging. It was May, and my weeks were still fragmented between work and home. Nothing much had changed in my hectic schedule, even though my life-altering trip was round the corner. I still packed for my 4 days in London, boarded the sleeper on a Sunday night and staggered exhaustedly through work until it was time to come home for the weekend and focus on planning for the trip. Teaching was my great passion, and I'd carefully created a life where I could enjoy the bustle of the city with interesting students but still return home to Cornwall for my weekends to see friends and be close to the sea. It had been perfect, but I had chosen to stay transient in London; living in a central city hostel in the week in shared dorms filled with excited visitors and school groups. I was becoming exhausted with the chaos, noise and lack of sleep, and I dreamed of woods with the quiet struggle of hard and rewarding physical work.

It was nerve-wracking to leave a job I loved, even though I knew it was right to step away. My student for the last 18 months had been James, a bright obsessive young man who couldn't flourish in school and who had absorbed my every waking moment for 4 days each week with his magnificent, mercurial character. We'd walked a long road together, and this job with him felt like a good career high – satisfying enough to allow me to step away from the profession for a while, and a role which had been so complex that I'd had a chance to finally synthesise all of my skills.

'Bears. Are there bears?' he asked one day, with a direct stare into my eyes across one of the many café tables we sat and studied at daily. James had struggled to learn in a traditional school setting. His quirks and differences had made engaging with learning a challenge in busy classes and also alienated him from peers and teachers alike. He hated to feel confined, and so we kept our routine deliberately varied. He felt free to move and change our learning setting should he want to, and to question me about *why* we were learning in a particular way. This helped him to feel in control and so better able to trust the process and concentrate on his studies.

'Yes, James. Bears.' I looked at him fondly. I loved this boy for writing large the fears, idiosyncrasies and tics that I felt myself but wasn't bold enough to speak about out loud. 'James. JAMES! Focus please.' Like a slow and steady ship at sea, he had a large turning circle. 'The comprehension isn't going to do itself.' GCSEs were looming for James after years of school refusal, mental-health issues and a type 1 diabetes diagnosis at the age of 13, the careful management of which was a huge challenge for James, clashing

23

with his Asperger's and oppositional defiance disorder traits. Coming out fully to me this year as a very confident and proud gay man was beautiful, but yet another complex piece for him to manage in the struggle to find his place in the world.

'WAIT!' Hand up, then flicked down with an effete remonstrating eyebrow. 'I am reading about the *bears*.' You couldn't force James. It would end in tears, tantrums, rage and refusal for days, so you had to work with him.

'Thanks, James, that's fantastic. Ummmm. Could you do 10 mins of research, then 45 mins to complete the comprehension, and *then* can you teach me all about the bear statistics over lunch?'

He glanced up from his phone. 'What about periods?' he asked. 'Will you let me research something personal about animals to make sure you're safe? And periods. You're still menstruating, aren't you?'

I nodded.

'Right. Then you'll need to know.' He scribbled 'PERIODS' down on the notepad next to his Laurie Lee extract. James didn't have the same filter that might usually be expected, and after nearly 2 years with him 1:1, 7 hours a day and 5 days a week, I knew which battles were worth the fight.

'Yep, deal. That'll be useful. You'll do your work and I'll get some info. Thanks, James.'

He grinned at me, happy to feel he'd won a negotiation but knowing enough to know it was really a compromise.

Kindnesses and compromise were not abounding in all areas, however: 6 weeks before my departure, I was stirred awake in my hostel bed by my phone chirping. Late – 23:45. It was my travelling-companion-to-be, Richard. I couldn't pick the phone up in the shared dorm room, so I put it on silent and tried to go back to sleep, but soon it vibrated with a text. Fuck.

Tried to call… No easy way to say this… Can't come… Have other projects… Sorry.

I mean, there was more, but that was the gist. That *bastard*. Bastard. He had let me down before and now *this*. This which was *so* important to me and to my parents, whom he knew and liked. A text message! What a shitshow. I couldn't believe he'd done this. It was a sleepless night before tutoring the next day, considering all the many fears that I hadn't had to think of yet: arriving alone, getting it wrong alone, starting alone, no advice or support if I became unwell with my condition at the very beginning. He was very aware of my fear about chronic pain flaring up again. I'd been so deeply unwell for *so* long, and after years of coping I had eventually found solutions that had enabled me to take on this huge feat, but I was still vulnerable to relapse, and felt anxious about the situations I might find myself in far from home and deep in the woods. Richard knew that as a medic, I was counting on him to keep an eye on me in the unsteady first weeks, and he had assured me that he would. I'd faced so many years of battle and trauma to get to this exciting jump-off point, and now here I was – ready to go but with a parachute that had failed. I knew I wasn't going to give up, but this felt like a serious, serious blow.

'Gail.' James had stopped me at beeping traffic lights the next day. We were stood next to a busy crossing into Hyde Park (he was never brilliant at picking his moments). 'Gail, listen.' BEEP BEEP BEEP. People jostling us on either side. 'I've been thinking. If you get frightened, just imagine you're walking all the way home. Just imagine it's Cornwall at the end. I know how much you always want to go home, so see it as the place you're going.'

He shoved both hands under each of his backpack straps on his chest, making his knuckles go white, and leaned down to me. 'You're just walking home.' BEEP BEEP BEEP – final chance to cross. 'And if it gets tough, just think you're me with my needles and blood sugar and my anger; not wanting to deal with my problems. You can think of what you'd tell me to get me through, to make me believe in myself, and then tell *yourself*, because look at me.' He gestured up and down his body with a serious face. 'It works.' He looked down, towering over me now, when I used to look down at him not two years before. 'And now…' He paused. 'I'm giving you a warning that I will hug you, so you have a chance to tell me not to.' He waited a beat. 'OK, I have given you a safe warning. I am going to hug you.' I grinned and welled up, and he did hug me.

In the following weeks I ummed and aahed about how to cope with my flaky co-traveller. I'd replied tersely to him and then cut off communications, having little energy to waste in duking it out. I put a post on social media explaining that I'd been let down and now felt wobbly about the whole endeavour, in an effort to seek advice and let off some steam. I didn't expect much to change, though strangely, it absolutely did.

Some days later, travelling above ground on the Tube, I was idly scrolling my phone when a message arrived. The name was 'Kate' and the content surprising. Kate was the girl who had mocked me at school and made life really hard, but in recent years she had become my friend. She had sought me out in adulthood to apologise – much to my surprise – and the friendship that never flourished in the past grew into something good and strong in our middle years. She had seen my post and her message read: *Hi, Muller. I'll come with you to the trail.*

I sat bolt upright reading the rest, realising that this was an incredible show of support and also that it was very important to her. To her, it was a chance to make good, to show up. She was protective of me in a way that was surprising, considering the past, and I was really grateful. My first thought was *yes*, but my second was quickly *no*. I was concerned. She wasn't particularly outdoorsy, and although I knew she loved the idea of the hike and the freedom, plunging in with just 5 weeks to go was a huge undertaking for anyone. She had asthma, wasn't in the fittest phase of her life and had two small children to consider. Perhaps I should politely decline, but who was I to say no to such an incredible offer? We'd had some good times together over the past few years, and having someone to share the journey with might be just what I needed. So I said yes and started to help her mobilise.

Once I had left London and my job for the last time, I was knee-deep in a last-minute repack and cull at my sister Nicky's house in Bath on the Friday night before my trip. We were besties, I trusted her opinion implicitly and she, having represented Great Britain in sailing all over the world, was very used to packing gear. She also has a pragmatic streak that I wish I had.

'No. Nope. Not that one. Why've you got this thing? Bin. *Out*. You can buy another one if you find you need it.' She wasn't even really looking at me, her head down and mumbling to herself with a determined expression, sprinkling a confetti of Band-Aids, gloves and extra underpants around the front room. She raised her head with a grin. 'Done. Here we go!' she said happily, presenting me with a little stack of items I didn't need. She was totally right – I definitely didn't need them. We then had a little back-and-forth over some Sudafed (I lost) and some extra leggings (I won), and then started triple-checking the haul and putting it into ziplocks.

Mum called us through to the kitchen for dinner. My nieces playing on the floor drew me goodbye pictures as I wiggled past them, bending for kisses atop their heads and cooing at their work. I squeezed in along the bench that backed onto the wall, and everyone drifted over to settle down to the meal. Nicky had sourced lots of my favourites for my last supper – pad Thai, ramen noodles... all manner of Asian delights – and we tucked in heartily, chatting over each other, listening, laughing and feeling grateful.

Partway through eating I stopped. I couldn't swallow. A huge lump in my throat had appeared from nowhere. Tears prickled the back of my eyes and my chest tightened. I forced the mouthful down.

'It's all going to change. I'll never be like this again.' They stopped talking and looked over at me. Allan, my brother-in-law; Nicky; Mum and Dad. The girls carried on giggling over their noodles.

'What do you mean, sweetheart?' asked Mum. She looked towards my sister. My dad cleared his throat and spoke next.

'Ahh, we'll still be here. Nothing changes. You know that. Always the same old thing going on every time you come back.'

Dad is a clear and logical man who knows when reassurance is due but gives it in staccato bursts. Emotions are murky waters for him, and he's kicked plenty of submerged rocks in his years of living with a strong wife and two feisty daughters.

'I know,' I said, unsettled. 'But I've got this feeling that it's me that won't be the same. I just have this dread – good dread, if that makes any sense – this inevitability. This is the last time with you when I will be the same.'

'But, Gail, we're never the same,' Mum said, reaching her hand over the table to cover mine.

My sister nodded. 'We're always changing, but we will also always know each other. We'll be here and we'll be excited to have you back. But for now we're sending you off. We believe in you.'

This was all too soppy for Dad. 'Allan, is there another of those beers? Mine seems to have a leak here.' He mimed looking at the bottom of his bottle and so the flow of dinner was restored. My moment of worry soothed to quiet. I was right. In the end I'd return changed. I just didn't know quite how much.

*

I stirred to a 2-year-old's inquisitive, gentle stroking of my cheek, rolled off the sofa bed and picked her up for a squeeze. Breakfast. Final bag-packing checks and then a hug for the girls and Allan. Easy-peasy. I turned to Dad and immediately choked up.

'Yes, yes. *Right*. Come here.' He pulled me in for a gruff quick hug, a scruffle on the back of my head and then a pretend little shove away. 'Geddon with you. Will go like a flash and you'll be back.' He turned to go, but I couldn't speak, my eyes brimming.

'Gaiiiiiil, I'll be fine. You've got to worry about bears and snakes, not me.' He smiled. 'Now come on, your mother's waiting for you.' He gestured for me to move along and I saw him slightly gather himself. I never used to see him emotional, but since his cancer diagnosis and treatment, his awareness of his own mortality seemed to have thinned pieces of his manly carapace and sometimes now I could see his heart on his face.

That quick flash of feeling in him was another hug to me, and so I gathered my things, threw 'I LOVE YOUs' over my shoulder and pinballed my way out of the house. Mum, Nicky and I piled into the car. Despite Bath railway station being just a 15-minute walk away, there were bags to haul and it felt expedient to drive there. Handbrake off, silence in the moving car, then handbrake on again. No one knew quite what to say. Parked and unloaded, I stood looking at my mum and my sister, the moment dreamlike. I was going away again, which was a normal occurrence for me. Saying goodbye to them was also something I'd done on many occasions, but this time it felt different.

This time I wasn't going for a job that was contingent on my brain and my savvy. I was going somewhere that was dependent on my body, and I'd never done that before. In fact, I'd never relied on my body for anything, not since I hit puberty. My love–hate relationship with it never really made it past the hate. The bully hordes at school made me fear for my safety and wish my body would disappear from the earth into a whisper of air rather than hear 'fat whore', 'stinky cow', 'fishy bitch' shouted at me from bus windows, across canteens or down corridors. I was a regular size for a growing young woman who didn't starve herself and who had hit puberty, but I was made to remember every day that I took up too much space with my body, my frame, my *being*, and I had long resented my physical form for not being extremely small. My breasts had announced themselves against my wishes, and I ran the gamut of pinged bra straps in lessons and nipple tweaks in corridors. My body betrayed me by being desirable and able to be seen.

Later, in my adolescence, when I was attacked, I was agog that it had let me down yet again. Too gross to be accepted in school, not gross enough to deter a forceful horror. My body hadn't ever really been my friend and this was evermore amplified when I was consumed with chronic pain later in life. I ended up detaching myself almost fully from my flesh. Things I did or things that were done to me were just 'happening' outside of my internal safe space, so that I wouldn't feel my body letting me down anymore. And now, on this very day, I was flying to the other side of the world to willingly walk deep into thousands of miles of forest where I'd need to rely entirely on my body. So I guess I was a little all at sea.

I posed for some photos next to my bag, leaning back against the big green Great Western Railway doors in all my bright, unsullied hiking clothes. Besides the clothes on my body, I had only two pairs of knickers, two pairs of socks, a vest, my shorts, a light hoodie and a sleep set. A hoarder at heart, it was incomprehensible to me to feel so 'light'. I figured I might float away without all my possessions to anchor me down, but then maybe that was what this whole process was about. Letting go... of my things, my frenetic drive, my deadlines, lists and the treadmill I'd found myself stuck on. Goodbye to them all – a deconstruction. A chance to rebuild.

*

'Mate!' Kate was already at Paddington. 'Fuck, mate. How was your trip up?' We'd been texting on the way but not much. She explained her heart-wrenching goodbye at Truro station when her son wouldn't let go of her and said he was very cross with 'Muller' for Mummy having to go away. Fair enough. I'd be cross too if I were him.

'All good,' I replied. 'You feeling OK?' I glanced at her neat and small pack. *Fucking hell*, I thought, *Kate is completely out of her element and even she can pack light. What the hell is wrong with me?* But I grinned. 'Love that pack, the design. Super nice choice.'

'Yeah. Love it. Feels OK on my back too.' She lifted my old suitcase by the handle. 'What the fuuuuck is in this, mate? Massive. Is your actual pack inside there?' She glanced down at my bulging colourful growth of a bumbag. 'And that too?' She looked back up at me with laughing eyes. Hmm, I wasn't loving this.

'Yes,' I said, swiftly changing the subject. 'Oh, look, the Heathrow Express is leaving soon – let's grab tickets.'

She grinned, knowing exactly what was going on in my head (as she always had the uncanny knack of doing), and we staggered towards the ticket machine and got on the train. Jabbering with excitement all the way there, I wasn't sure why I'd been nervous about talking. It wasn't because it was *Kate*; our dynamic was very different from our early days, but I knew I was feeling something I couldn't quite explain. This trip felt so important that I needed to dive inwards to find the resolve to focus on what I was going to attempt. Like an athlete who focuses before an event, or a job candidate before an interview. Kate and I were embarking on an adventure together, but although we would begin at the same place, our journeys there and beyond were very different. I began to lightly wonder whether this was cause for worry but pushed the thought aside as we pulled into Heathrow.

So excited! I checked in and glided through security with only my bumbag – such a change from lugging the usual over-stuffed cabin bag with me. With my hot hands on the cold counter, I made an impulse decision to use all my airline miles and upgrade to first class. These miles had been gifted from a previous trip to volunteer to 'teach teachers' in Guyana when the airline's mistake found me stranded in various different locations without a seat on any of the planes that were assigned to my ticket. Guyana, Trinidad, Tobago *and* Miami – refused boarding and stranded at all of them on the same leg home, with the extra blessing of extreme gastroenteritis and suspected Chikungunya virus. So I felt like now was perhaps the moment to enjoy some comfort ahead of the mud and black flies to come. I texted Kate some photos from the lounge, courtesy of the air miles, and she texted me back the bird, which I considered to be excellent and entirely appropriate. And then we went dark on comms and retreated into our heads, both careening over the oceans to the start of something quite extraordinary.

CHAPTER TWO

Arrival

London Heathrow Airport UK
to Boston Logan Airport, MA, USA

3256.9 Miles of Transit

An American airport has some kind of thrill to it: oversized, busy and exciting. Kate and I convened in Arrivals at Boston Logan with our bags, then headed to get a coffee and figure out what the heck happened next. We had a bus booked, but it wasn't at all clear where we'd get it from. I looked at the paper in my hand and rubbed my tired, itchy eyes – some sense of urgency came from the stern words on the booking confirmation: 'This booking does not confirm a seat on this bus. Please arrive in good time to ensure your place.'

'Well where the fuck does it go from? This map doesn't make any sense.' I'd printed out the map from the bus website, but it wasn't helping and didn't seem to give any indication of where we needed to go. 'I reckon we try to find an information desk?'

We both swivelled our heads, but all around were cavernous corridors and high ceilings, empty escalators and walkways leading up to double doors and more halls. We hustled along, trusting our guts that we might somehow emerge in a central atrium. Both of us were feeling the effects of a very early start and long journey. My skin crawled and prickled from wearing the same clothes for so many hours. I saw myself reflected in a glass walkway wall. Rough as shit. I guessed I was going to have to get used to that.

'Down here!' Kate had spotted a sign for transit. And then another and another. Then a coffee shop. 'Right, let's get a drink and think properly,' she said. 'We've got time, and I need to call Chris and the kids, so they know I'm here safe.'

'Yes, yes, of course,' I said, but worrying slightly that we wouldn't make the bus and we'd be playing catch-up from the get-go. I knew I needed to start at Mt Katahdin on 15th June. I also knew that we had a bunk in the hostel for only one night and that they were rammed with the later opening of the park this year due to heavy snow and late thaw, so there wouldn't be space for us tomorrow. And finally, I knew that my frenetic worrying and anticipating the problems ahead wouldn't get me anywhere. I was so used to travelling alone and had spent years planning and executing adventures in far-flung places. Always happy to plot short visits to overseas friends into my itinerary, I spent the bulk of my trips moving around by myself and enjoying the fascinating people and experiences that can often only be found when you're solo. I had also shaped my working life around my love of travel; tutoring overseas for wealthy families and also using my school holidays as a way to immerse myself in different locations overseas for more than just a week's vacation. This independent and autonomous way of travelling was deeply ingrained, and meant that sharing the experience was a learning curve. I needed to dig into partnership and stop feeling like I needed to hustle along. I sat with Kate, sipping coffee, and checked in with myself.

I needed to find a spot between now and hiking to deal with all the meds that were in my bag. All still in their boxes – blister packs of co-codamol and naproxen for my chronic pain and lymecycline for my skin – stacked neatly in rows and taking up incredible amounts of space in an effort to show any customs officials that the medicine was official and I was not trying to smuggle drugs into the USA. I even had a letter from my GP explaining that the drugs were prescribed by him and running whoever read it through some of my medical history to show why I needed meds for this trip. I was only able to take 3 months' supply with me for this 5–6-month hike as my doctor didn't want to prescribe me any more in one go. I would have to eke it out or find a way to get further supplies (at a US doctor's office or get them somehow sent from home) or see if the trip could be the means towards me no longer taking them. I didn't quite understand that at this point. How was a painful 2,200-mile physical ordeal going to be the way in which I didn't need pain meds for my dodgy, mercurial body?

I took a moment to ask myself how I was actually *feeling*. Head check: all OK, if a bit tired, fuzzy and stressed. Body check: I probed all the corners that usually hurt the most, using the methods I'd borrowed from yoga and meditations I'd tried in the past, including the full body scan. My body told me that it was hurting from being on the plane. My right hip and SI joint ached and didn't like me pulling my right leg forwards as I walked, but this was familiar territory for me. I lived with pain all the time and, like a bad smell, soon you become accustomed to it and barely notice it. I was doing OK.

I didn't feel like making my pain status clear to Kate at this point. I wasn't about to acknowledge it, because I wasn't going to let it have a seat around the table yet on this trip. I was used to squashing mention of my pain and belittling it when the subject came up. The specifics of it have become mindless in the telling, sometimes rattled off with an incongruously happy tone, like a kid answering the phone by rote. Either that or I simply forget to include it in my introductions. I mean, when do you throw that little party-pooper grenade into the chat?

'Hi! Yeah, nice to meet you too! I'm Gail. Oh, I'm a teacher. Yes, yes. *Oh*, also chronically ill most of the time and unable to walk a lot. Hmm, oh no. Don't look sad! I'm OK. It'll be alright. What? Oh, these stretchy loose trousers I'm wearing? Yes, yes, ugly aren't they? It's because I can't have the fabric touching my skin because of pain. Agony actually. Let me just lift my left leg over my right here a moment as… ahhh, FUCK IT… Yes, that's better. Won't move by itself at the moment you see. Look, it's even numb in places! Oh. Sorry… What's that? You have to go? Oh, gosh, sure, no problem. Well, was nice to meet you.'

No. Discussing pain was not a successful social strategy, especially in the territory I was heading for, where I'd be around ruggedly fit folks who'd trained in readiness for this adventure. I bet they'd smell weakness at ten paces. No, much better to sit on it and pretend I'm like everyone else. The thing is though, no one *is* like anyone else, are they? We're all hiding things that we don't want to be judged for. But it's strange to absorb a medical condition like this so deeply into your being that it becomes just another part of you that you don't consider even mentioning anymore. I would forget to flag it to people even when it was vital. I'd even forget sometimes to explain it as the reason for my slowness, foggy brain or irritability, and eventually ended up believing that I *was* those things, rather than being someone who was suffering *from* something. Don't we all risk this with our silent struggles, masking our anxiety, depression or litany of physical pains – subsuming them into our very identity so we can't tell where we start and end anymore? We shouldn't confuse our identity with our suffering – you *aren't* your illness, but you are sharing the same body, so you need to work with your condition, but you don't ever need to let it define you.

I had been a robust, lively and fit teenager. As a young woman I had been a gig rower for my local teams in Cornwall, a cross-country runner and an extremely enthusiastic dancer in our Cornish pubs and tiny nightclubs. I had suffered no noticeably difficult health issues while growing up, but there were some grey clouds over my head from a smattering of damning expert diagnoses in my childhood years.

When I was born, my feet turned in quite severely. I'd had them tucked up under my butt in utero in some awkward position which meant they weren't really fit for purpose when I emerged into the light. So for the first year of my life they were nestled in little white casts. The casts came on and off, growing with me. As a toddler I recall being lifted onto a long boardroom table and being coaxed to walk down the middle so that the specialist next to me could see my gait and watch my feet move everything above them: knees, hips – all the stuff I took for granted as a child. All was well, they said. I was fit, clear and just like every other little human gambolling around playgrounds and gardens.

My feet still turn in, bless them, the little bananas. My ankles roll over nothing and I even tripped over my schoolbag as a gawky Year 7; trying to play a game with my pals, my toes would trick me as they collided with their opposite numbers on the other foot; and I once broke my arm rolling down a bank. My goofy feet were annoying but their effect on my body wasn't noticeable in childhood, mostly providing amusement and later some bullying rather than any physical hindrance to my running or swimming in school. My parents were still a little concerned for my later years, and my kind Uncle Ian sent me to a consultant in London in my early teens to check how I was doing. Cue more memories of walking in front of specialists, but this time with much more awkward self-awareness as a teenager, hitting puberty with encroaching puppy fat and desperate horror at budding breasts, having to slip out of my trousers and expose my pale legs in my M&S pants to walk slowly along a treadmill under the eyes of machines recording my legs and hips moving as I walked to nowhere.

'How was it all looking?' I asked.

Not great as it turned out. My mum wasn't in the room when the specialist told me what he thought – I hadn't wanted her there, hating this attention and hating to see her worry. I remember sitting with my head turned to him but my body turned away, smiling at him in the way that I still do when I'm nervous. Being charming because it feels like my only defence, naked legs sticking to the red plastic chair. He cut to the chase, I think. I don't remember word for word what he said, but I remember how it landed and what I absorbed: 'If you don't get your feet broken and reset, you'll be in a wheelchair by the time you're 40 years old.' I

39

write that now in some kind of awe that I ever heard those words as a young person.

I think that's where I started just swallowing bad news and deciding to put it away and not think about it. I didn't realise that it was still inside, and it would have its effect one way or another. But sitting there in my undies that day with the cold air prickling my skin and my feet skimming the '80s lino, I knew that there was no way that on top of the adolescent red flags of having pigeon toes, being smart at school, not enjoying or understanding netball and having a mole on my chin, I was also going to have to absorb and deal with this wheelchair crap. So I nodded and promptly ignored it. I didn't discuss it and absolutely didn't tell my mum, who I imagined would have been told by the doctor too.

I remember waiting fearfully for a long time for her to bring it up so that we'd have to *do* something about it. I was scared and didn't want to be further stigmatised in school, but she never did bring it up. I thought it was because the situation probably wasn't as big a deal as the man had made out; or maybe it was, but she knew I couldn't take anything else on top of how traumatic school was turning out to be for me. (I was bullied so much by one girl that I almost reached the point of school refusal. She had made destroying me her self-professed project.) But many years later when I mentioned the appointment to my mum, when the pain had become terrifying and I wanted to die, she told me that she had never known, that the doctor hadn't told her. I realised it must be true, because of course she would have done something about it. She who held my hand whilst weeping in frustration that there was no magic wand to wave to take my pain and despair away.

She who felt my pain in her own body. So it had been my doing. I had decided to ignore my prognosis and just barrel on through my life. Life's ups and downs. The usual stuff that feels like you're living… until it doesn't.

I struggled to shove the memories aside. I mean, it was clear I was living *now* and I didn't feel like hashing up all the trauma of the past just yet. After all, I was sure I was going to have to confront it soon enough, either by revisiting the pain physically when hiking, or as my thoughts swelled up in the woods by myself. Right now, it was more important to be present and get where I was going.

I refocused my tired mind. Coffee and calls done, Kate and I roved further through the airport and finally found the long queue for buses snaking around a corner. I felt freaked about never getting a spot on the bus, but over the course of half an hour it was clear most of these people were getting on the different buses that pulled up outside. Hissing hydraulics and some luggage Tetris and they left again. The queue thinned. I was bored standing after being bored sitting not an hour before – so mercurial. Our bus eventually came and we boarded. It wasn't busy; there were seats for all.

We rumbled away from the city, me with my face glued to the unreal view from the window. Iconic fast-food restaurants with bright gaudy signs made even a simple suburban highway feel like a tiny piece of Vegas to my eyes so used to British austerity. Cluttered chain-link lots gave glimpses of folks perhaps up to no good, there were kids throwing basketballs across outdoor courts, and then convenience stores gave way to out-of-town storage depots and industrial units until the driver indicated, turned and settled down onto a regular grey strip that held us apart from either town or city life – the tarmac ligaments stretched between the sockets and sprockets of life.

With a long ride ahead, I dozed and Kate listened to music until we were at the next stop: Bangor. From Bangor we took a smaller bus to Millinocket. Sitting up front, I enjoyed a chat with the driver.

'You're all from England!' he exclaimed happily, with his hands gripped what seemed like a metre apart on the wide steering wheel. He didn't turn around, thank God, but eyeballed me with delight in one of the many mirrors around his station. 'Where are you from? I don't meet many of you out this way!'

'Cornwall!' I exclaimed with pride, like I always do. 'The best part of England!' I was a little taken aback as he gave a joyous yelp.

'POLDARK! Oh, my LORD. POLDARK!' He seemed agitated. 'Those mines? The sea. THE SEA! Is it really like that? Does it look like that and are people like that? I'll be gosh darned. I love that show and now I've met a Cornish person! Sure made my day.' He muttered happily on like this for a while and I duly discussed the wonders of Cornwall with him, then tailed off, distracted by a grey-haired lady in her mid-80s next to me who had been gently nudging me with her elbow for a little while.

I smiled at her. 'Hi, how are you?'

Her twinkly eyes smiled back. 'Well, dear. I'm visiting my boy.'

'How lovely,' I replied.

'Sure is.' The twinkles turned mischievous and she waggled an iPad at me in her frail hand. 'You see, he gave me a website address to see my shows without having to pay.' She paused. 'Would you be a dear and help me set it up?'

I smiled and got stuck in.

CHAPTER THREE

Entry

Boston Logan Airport to Millinocket, Maine

303.6 Miles of Transit

The landscape through the windows altered between each bout of dozing and chatting. Buildings got lower and trees higher, grey receded and green stepped up, as though we were edging back into Eden. Lakes appeared on the left and right, silver slivers in the green.

Unlike the roads back home, which always seemed to take you to a new place so quickly – the next village, town or shopping hub – these roads just kept *going*. I was beginning to understand the scale of this country. It was a land writ large, with no urgency between places and enough landscape to fill every gap. Maine was already showing itself to be a full *in-breath*, a swelling lung of green fresh air; so different to the rapid, ashy panting of London's city streets or the cluttered, clogged arteries leading out into the rest of the UK.

I peered, hoping for wildlife, but any sensible creature would have sunk from the blacktop into the deep woods. It's what I would do, what I was *going* to do.

After what seemed an eternity, we disembarked in Bangor, Maine to await the next stage of the journey. Between coaches we found a diner to eat at, paused to read patriotic signs smattering the roadside (saying things like 'JET NOISE IS THE SOUND OF OUR FREEDOM') and enjoyed sending messages from my Garmin inReach® to both our families so that we knew we'd be able to be in touch once we disappeared into the wilderness. After filling our boots with a huge breakfast, we went to the store to try to fill our packs before the next transit turned up. *More* than fill, it turned out, as I struggled to carry my cache of supplies back to the bus station. My panic buying of tuna packets, beef jerky and Nutella didn't bode well for when I had to put it all together and carry the whole lot up mountains. Would I ever get past being 'too prepared'? I knew I needed to live a little more in the place of scarcity, but at this point it was all too much, and overpacking seemed to be the final comfort before I let go of it all.

*

Hot, foetid air, and food wedged between bunkbeds that no flossing brush had attempted to dislodge for many a month; the dorm at Old Man's Hostel in Millinocket was like walking into a mouth. The beginning of thru-hiker season in the far northern wilds of Maine was about to open its gates and the hikers were champing to be released into green freedom. Thru hiking is a pilgrimage to many, a way to escape real life and disappear into the woods along trails for months at a time. Not aimlessly but along a prescribed and often famous long-distance trail, relying on wits, navigation, the friends you make and the gear you carry with you. Each season, thru hikers wait excitedly until they can start, watching the weather. Heavy snow had precluded Mt Katahdin from opening thus far. The tiny town of Millinocket was a bottleneck of rabid walkers careening around like mindless zombies, bouncing from hostel to café to bar with little direction until tomorrow, 15th June – the date that Baxter State Park had agreed that Katahdin would be safe to open for summit. Pre-hike adrenaline was high on Facebook groups and reddit subs, but not here in the hostel tonight. Tonight was mostly snoring. Peppered around the dim room lay an array of soon-to-be outdoors folk from all walks of life, drawn to this pilgrimage for many reasons but united by a kind of masochism, forest-style.

The boards squeaked as I tiptoed my way through the thick cooking air to the tiny slice of grey upper-bunk mattress that was mine, my very flesh vibrating as I moved past one huge snorer – spread with abandon across his bed like a slowly melting butter stick. Picking over food bags, stray limbs poking from sleep pads and pages ripped from books (already read and abandoned so that no extra weight was carried into the wilderness), I eased myself towards the ladder. Kate lay below me, already sensibly ensconced under her shiny new sleeping bag, face glistening in the stinking dead ether and headphones in. She winked at me, then turned and settled into her own fears for the morning, as I squeaked step by step above her and unrolled myself onto the noisy springs.

I slipped my pack behind my head and gripped my phone and purse tightly in the dark, not through fear of theft but my general fear of letting go. Of it all: my pain, my past, my traumas and the safety of a me that I knew. The person I would meet in the mirror after this night wouldn't be the same, I was sure of that. So I didn't sleep. You wouldn't have slept either. The ladder to that top bunk was really the staircase to the top diving board, and tomorrow I'd

45

be shuffling to the edge, ready to cannonball into the rapids that my life had been meandering towards for the last 20 years. I closed my eyes and settled into a few fitful hours of night-time overthinking.

*

Morning had come like a cold flannel down my neck.

'Who the heck's pack is this?' Compass asked, running gnarled knuckles across his already beading forehead. He hiked and then worked here in alternate seasons. Hiking then saving to hike.

The nine of us subtly eyed each other across the gravel parking space. It was 7 a.m. and I'd slid out at 5 a.m., which was when the tiny town's café opened, so I could take advantage of my hostel discount and try to muster confidence about all the climbs ahead of me that day.

The wiry man continued to lean at an angle off the side of the massive truck. He'd already overhanded a number of packs snugly into the roof bars, but this one had clearly piqued his interest. 'There's a damn axe in here. Seriously. Come on, you guys, who brought the hatchet? This pack must weigh upwards of seventy pounds.' He scanned the small crowd and looked disappointed, as though we'd already let him down with this egregious error – *the too-heavy pack.* This man; this stranger who had already thru hiked, and whom we could only look up to in awe.

No one answered the call, and he dropped the bag with a disdainful thunk to the dusty ground. There it sat for a moment, all dark green fabric and straps, looking ashamed at being so full.

'Sorry I was late,' I mumbled. 'That one's mine.' I pointed to my brand-new Gossamer Gear pack, chosen after sleepless days and nights combing the internet from my perspective of 'utterly clueless hiker' in my months of AT prep in the UK.

He hefted it up. 'Pretty good,' he said, running his eyes briefly over my shiny everything, as I tried to look like it was all just new gear by accident, and not because I'd never really used any of it before.

'Sweet,' I said, beaming internally but keeping the straight face of an old hand.

At that moment, a tall, young man loped onto the scene. I remember his name was Lee. He tipped his head back in the morning light and scanned the bags on the roof rack, then looked towards the pack left on the floor. The one in the dust with the axe. We all looked at him, the hatchet man. We knew it must be his.

'Dang son, is that a hatchet in there?' Our heads all swivelled right as one. It was Old Man himself, out into the car park from his eponymous hostel. Short, powerful and bearing all the hallmarks of a '60s Deadhead, we were all a little intimidated by him and his brusque style. He was the start-gun for our southbound hike, and the welcoming committee for those finishing their northbound, the thrumming fuse holding both ends of a hiking circuit board that pulsed with hopes, sweat and big characters. He didn't suffer fools or spare his words, which didn't bode well for Lee.

'Every year, every time, someone comes with too much stuff and I hav'da tell 'um to get rid of it. No problem though, young man, we can give you a shakedown for that bag right now and you can tell us whether you want your extra gear shipped or given away.' He paused to think and touched his short ponytail thought-fully. 'There'll be Sobo hikers coming through here for a couple months now – it'll all get used.' He leaned over and picked up the thick canvas army-style pack from the floor. It was the type of bag that looked ready for anything – except carrying it very far without swearing a lot.

'No,' said Lee. Now still as stone and clear as a bell. 'No, I don't want to take anything out.' We all looked at him, awed at his certainty.

Old Man paused and appraised Lee. Tall, slim and clearly very sure of his decision. 'OK, son. Well that's on you.' He tipped a nod at the bag-swinger, who loaded it in. 'Let's get you lot gone!' With that, he was inside the van and started it up. We'd gone from being ready and ahead of the game with our packs in the lot to standing outside the loaded van that was revving to leave – from prepared and ready to playing catch-up in a heartbeat. This was to be the trail all over. We dove in.

PART TWO

Into the Woods

MAINE

281.4 miles

CHAPTER FOUR

Are We Hikers Now?

The ride into Baxter State Park took just under an hour. Old Man warmed up and used most of the ride to impart useful wisdom about near enough everything, including how much water we should carry (not much as the snow was melting and the rivers were high) and what we should do if we encountered a big, angry moose. I stared out of the window, trying to glimpse some majestic beasts, and marvelled that it was still over an hour until we even got to the ranger station which would mark the *beginning* of the park. We were already in deep woodland not moments into our journey. How vast could this place *be*?

I felt suspended in the safety of the vehicle and the confidence of my fellow riders – as though I could count on them and they on me, as if our chatter on this morning had bonded us deeply and into a place of security, but I knew deep down that this was not true. The one couple in the car would have each other, but the rest of us were going to be turfed out of these last vestiges of real life and into the woods alone. The Appalachian Trail 'Hunger Games' would begin and we'd be fending for ourselves.

I turned back to Old Man and listened as he continued to talk about how to save fuel when boiling water, while still making sure it killed any nasties inside. He wound up the latest hiking parable and went quiet, leaving the van silent and us all in a state of anticipation. What was coming? And then, as we started to turn a corner in the road, he slowed, fumbled with his CD player and asked us, 'Are you ready?'

'Yeah!' we all shouted, so excited and buoyed up with anticipation but with no idea what we were ready for. He pressed 'play' and accelerated slightly. As we all leaned left around the corner, we caught our first breathtaking view of Mama Katahdin, and the car filled with the sound of 'Eye of the Tiger'.

She was vast, rising up from the forest and filling the windscreen. It seemed momentarily that my attempt at this trip was a joke, a gag and a ruse. I got that familiar wash of humiliation that I was going to be exposed as a sort of 'sporty-fraud' and told to sit back on the bench. No way was I going up *there*! Who, me? No, definitely not taking the risk. Time to spin the car around and back to the airport please.

But then shame and self-doubt were nudged aside by a different voice, one that I'd been working on making louder and louder these past months and years. I *could* do this! Yes, *me*. I *was* outdoorsy. I had beaten huge odds to get this far. I was going to do it, and if I was going to have to do it on my knees, I was still going to do it. And so I breathed the magnificent mountainous sight in and out, let a grin spread across my face and turned to look at the others. *Yes*! The whole gang was grinning, everyone feeling pumped to get up there. I went back to staring out of the window, singing along to the hiking hype music and giggling at Lee giving it his all in the back seat, fists pumping and head thrown back in song.

I noticed a number of stickers on Old Man's water bottle, which was shoved in the centre console. One was a sketch of a hiker at the top of Katahdin with the words 'Save Alcohol For Later' underneath. Puzzling, but it wasn't until later that I realised people had been taking champagne and beer up to the summit to celebrate the end of their hikes, but some left smashed glass and trash up there before they descended. Totally shitty behaviour, and it made me wonder why some who say they love the outdoors seem to think it's OK to trash it.

Deep into the woods we drove, the van slowing to crawl over potholes and down-deep dents in the backcountry track. I thought I'd miss Kate, as she had decided not to summit Katahdin and instead to meet me back at the shelter that night, but I was glad to feel like a lone wolf again for a time. I kept trying to be in the 'thru-hike' mindset that I'd been working towards for so long, but then realised Kate needed me to be in the 'short-trip' mindset too, otherwise how would I understand her totally valid fears and concerns and be supportive of her venturing entirely out of her element. It was hard, and I knew it was going to get harder, but for this moment I was glad to have the space to sink back into my thru-hike head and begin to feel like the lone adventurer I'd been hoping to be.

Eventually we pulled across a dirt parking area by Katahdin Stream ranger station and disgorged from the van. No sooner had I unfolded my body and stretched out on the dirt than I was attacked by flies and mosquitos. They flew and tangled into my eyelashes, up my nose and onto my hands and neck. I spluttered a few out of my mouth and tried to yank my head net out of my bumbag (soon to be 'fanny pack') with one hand whilst swatting my face with the other. 'Shit, shit, shit. These are ridiculous!' I exclaimed, pulling my net over my head; cap and all.

'You ain't seen nothin' yet,' a man standing in the lot said, grinning. 'They're thick like storm clouds in there.' He was pointing at the woods.

Great. Thanks. I smiled in a polite 'Hoooo, that's rough, hey!' way and turned to the rest of the van crew. They'd vanished. In the time I'd been fussing around, they'd been doing something more important like listening to Old Man tell them what to do. I flailed around inside my head net, trying to see where everyone had gone. I couldn't be falling behind on Day 1! But that in itself wasn't even a correct thought anymore. Falling behind who? I was on my own. But I wasn't on my own. Oh, heck, I would have to get used to this. Making friends with people, hiking with them, creating bonds but having absolutely no guarantee that you'd ever see them again or that they'd wait for you anywhere. Not even knowing if you should wait for them. I didn't know the etiquette and clearly needed to get up to speed damn quickly.

Tramping up the wooden steps, I followed the small group inside the ranger's office and noticed people's packs were already piled up in the porch area. I dumped mine on top and got the last spot in the line. Hiking Katahdin could take a person 9 hours to summit and descend, so everyone would have to stay the night here in the campground. Most people had already booked a pitch or cabin online months before, but many were sharing their large pitches with others – it was an unusually crowded time with the late thaw. It was the day after Katahdin officially opened, extremely delayed, and many hikers had been waiting with their cancelled entries from the week prior so that they could slide into any spots available. Of course, those with spots were very happy to oblige. That was the way it was with hikers I was to learn – everyone wanting to help. Some hardy souls had suggested they might summit, descend, then carry on hiking on the trail to make a few extra miles that day, but Baxter didn't let people camp anywhere but Katahdin Spring on this route out. So if you wanted to leave this campground, you had to make damn sure that you hiked allll the way out of the State Park and made it to Abol Bridge, the next good feasible spot to stop for a night. That was another 10+ miles though, so a hard 'nope' for most after the exertion of climbing Mama Katahdin.

As folks were forced to stay the night in Baxter, it didn't make sense to carry full packs up the mountain and back, so we swapped them for day packs at the cabin after we'd signed for our permits. I nodded a smile at the person before me as she picked up her bright yellow permit card and watched her step outside with a bounce of excitement. I think her name was Kelly; a curvy, laughing girl with joyful eyes. I knew immediately I liked her.

My eyes glided across the wooden walls of the station, full of racks bulging with leaflets about the various trails and park initiatives that are run by these wonderful people. The ranger's voice pulled me from the moment and I chatted happily with her, signing my form and singing cheery goodbyes over my shoulder as I hit the porch, then the dirt, double-checked I had my two water bottles, stove, snacks and first aid in my day pack, and set off.

Well I kind of set off, because in my moment of bravado I'd got turned entirely around and didn't know how to get out of the car park. For a moment I pretended to tie my shoe lace in order to watch Lee, who was dithering, and decide where he was going to go so I'd have a route to follow. Christ, I wondered if I was really cut out for this, questioning my skills as I watched Lee set out in a move that bemused me because it was very obviously the wrong way.

I sat back on my heels to see how this would roll out. How could someone with an army-style pack and who carries a hatchet in their bag not know what they're doing in the great outdoors? Luckily, the ranger spotted him and came to her door, gently stopping him with a little shout and pointing out the right route. Thankful it hadn't been me, I waited a little longer to give Lee space and then I started hiking – over a wooden bridge, past my first wooden 'Appalachian Trail' sign with arrows, places and distances written on it. It was as though my dream had stepped out from the screen of my computer; the countless research, reading and groups I'd dived into to get ready had become *real*. This very image that I'd seen before on other people's social media was now here, in front of my eyes and there for the touching. My journey to get here had methodically closed all the tabs on the browser of my imagination and now I was standing in front of my own home screen. Real life. Shit. Was I really going to do this?

I swallowed, pressed my hand on the scarred, mossy wood around the lettering. Hell yes I was. One step at a time. And setting my shoulders, I pushed myself up into the deep green tree cover towards my first white blaze.

*

I was worried I'd catch up with someone or that someone would catch up with me. I didn't feel ready for small talk or politeness, or for the pressure that my overtaking someone would put on me to maintain a steady faster pace, but, confusingly, *also* not the embarrassment of someone else overtaking me. Already my stupid busy brain was worrying about all these things at once, instructing me to speed up, slow down and maintain my current pace all at the same time. If this hike achieved anything, I hoped that it might slow down this slavedriver in my skull a touch. I mean, it's great to be able to see all the angles, but not when you then decide you have to worry about or try to control them all at once.

Luckily though, it took me a long time to see anyone, and I very quickly didn't give a toss about it anyway because the meandering green path soon turned into a slippy, boulder-riven shitshow. In small 5-minute segments it would have been ace, a little adventurous section filled with rocks and tree roots to squeeze up and through between smooth paths on a little incline, but it was not that. It was all hard. I had kind of been fooling myself when I read the warning in the books and on the signs – oh yes, I know it's tough but I'm going to be one of those people who can just *do* it. What a dick. Forty-one years old, years of chronic pain, body issues up the wazoo and heaving plenty of extra chunk around with me.

I'd always had to pretend I could do it, because my pain was invisible and I didn't have a glaringly obvious reason to duck out of anything without a laborious explanation, which, quite frankly, I was fucking *over* giving out to people. It was also super traumatic. Imagine having to explain the background of your mental-health trauma every time someone asked why you were feeling a bit anxious. But for invisible illness sufferers there seems to be some expectation to 'justify'. I didn't want to anymore. I just wanted to be in the chorus with the rest, not front and centre explaining why I wasn't like everyone else.

It's part of the issue with invisible illness that often its sufferers are able to function. The general consensus seems to be that if you're able to *do* stuff then you're clearly not actually that ill. It's such an unhealthy way to structure our narrative around being unwell, and we do our society a disservice by needing to see wounds in order to confer compassion. Things seem to be improving, but the rate is slow and people are silently suffering more than they need to.

You see, the dichotomy is that if you're in pain, fatigued or otherwise suffering inside your body, then chances are you're also very likely to be facing some mental-health issues. The body, in my opinion and experience, is a whole – not separate 'pieces' that need treating as individual elements. Everything we have is joined to something else in the whole; therefore any issue is connected. So it is with our body and our mind. Should you, therefore, have some physical ailment that is not immediately recognisable or visible, and the concurrent depression or anxiety that can go with it, then you probably would like to be doing something nice to take your mind off it. This, however, could become an extremely risky enterprise for your social standing, workplace trust and relationships with your community.

If you had a broken leg, then your community would be able to see that you can't walk well, or run, or swim, or do Zumba. And if they saw you out having a coffee with a friend who had driven you to the café and helped you to your seat with crutches, they wouldn't judge you as being a liar or a fraud who was looking for sympathy or skiving work. On the contrary, they would probably applaud you for making the best of your injury and keeping your spirits up. They might even be impressed at your pain management or resilience. If though, like me, you were in chronic pain that is entirely invisible, and went for the same coffee with a friend, you might find the responses to your being there to be quite different.

'Thought you weren't feeling well?'

'All fixed? Glad to see that.'

'Hey! Ahh, you're out and about! Why didn't you come to my birthday dinner a couple of nights ago? I was so sad you couldn't make it – we had such a good time dancing. You missed so much fun!'

And so on, and so forth. You can't be seen to be upbeat, like you might be with a broken bone! I have a pretty ebullient personality so that even when the chips are extremely far down, I can still raise a smile and laugh about it – my way of coping. But it doesn't seem appropriate to use these coping mechanisms when you have an invisible illness, as it apparently comes across that you're 'taking the piss' by trying to be upbeat when you're 'supposed' to be unwell. So here we come to the very frustrating core of this situation. Not only are you suffering, but this is compounded by some societal need to keep yourself humbly isolated, in keeping with traditional ideas of 'suffering through illness'. You're to keep some serious gravitas around it all, playing down the smiles and attempts at joy. Well, sorry, but the word 'chronic' should help you understand that the illness isn't going away, so the expectation to conform to how people behave with 'acute' illnesses isn't going to cut it for us 'chronics', unless you want us to truly give up on the quality of life we *can* get in order to fit what you think looks right for an 'ill' person.

I had been 'invisibly unwell', but I certainly became 'visible' on my journey back to wellness. From gentle strength training to learning deadlifts and eventually participating in trail-running events that had previously seemed forever out of my reach, I was making a noise because it was better than the deathly silence of suffering. After finding a solution to my chronic condition in Italy, the journey to wellness took years. It was my side project that travelled with me as teaching and tutoring work took me through Alps, valleys, across Hong Kong, Bali and beyond. I built my fitness slowly and couldn't do it alone. I knew of a friendly and knowledgeable team of outdoor trainers at home in Falmouth called 'Fitness Wild', so I called them from my kitchen in Italy, feeling excited that I might now be able to exercise without pain. After I explained my history and background to them, Ben and Jimmy assured me they could help, and worked with me both in person and remotely to build not just my body but also my confidence. We inched forwards, even taking steps back to relearn movement and techniques. I started at the beginning and embraced the humility of being at the bottom rung again, dili-gently doing the work to rebuild myself – from small exertions to big lifts and longer distances. I was laser focused with one goal in mind – to live the lost years with all my might, which is how I ended up right here, huffing and puffing through the trees with my fresh rosy cheeks and eyes wide with awe, fear and wonder. I was going to struggle, but I was going to fucking do it anyway.

It was clear, though, that I wasn't going to struggle as much as Kelly. Kelly was firmly on the struggle bus when I caught up to her, lolling on a rock in the sun and exclaiming good-naturedly that it was super damn hot and she was knackered and thirsty. I agreed. She glugged some water and we took photos of each other and chatted briefly before I asked if she needed anything and carried on past her into the next section.

The silence was already interesting to me. I'd been craving silence for so long and now it was all around. The atmosphere seemed dead, and gradually my ears tuned in and the swell of the natural world rose to fill it. The trickling and dripping of snow melt, pine needles dropping, rocks and pebble shifting, and the deep ragged breaths that were coming out of me. I stopped regularly, wondering how far the final summit was and being totally unable to work the Guthook Guides app I'd downloaded. That could come later. At this stage I figured, yeah it's tough, but it's not super tough and I don't know why people were saying it's such a difficult way to begin the trail. Soon though, the path gave way to more boulders and my angle of ascent changed from leaning forwards to scrambling on all fours. It was clear that if this were a platform game on an old Nintendo, I had just cleared the basic level and had now ascended into a different league. I was left wondering what the big boss at the end would be like.

About an hour later, I was clinging to the side of a huge rock on a piece of rebar (iron) with my feet inching around the bottom ledge and my butt swinging in the wind. I felt the cold draft that chased up the side of the mountain lifting my top and whistling around my bra as my cheek grazed along the stone. I thought, *Good God. How the* hell *is this allowed? What about health and safety? Surely only proper climbers could come up here? What about a top rope and a harness? This isn't OK. I must have taken the wrong route*. I stopped and tried to sucker my whole body to the surface for a moment and catch my breath, this time shallow from anxiety and not from exertion. As I did so, I heard a scuffling and a pair of sneakers materialised above me. Someone was coming down.

'Hey! You doin' OK?' he asked as he nimbly shimmied past me. A tall and rangy man in red shorts and a slight tee, a tiny bag with water slung on the side, looking quite at home in this mountain-goat territory.

'Yes, yes, sure am.' I smiled at him with a rictus grin and wide eyes. 'How much farther is it?'

'Oh not far!' He smiled. I would soon come to know that these descent-folk measurements of distance are a total fucking lie, but I was still fresh and green at this point. 'Well, not far until the end of this field, then there's a sharp ridge like a knife-edge for a while, and then... Hooo! Then there's a steep bit! And after that the Tablelands, then the summit. So all in all, another few hours? Not far at all.' He beamed at me, totally sweat-less and fresh, and I was consumed with the urge to shove him off the side. Another few hours? He had to be fucking kidding. I'd been at it a few hours. This was a joke.

'OK, thaaaaanks!' I chirped and waited until he had gone before telling myself to buck up.

Detaching from my perch, up I went, over and around more boulders. The tender insides of my upper arms were scratched and grazed from reaching up and dragging myself onto ledges, with my feet precariously balanced on different edges and ledges to stop me from slipping between Ice Age cracks. Spreadeagled. The knife-edge was no joke. I kept my body low from the wind in case a gust cast me off like a finger-flick from the gods, further bruising and scraping my shins.

Finally I made it up the acute angle of ascent with a heave and a huff, pulling myself onto a flat plain. I paused and lifted my head, now fully understanding the gut-punch of a 'false summit'. You think you're aiming for the top, and even though you're knackered, the very sight of it is encouraging, so you exert every ounce of energy to get there, knowing that it's the end. But it's not the end; it was just the end of a section that blocked the view of the next section. So now I faced a long flat piece of trail called the 'Tablelands' and a further ascent in the distance. I was tired and discouraged by this point, but people were close and I didn't want to look like the useless, pain-addled woman that I was trying to shed, so I pulled myself together and set off again.

I realised that the people I saw around me were actually working. I was to learn they were 'trail crew' and I would meet many of them along my route. However, these were the first, gently placing pegs and twine around areas of alpine greenery that had already suffered from the snow melt and then the footfall of eager hikers keen to get started. I nodded and they reciprocated as I moved through them.

My feet begin to hurt from the small sharp rocks through my zero-drop, thin-soled shoes. Bile rose and I felt dizzy and seasick from constantly needing to look down but simultaneously ahead to judge where to place my feet on the desperately uneven terrain. One false move at any kind of pace and I'd be done for before I began.

I turned to look over my shoulder – no sign of Kelly. No sign of anyone I recognised actually. In the swivel I realised what the views around me were like: the true definition of epic. Miles of green in all directions without even the hint of a conurbation. Trees and more trees punctuated only by the silvery slashes of lakes and rivers in the afternoon sunlight. Such *space*. Such peace. Such a big job. It made me well up.

As I approached the summit I could see more people than I expected, sitting around and admiring the views, eating snacks and chatting. In the middle of them stood the iconic 'Katahdin' wooden sign which I was super keen to drape myself over in relief. More folk approached from ahead of me, which gave me pause and a momentary panic that I'd screwed up, but they'd summited from a different route – the *real* Knife Edge. I glanced over at it. 'Phew,' I said to no one. 'Fuck that.'

'Hey, guys.' I approached a friendly-looking group of three men who were hovering near the summit sign, that iconic sign I'd been staring at online for the past 12 months. 'Would you mind taking some photos of me on the sign?'

They all turned and smiled, looking at my day pack and figuring me as a day hiker. I wasn't to know this yet, but there exists a definite divide between day hikers and thru hikers. Not an unkind one, but some element of comfort versus arduous privation that would become much clearer once I was more blooded by the forest and coated in weeks of filth. I would pass sweet-smelling day hikers and turn like a zombie to inhale the fragrance of a daily shower and laundered clothes. Like a dog smelling a treat 500 feet away; thru hikers could smell day hikers around corners.

'Sure we can!' And the biggest guy put down his sandwich on a rock and ambled over towards me. I have visited the USA many times, and every time the common thread is kindness and a willingness to help. Sure, a woman with nails at a check-in desk in Miami airport was once a belligerent witch who made me miss my flight even though I was there 3 hours early, but aside from that and the occasional barging for the metro, everyone had been angels to me. Little did I know that the angel-ling had just begun. This trail was full of them.

The day-hiker fellas and I enjoyed the usual chat about where I was from. 'England! Wow! What brings you out here? Whoa, a thru hiker! Neat. What's that flag?' And then they ambled back to their lunch and left me examining the sign.

With my Cornish St Piran's Flag gripped in my left hand, I placed my right onto the scarred wood. So many people were on their way north right now, striving through woods and over mountains to end their hike at this very sign, and I was just beginning. It almost didn't feel right to have had my photo taken with it, having done less than one day, but I knew I'd be earning the moment in the days to come.

Balancing my feet on sharp rock edges, I moved around to the back of the sign, hand over hand on the wood until I could climb up the wooden struts on the reverse. Clambering as high as I could, I swept my vision left and right. Breathtaking space, sharp air like wasabi in my nostrils, unbelievable amounts of pure nature with no cities or towns anywhere. I'd be in there tomorrow. Deep and irreversibly in the green. With Kate. What could possibly go wrong? I brewed up a quick cup of coffee and broke into some oatmeal packets while I pondered.

*

The way down was hard and I was more fatigued than I had realised. Getting to the end of the Tablelands was OK, going past Thoreau Spring, named for the great naturalist Henry David Thoreau, who ascended Katahdin in 1846 as part of his quest for a life deliberately lived, and who wrote *The Maine Woods*, capturing the wilder side of America in his forest excursions. Much, of course, as I was planning to do if I could reverse my big arse back down the steep scrambles in my current giddy vertigo whirl.

I repeatedly peeped through my arms down to where my feet should land, trying to make sure that I wasn't going to catch just a toe-tip, then lean my weight on nothing but dust and gravel, careening down the side of the sheer drop. My fingertips were raw from gripping the rock edges over my head. I gingerly lowered myself down each rock, the flimsy brim of my cap catching on the edges, pushing it back over my head. Every time it happened, I absentmindedly risked death by letting go with one hand and grabbing the cap to force it back on but then panicked and flailed to grip the rock again. What an ignoble way to go. Maybe I wasn't cut out for this. I didn't even like the bloody hat. The wind had picked up and brought voices to my ears from far below, then whipped them away and gave me only static. I continued steadily down.

It wasn't long after I descended into the green forested section of the lower mountain that I glimpsed someone ahead. The back of a pale shirt between branches, then gone again down a lower switchback or behind a set of huge, monolithic rocks. Incrementally I caught the cypher up, very happy to see another face once I had realised from his gait and frame that it was Lee. I was surprised to have caught up with him. He was so fast in the morning, disappearing like the bullet from a gun, and I had surmised that he was an extremely experienced hiker. He didn't have his full green pack with him so was without his hatchet, but his day pack still looked full and weighty, with lumps and bumps protruding. If I wasn't such a novice, I might have thought that it even looked a little… poorly packed.

'Hey! Lee!' I shouted, my words absorbed immediately by greenery, branches and earth. He didn't hear and I speeded up, kicking brown pine needles and hanging on to tree trunks as I swung around path corners to move faster. 'LEE! Yo! Hold up, buddy.'

He turned quickly, putting his further-away hand out to brace against a boulder and slow his pace. He saw me and his face lit up into a relieved smile.

'Hey! Gail! Oh, how are you? This was hard right? It was steep. I'm really tired. Taking it slower coming down. Are you OK? How'd you find it?' He spoke softly but quickly, his words tumbling gently out. It was clear he had found the day harder than he expected.

'I'm good. Yes, it was really hard. Your pack looks super heavy though. What do you have in there?'

He shrugged. I clearly wasn't getting pack secrets from Lee just yet. 'Nothing much.' He paused. 'You want to walk together?'

Yes. Yes I did. For all my craving of solitude and silence, I now really wanted to be in someone's company. The wood section was short, but I was still uneasy with the lack of peripheral vision it gave me, like being in murky sea water far from shore. You know nothing is probably in there, but you can't see clearly enough to be sure. My hunter-gatherer hindbrain was probably propping itself up out of bed on one elbow and trying to gather its wits about what danger there might be, after snoozing for countless years whilst I sat indoors doing jobs on computers or safely in steel and stone buildings. I think its default setting before it fully woke was to press DANGER until it could get something more nuanced together after a coffee. So, yes, company felt good.

Lee was an interesting character. He spoke at length about politics, technology, data collection and topics as diverse as astrophysics, consciousness and weapon sales. I hadn't expected my brain to be quite so stimulated at the same time as my body, creating a jerky gait as I thought for a moment and stumbled, or walked fast and nimbly but sounded dumb. Eventually, I just let Lee talk, hmmming and ummming to chivvy him along. I just knew he and Kate would hit it off, with their physicsy, mathsy brains, and was keen to get them together.

We stopped at a waterfall and river that I'd barely noticed on my way up, excited as I was to get going. Our thirst was raging and we both carefully lowered ourselves down the slippery mud banks on either side of the wooden-planked bridge over the torrent. One hand gripped a flimsy branch and the other waved my silicone water pouch in the river, trying to get the mouth to open up without my being able to finger it open. My right foot slipped backwards in the gunk and I landed on one knee with a heavy 'Ooofff'. Oh well, I was in it now and sat in the mud, prising the water container open with both hands, watching with tired satisfaction as it swelled immediately. As I screwed the water filter onto the nozzle and secured the bag, I heard my name over the torrent of water. Kate had arrived!

Chatting happily about her day and mine, we descended towards the campgrounds and I collected my pack. Somewhere along the way, we lost Lee, gathered an armful of firewood from the ranger station and found our shelter for the night: a three-sided structure built with logs, a slightly pitched roof and an open sleeping platform set back inside which stretched about 3 metres wide, the wooden planks faded but mostly clean. Along the front edge of the shelter there was a gap and then a long log fixed as a seat. I guess you could sit on the edge of the sleeping platform with your legs dangling in the gap if it was raining, or sit out on the log if it was fine. It also gave some room to unpack and then hang your bag if the weather was torrential instead of doing it outside the shelter and making all your dry stuff wet. No one wants to do the wet unpacking when the shelter's full of other people; not good etiquette.

Speaking of good trail etiquette, Kate and I didn't know shit, so we put our tents up *inside* the wooden shelter, without the fly of course, so that we felt safer sleeping. I mean, this was lunacy, but we couldn't quite get our heads around the fact that if we just lay in there in our sleeping bags, then the armies of black flies and mosquitos would just eat our bare faces. We were also still in that transition period of feeling secure behind walls and a little vulnerable sleeping in the woods without them. Mix some bears into the equation with novice Brits and you get tents inside a shelter.

I gazed at the tents and felt that this definitely wasn't the adventurous image I'd seen for myself. The tent frames didn't quite fit and pinged their feet out over the lip, causing the tents to lose tension and sag one after the other, despite repeated fixing. Fuck it, I was too tired to care. Fire lit, we drank a celebratory beer that Kate had brought with her.

She drew deeply from the can and fixed her eyes on me. 'How did Kelly get on?' she asked. She and Kelly were of a similar fitness, and Kate had been worried about her own ability to get up and down Katahdin in a timely fashion so had some concerns for our new friend.

'I saw her on the way up.' I thought for a moment and then felt a little guilty. 'But, weirdly, I didn't see her coming back. I thought maybe she'd stopped at a lookout for a snack or something. Didn't ask Lee if he'd seen her either actually. Hmm.' I paused.

Kate was quiet too. I thought about how thirsty I had been on the way back, how tired I had been, and the dusk creeping into the trees even though the sun was far from fully dipping. I remembered that Kelly hadn't taken her water filter, thinking it was a bit unnecessary. I furrowed my brow trying to recall how much water she'd shoved in her bag before disappearing up the path that morning. Not much, I thought.

'She'll be fine. Won't she?' I really wasn't sure. How does it work out here when you're on your own but not *really* on your own? Who assumes responsibility for wondering where you are, and how *do* you worry about someone when we're all out here being wild, free and strong, so you don't risk looking like a clucky mother hen. It was slowly dawning on me that this hike was going to be a navigation of more than just woods. 'We could go and check the register, I guess?'

'Let's go.'

We jumped off the shelter ledge and walked back to the trail-head in the cooling early summer evening. It was still light enough to see. People in pockets of woodland were setting up fires and talking in hushed tones. Peals of laughter reached us and made me momentarily grieve for being alone and that forcible need to go and make new friends that solo travel gives you, but I knew that it would all come soon enough. For now, Kate and I were a team, and we needed to find Kelly.

*

'Haha, yeah, I just tooootally didn't bring enough water. He was just so great helping me out like that.'

Kelly was safe and well, reminiscing about the dreamboat we only knew from her as Kit, but who we would later know as Baby Milkshakes. Her Katahdin tale involved heroes (Kit), villains (the mountain) and an unreasonably hot and hard hike. It was a gripping yarn, but later, as Milkshakes and I crossed paths and hiked together through Virginia, the story would flesh out to include stopping her from drinking from a filthy puddle without a filter and helping her through rocks in a delirium to ensure she got down OK. Kelly was a card alright, but sadly we weren't to have her on trail for long.

'He was, like, soooo hot. Do we really have to move again now?' She sat fisting in peanut M&Ms from her gargantuan bag of trail mix. We'd been sitting awhile already and I was feeling frustrated with all of the stopping and starting.

'I think we need to move now to get to the campsite before dark.' I glanced at Kate for confirmation, and she nodded.

We were on Day 3 and moving slowly. Lee had also already had a nightmarish couple of days, and we were well updated on his misery: a tent that wasn't waterproof that he'd bought second-hand, holes in the netting too large to deter the swarms of mozzies we were up against and that (Shock! Horror!) tins and jars of supplies might actually turn out to be too heavy to carry for 10 days. We had found him that morning with wet kit, a soaked pack and a useless tent. 'I just kept going into the night and found an old boat, which I crawled under in the rainstorm,' he said. An old boat? What the hell? We were in the middle of nowhere. 'I don't think it was on trail,' he mumbled.

'Your *face*, Lee. Do you want some antihistamines?' I started to pull my pack off.

'No. It's OK.' He lifted his shirt and there were at least thirty more angry welts across his chest. 'I took off my wet clothes to sleep under the boat and then the ants got me as well as mosquitoes.'

I had never seen anyone more miserable, so I pressed the tablets into his hand with some Anthisan Cream and shook my head.

'Take it all. I have too much stuff anyway,' I said, walking away so he couldn't refuse. I left him smearing on cream and hefting his huge pack over his shoulders.

Lee: great to know but tough to be. He was determined to make the hike harder than it already was, and it was already pretty taxing.

The next evening I got to camp behind him, only to hear his screams and rants through the deep thickets down by a river. Pure pain and irritation; loud fury and disbelief. He couldn't seem to hear my yells to see if he was OK and so I marched down the blue blaze trail to the river to see if I could see him. There he was, across the river, scratched and defeated, filling up a bottle. He still couldn't hear or see me, so I filled mine and made it back to camp long before he emerged. He looked at my bottles and then at me. 'What's that?'

'Umm, water.'

'Where the heck?' he said, his face scratched and wild. I pointed meekly to the blue blazes. His shoulders sagged. 'I didn't get far enough in to see that. Urgh. I just wanted water so bad so I went through there – I could hear it!' He gestured to the thick bush, arms scratched and bleeding on top of his bug bites. With enormous defeat he grabbed the top of his heavy green pack and dragged it towards the shelter ledge. His axe fell out of the side onto the dirt. 'I'm so tired,' he mumbled. 'My pack's so heavy. I can't go as fast as I want and my knees hurt.'

I nodded at him, wanting to put my hand on his shoulder or offer some words of support, but we were deep into the 100 Mile Wilderness with no easy way out. Everything he brought he was going to have to take out. It wasn't possible to dump food in the woods – 'Leave No Trace' was serious, and even cooked food that you buried was enough to disrupt the natural order of things. I didn't want to give him any false hope.

Leave No Trace has seven principles that were made to help people who visit the outdoors to understand how they can leave the least impact. Three of these principles are to leave what you find as you found it; to dispose of your waste properly and respect wildlife – all things that are disrupted by dumping food in the woods behind you, even if it's without packaging and cooked. You might think you're helping feed wildlife, or that it'll biodegrade, but I had learned in my research that it might attract wildlife to humans or pollute a water system. You just don't know, so the best thing to do is, literally, leave no trace that you were there. Lee needed to saddle up and carry all his shit out, which of course he was always happy to do. Well 'happy' might have been a stretch.

'It'll be OK,' I said. 'You can push on through.' I wanted to laugh so hard at the thought of him screaming fury at the woods, but this was more indicative of my level of hysteria. At least he was honest and out loud. Kate and I were making things hard through our bickering. We were so different. We loved each other and had trodden a long road, but I was the eternal bubbly optimist and she the dour realist. In real life it was a clash made in heaven as it served to balance us, but finding that balance out here was proving agonising for us both.

Three days into the 100 Mile and the pressure was building on both of us not to lose our tempers and break down into swearing and the kind of sobbing that shoots big snot bubbles out of one nostril. Despite my preparation, I was beginning to feel fatigue with the intensity of focus and energy that the trail took: roots to step between, slick rocks to navigate and the weight of an overfull pack. I felt for Kate, as we had quickly learned that she was allergic to the pine trees we were surrounded by. Yet still she kept coming, strong and focused despite not getting the breaks that I did when I paused for her to catch up. We rested briefly and often, then forged forwards together, finding it hard in the misty light to see where the slippery roots began and ended underfoot. Both of us regularly took knees to the forest gods, filling the air with our thunks and tremendous sighs of resignation as we struggled back up to our feet and pushed on.

I felt a lurch in my gut when I realised that Kate was struggling and pushing herself hard. It was to be expected with such a short time to prepare, but she wasn't one to give up and I knew she didn't want me to worry so I continued to hike a little ahead and not crowd her. I was so glad she was here, out of character as it was, but I was beginning to suspect that it might have been a little easier to have taken being let down by Richard as a sign to come alone rather than agree to Kate's suggestion to wing-woman me. I had a feeling she might think the same.

I strode forwards at my natural cadence, dodging roots and heaving myself over blowdowns until I got into a rhythm and was trucking along pretty pleasantly. Regularly I'd notice she wasn't anywhere behind me so I'd stop and wait, terrifying myself by imagining scenarios where I had to tell her husband and children that she'd been lost down a deep crevice on a wild mountainside and I was sorry that I hadn't kept a closer eye on her. Then she'd arrive and we'd continue. In rain, drizzle, mist and storms she powered through without stopping. Her cadence may have been slower than mine but her strength of mind and steady rhythm meant she would appear in good time. She would stop to reach in her pack for a drink or snack and then plod forwards, urging me to go on ahead and stop waiting because it made her feel bad. So off I'd go, and our pattern would run again. I didn't think about it then, but later, when *I* joined a crew and was the slowest, I realised how shit it is. No breaks, no rest – using every ounce of energy just to keep up. Then, as soon as you arrive everyone heads off, finishing their break as you sit down, feeling like the slow, crap hiker even though you tried so hard.

The 100 Mile sounds pretty daunting but isn't as wild as it sounds. In reality, it just has no paved roads or services, but you can get access to trailheads for day hikes if you want to by utilising the dirt gravel logging roads into the interior. However, for us naive and 'just been born' hikers it might well have been the middle of the jungle in the 1800s. Just two nights previously things had been looking OK, but now we felt remote. The number of people we were seeing had thinned out dramatically and the trees seemed to crowd us when we took our eyes off them, sneaking closer into our peripheral vision like people hiding in tree suits shuffling up to shout 'Boo!' It was time for some space, and we found it.

On night four in the wild we pitched at Antlers, a camp space next to a glorious lake. There was room enough between trees on the flat, dry ground for us to set up away from others who were arriving. The solo hikers who hadn't found buddies or who preferred to be alone dripped steadily into camp until there were almost ten of us scattered around the lake shore, including a small group of giggly schoolgirls on an outdoor trip with their teacher. They set up in a central, obvious spot, but hikers arriving tucked themselves away in naturally screened tent spaces surrounded by greenery that had been clearly smoothed and flattened by the countless tents that had come before.

Sweeping away dry pine needles and cones with our hands, we set up shelters and started to cook. Eating was number one on the list – we were famished. After that, it was a couple of fistfuls of sweets, and then to the lake itself. Was it worth a dip? I had gone 5 days without a wash and felt grimier than I had ever remembered being. Lakes gave me the creeps for swimming, but this one was right there, glistening and beautiful, and I was feeling extremely in need of ablutions. So in I went in my knickers and sports bra, which I then took off underwater and washed as best I could. I didn't use any suds or chemicals so as not to pollute the water; a good rinse through was still going to make a difference... I hoped. I then jumped out so Kate could hop in and I could photograph her escapades in the lake for her children. It was too beautiful not to, and the dusky sunset with calls of birds and coyotes made us feel humble and happy.

I rested alone in my tent later that night, marvelling that I'd got up Katahdin, down again and now was *actually* in the 100 Mile. My hip hadn't popped out of place, my legs were working OK and my pain levels were really manageable; perhaps only a little higher than you'd expect anyone's to be after this quick immersion into physical activity. How had I got away with it? Had my body not caught up with what I was doing yet? Perhaps the pain was going to creep up on me slowly – it had before. In fact, I shouldn't be surprised if it did. My original illness had all started with only a few days of aching that... just... never went away.

In my 20s I got a twinge in my lower back. I ignored it and didn't go to the doctor. You don't bother the doctor unless your leg has fallen off. Life was fine; I was the stroke rower for my local gig club, I ran distance, I was trying to learn to surf and I was as fit as a fiddle studying for my PGCE in Exeter. But the Twinge wouldn't go away. I didn't moan. I perhaps mentioned it a few times, but I didn't moan. What's a bad back, eh? Every boring bastard has one of those, and those that do just moan about it. *I don't want to be like them*, I thought. *I don't want to be a moaner.*

My mind occasionally threw me back to my years working at a coastal hotel at home where one of the handsome young men who worked there in the holidays, like me, was always getting out of hoovering. Just the hoovering. Always moaning that his lower back hurt. I was convinced that he was just lazy, until he had a spinal tumour diagnosed and died a few weeks later in his early 20s. Sometimes I thought about this but shoved it back down. No space for that in the day-to-day.

The pain nagged me until I was struggling to lean over school desks at work and to get my shopping out from the car. I couldn't really row anymore, but the team were counting on me for the Gig World Championships on the Scilly Isles. I was eating ibuprofen and paracetamol like sweets to get through the days, and sometimes the pain would surge enough to make me vomit. But I couldn't give up on these things, the relationship I was in, the running, the rowing and my teaching. My body needed to buck the fuck up and get with the programme.

This is really where my pain story divides like sliding doors. In one direction is a sprain or a disk bulge that heals and I return to my normal life. The other is, unbeknownst to me at the time, the dark path into the woods of my life where I can't go backwards, only further in. This is the same for all of us who suffer from something chronic – in our minds *or* our bodies. Each week of pain, each therapy, each disappointment, each sacrifice closes a door behind you. This is the slow creeping beginning where you don't even realise that your life has started changing, but when you look back you realise, fuck, it was *then*. That moment. *That* was the last time I was my old self, my real self. Chronic illness is like the child catcher – it sneaks in under the radar of an ache or a pain but puts a bag over your head, slings you in the wagon and drives you away from yourself. By the time you've realised what's happened, you're abroad from your old life and there's no way to return. It's possible to come back sometimes. I know I did, but your original self is no longer there. It's moved. It's an empty house. And if you want to move back in, you've got to furnish it with all the new luggage you carry – stuff that's almost impossible to throw out.

Maybe this was the place to throw the luggage out. Maybe I could walk along this trail if my body let me, shedding bags and bags of the pain of the past as I moved through it, and go back to my old self. A kind of Leave No Trace but of my trauma not of my physical presence. Maybe by the time I reached the end I'd summit Springer Mountain as a tabula rasa, scoured and empty of all the old baggage. *Wouldn't that be nice?* I thought, rolling onto my other side, my Thermarest crinkling like a multipack of crisps as I did so. I smiled at the idea of being scrubbed clean and luggage-less, and fell asleep on the honest earth, listening to the crickets with a heart full of hope.

*

Rain was set to come in over the next few days and I had been asking my Garmin inReach® for weather updates sporadically. I wasn't looking forward to getting drenched but knew it was coming, and I also knew Kate wasn't going to like it much. I'd wondered how quickly I was going to be learning lessons about myself out here, and the answer was clearly pretty goddamn fast. I now realised that my positive nature wasn't just how I was but something I had unconsciously cultivated to get me through all the shit I'd experienced. It wasn't a choice but a need, and Kate's need to be scientific and deliberately realistic was pissing me off.

'Don't worry, Kate,' I said on Day 5. We were both careening towards 'broken, tired, bitten and in pieces.' Exhaustion was making us both drag our feet – we weren't strong enough to lift them up and over rocks, and we were swearing constantly as our shins ground into sharp edges. We had both fallen more times than we could count. I would try to keep spirits up. 'Don't worry,' I would repeat ad infinitum. 'I think we'll get into camp before dark tonight!' Big smile even though I didn't feel it. 'I can light a fire and make you dinner. I could go get water. It'll be early enough for eating in the light and setting up easily!' I arranged my face and set about getting behind my own optimism.

She would grimace and reply along these lines: 'By my calculation at the rate we're hiking and the terrain we are covering currently, we will take another 4½ hours to get to camp, *Gail*. Then part of the next route on the paper map shows we are going *up*hill more, slowing us further. That'll put us an hour after dark, and the water source at the next camp is another 0.3 miles down a steep track. In the dark. It will probably rain, based on the forecast, and so we'll be arriving wet, and in the dark. Let's be realistic.'

Oh, for fuck's sake.

'I don't WANT to be fucking realistic, *Kate*. I want to be a bit fucking positive. I want to *imagine* that it might all be OK, or I won't get through the next three fucking hours before it even gets dark.'

I threw a pole on the ground, clearly crosser than I realised. 'Why can't we have a bit of cheer? Why can't we *pretend* it's going to be great and ease up?' I frowned my dirtiest frown at her. Useless in the face of her obstinacy. I was just as annoying to her in my Tigger-esque idiotic hopefulness as she was to me in her hyper-logical realism.

We were escalating in moments like this. Sparking off the old relationship from school and moving to our established positions – ones that didn't work out well for me back then. But now things were a little different. I was more able to find resilience and not back down. I didn't like how it felt, but in this situation I was probably being unkinder to her than she was to me. Perhaps fair enough in the grand scales of our lives, but not someone I was comfortable being. My patience was becoming short, my excitement to dig into my epic journey nipping at my heels. I didn't *want* to be brought into a negative mindset about the whole trail by my friend who got to go home in just under a week. I had to try to keep my idiotic optimism going or I wouldn't ever make the distance. I needed to find a way to make it work for both of us or we were going to hit the skids. That's how I felt anyway, and we weren't even halfway through the 100 Mile. Christ, I needed to get a grip.

CHAPTER FIVE

No Shining Armour

I winced, my shin scraping the sharp corner of the jagged rock step for the second time that minute, my usual painkillers not touching the raw immediate injuries my body was sustaining through each day. I was getting angry thinking about it. Why was I going *backwards*? Why was I here in the dark and rain, 70 miles into the 100 Mile Wilderness and ascending elevation that I had already completed and descended an hour before?

I tripped, falling sharply forwards but saving myself, braced on slick, cold rock. I'd done this – White Cap Mountain, the highest in the 100 Mile – hours ago. At the top I'd sat watching storm clouds gather as the incredible views of Maine and endless pine forests were gobbled up by mist and the incoming evening.

*

Earlier that day I'd reached Logan Brook shelter and scooted my butt onto the wooden base of the three-sided hut. Only one other person was inside, and I gave him a smiley 'Hey!' I was still in the phase of enjoying the double-take I'd get when folks heard my British accent.

'Hey,' he replied coolly. I vaguely recognised him and asked if we'd met before somewhere in the past few days. The only people we passed were usually going north doing a section hike; it was too early in the season for northbound thru hikers to have made it up here yet.

'Yeah,' he said. 'You and your friend helped me out when I got turned around up there by Potaywadjo.'

Fuck, I remembered now. Oh, man, this poor guy. I had first passed him going north when I was on my way to stop for the night at the Potaywadjo Lean-To. He had hustled past me with purpose about 40 minutes out from the shelter, going down-trail as we were going up. Just a nod and a hello. That's all. A little while later (this was just after Lee's water fiasco, when he was settled into the shelter for the night and Kate and I had set up our tents by the big pines), we were all sitting with our butts along the edge of the shelter lip, eating our food and listening to our muscles groaning as they unwound from the day. It was then that we heard a rustle. Out from behind the shelter, from a direction we hadn't yet explored, came a man in the dusky evening.

'Ummm, hi,' he mumbled. 'Can y'all tell me the way to leave camp southbound?' 'Hatchet', who was really Lee with his new trail name, jumped down off the edge of the platform and walked over to him, explaining that the camp layout was a little confusing, something which I, feeling lazy by this time of the evening, hadn't fully realised. Apparently there were three exits and entrances, with one of the clear-cut paths being a loop around past the privy, and then back onto the northbound trail. The tricky part was that it initially headed off southbound to hit the privy first, and then gently looped back to the northbound trail. It was easy to go the wrong way and not even realise. The hiker, whose name was Dan, had apparently fallen foul of this over 2 hours before.

'I've been here already,' he said miserably. 'Damn hiker in here before told me thataway was south. G'tting dark under these here trees and I didn't realise I'd done a goddamn loop back to the same damn place. I saw this shelter comin' up and I was just so happy I'd made it, but it's the same one I was at two fuckin' hours ago.'

I couldn't look at the guy – I didn't want to add to his obvious embarrassment. Hatchet, in his matter-of-fact way, pointed out the correct southbound route and, to my surprise, Dan just turned and walked towards it, disappearing into the gloom without a word. There was not another camp spot listed on my map for 10 more miles. Jesus.

'Oh, that was you,' I said, with a wry smile. 'Sorry that happened. You camp OK?' He said yes and asked where my friend was. 'Good question,' I replied, remembering that I was a bit worried about how long she'd taken to catch up.

Dan and I kicked our heels at the shelter for a while. I went to filter water at the stream nearby and wandered back. Digging into my pack I pulled out two Cliff bars and offered him one. We ate in silence, listening to the breeze through the pines and keeping out of the hot sun. It was about 40 minutes later that Kate arrived and filled her bottles at the stream. We agreed that she'd rest a little and I'd go on ahead up the mile of elevation to the top of White Cap. It wasn't an easy climb, but the trail was beautifully maintained – no mean feat when it was so deep in the woods. Steps had been cut into the mountainside, which made things slightly easier, but I still found myself leaning on my poles and gasping for breath, cursing my too-heavy pack. Peeking through the thickly needled branches, I guessed that I was in for a big view at the top. I was learning that such is the way of Maine (and probably the rest of the trail ahead) – the foreplay of mud, sweat and claustrophobic tree cover gives way to an explosive mountaintop view at the summit when you emerge from the green gloom.

I could feel the hot, wet chafe of pack straps where my vest had ridden up on my back, pulling back the pale, juddery flesh on my love handles and exposing tender skin for the tag-team of mosquitoes I'd been amassing since Katahdin. I knew I couldn't give these things the slightest bit of attention or they'd utterly overwhelm me, so I just kept pushing up, tired legs taking missteps and my clumsy feet skittering rocks off the edge into the seething morass of wild woody fingers below.

You know when you're getting close to the top of a peak in Maine because the soupy thick branches begin to thin out and more light gets in. You'd think that seeing skeletal branches and spindly brittle trunks would make me sad about nature, but no, I was just maniacally delighted that this meant the end of the climb and some big boulders to place my tired ass on at the top.

And it was worth the effort. Popping out of the tree cover like a grasping hand at the end of a tight sweater sleeve, I breathed a huge lungful of clear air and looked for miles in every direction. I could see nearly 200 miles of the Appalachian Trail from up here, stretching from Katahdin to the Bigelow Horns in the distance. Little did I know how much was to happen between now and those peaks, which looked so insignificant to my tired eyes.

Settling myself on a rock, I opened my maw and fisted handful after handful of the sugar-rainbow inside it: M&Ms, Skittles, trail mix and Cliff bars were thrown down, which made me regret only having half a litre of water left to follow them with. Sitting still awhile, my internal barometer moved from elation, to calm, to cold, to annoyed and worried. I watched the dark clouds play Grandmother's Footsteps with me every time I looked down or turned to dig in my pack for a sweater, and the first fat drops of cold rain down my neck told me that I shouldn't have been so eager to push on and upwards without checking the weather for us.

Once Kate had arrived, we didn't spend long at the summit. We were both tired and the weather eclipsed what could have been an argument as thunder grew ever closer. I estimated it would take 45 minutes to get down, maybe more. It was definitely going to feel like more when being chased by a storm and fork-lightning up on top of a bald. I was still learning how to estimate distance and speed over tricky ground so at this stage my guesses were worth as much as my opinions on how to make Baked Alaska (poor at best), so we just set off.

As the rain started to belt down, Kate yelled at me over the thunder to, 'GO, GO, GO!' She was right. The top of a mountain in a storm was not the place to be, and the sooner we got down the sooner we could find better shelter.

The flat dirt of the top quickly moved into a slimy stream downwards, keeping me heel-skidding and holding on to spindly trunks to stay upright. Next: rough-hewn, deep stone steps covered in pine needles and rotted mulch. Perfect for toppling down with a heavy pack in rain and poor visibility, to be found weeks later lodged head-first between some boulders and undergrowth at the bottom of a ravine, nibbled by woodland foragers. Fuck.

Laser focus and a seat-of-the-pants madness propelled me to the bottom after about an hour, with skinned legs and blisters pretty much everywhere that something had touched my sad, wet body. It was dusky as the trail levelled out at the bottom, and what felt like a perpetual descent into the bowels of a beast became less panicked and much safer. I readjusted my straps, flumped my pack up a bit with some pride and had a word with myself, accepting that we probably wouldn't be going the further 4 miles that I'd planned to get to the next shelter.

Hmmm, where would we sleep? I pulled up the map and looked. Just around the bend by about 5 minutes was a flat camp space, affording me a little bit of relief. It felt like it was my responsibility to check out and make it nice for when Kate arrived, so I took the risk of going a bit further without her. I didn't expect to meet anyone this late between shelters, so I couldn't quite make out what I was seeing set back from the trail in the thickets of deeper forest. Twinkling lights and soft voices. Not the noise from a hiker or two settling in for a sleep. A group. How?

It faded out as I rounded a corner only to appear again from what seemed like a different space back inside the woods. I was reminded of Wood Elves firing up their feasts deep inside Mirkwood in Tolkien's *Hobbit*, only to lure unsuspecting walkers deeper into the maze. Fuck that. I was going nowhere near it. Jesus Christ, why couldn't I just have an easy day? Now I had to deal with *elves*? Maybe I was hallucinating in exhaustion.

Seeing the sign for the old campground loom out of the gloom ahead, I sped up, only to howl at the 'closed for trail maintenance' sign plastered over the top. So this was it – a trail crew. Volunteers come out to the trail all summer and spend weeks living deep in the backwoods to repair and renovate steps and paths for hikers. Amazing, but today their benevolent camping closure was possibly going to push me over the edge.

'Hello?! Haloooo?!' Gently pushing through the branches towards the light, I figured that a bit of British-accented politeness might get me what I desperately needed – permission to stop and camp for the night. 'Errr, excuse me?' I edged through into a clearing and the circle of hardy mountain-ready folk standing around a warm fire all turned to look at me, a bedraggled goon who had most of the gear and definitely no idea. It was, remember, still only Day 5 of my hiking career.

After a little negotiation and some incredible kindness from the crew, I backed out of the clearing and onto the trail. Picking a little clear spot for us on the side of the path, I set about putting up my tent. The campground space itself was filled with the maintenance folks and their gear, but they had no objection to us setting up trailside. This put me right in the pathway of the murderers and rapists I generally thought were always hot on my heels, but I didn't have many options and wouldn't be alone, so it was all fine by me. Deciding that my priority would be offering to cook for Kate when she arrived, I sought out a water source to replenish my bottles. This was, of course, 300 metres down a slippery off-trail blue blaze where I'm sure bears were sizing me up, but I grabbed 2 litres of ice-cream-cold water from the spring and dragged myself back to the top, fully expecting to see a cross Kate waiting by my tent. But no.

And so it was that I found myself heading back up those sharp-cut White Cap steps into the darkness, skinning my knees to find my friend.

*

Bone tired, we stood on the path after I'd located her stepping down what she termed as 'Stonehenge fuckers' towards the bottom of the mountain. She set up her shelter, and some unpacking, mud-scrambling and stove-cooking later, we both sat in our tent openings, looking at each other with a little more kindness and trying to find the good in our day of achievements, which felt a little more like a day of survival. Despite being only around 8 p.m., it was fully dark and there wasn't much left to do except crawl into bed and sleep.

In the stillness of thinking about asking our bones to move, we heard footsteps. Not the steady steps of someone heading down to the spring from the maintenance team, and not the weary slop of someone exhausted from a day of hiking. It was a... bouncy stride. One full of mischief and coiled energy. Then a figure all but skidded sideways into our little camp. Someone arriving with a palpable energy field around them, who stopped dead centre between the tents.

'Yo!' it said. Six feet 4 tall and built like a brick shithouse. 'Yo, girls! What's happenin'?'

With a backpack smaller than Fievel's, the mouse in *An American Tail*, our new trail friend stood grinning at us. In the dim light of our head torches we appraised him: long, brown hair, a big bushy beard and a charismatic grin that seemed to lift the mood of our tiny camp a number of notches without doing anything particular to earn it.

Kate raised her eyes from the dirt and old firepit she'd been staring at. She knows a dickhead like a fisherman knows the tides, and I could see from her face she wasn't sure.

'Wooof!' he said. 'Damn, that was a good day.'

'How far have you come?' I wondered whether our valiant attempts to scale mountains *and* do distance today had been anywhere near comparable.

'Oh, just since Antlers.'

What? 25 miles? What was this guy about? I was already feeling that familiar rise of interest in someone so unusual. He was disarmingly friendly and, more than anything, had an air of capability that in this moment I was desperate for. Like someone had slotted a chair underneath me as I was about to collapse from standing and encouraged me to sit for a moment, to rest with the support of something stronger. I became aware that I had a dumb grin plastered across my face looking at him and snuck a glance to my right at Kate. *Ha!* She had exactly the same look: a half-smirk and sparkly eyes. Good. This was good.

In the dusk I asked him a couple of other brief questions about how long he'd been on trail. He was still standing and we were sitting, still emerging with our heads and legs like turtles from our tent shells. I felt briefly desperate – I didn't want this ball of energy to leave and burn through the dark trailside camp we'd made. He dumped his bag into the grass on the side of the path and gave the old fire between us a little nudge with his foot.

'Better get some sticks for this, hey?' He grinned, and I knew he was staying.

I watched in awe as he gathered some wood, started a little fire and then sat in the dirt, not at all worried about getting muddy. Peeling off his damp socks, he lay them on stones around the fire and settled back down with dirty, slightly steaming feet, and pulled his purple hood over his long dark hair. 'What's your name?' I asked, mesmerised.

'Buckshot.'

'Haha.' He had said it '*Buuuuck-Shaahhht*', and the accent tickled me. 'You look more like a Viking with your big beard and being 6 feet 4!' I said, laughing.

'Well that sounds good to me,' he said, grinning right back.

He tipped out his tiny bag. Packets of tuna, ziplocks with a range of mystery ingredients and some snack bars tumbled out, alongside a few other essentials and some fluttery bits of fabric.

'Is that it?' I asked incredulously. 'Where's the rest of your stuff?'

'Ha! That's it. I don't need any more. Well, actually, to be honest I mighta fucked up on the food, but that's OK – I'll just go without and crush those miles to get outta here in a few days anyway.'

I thought about my pack and cringed with embarrassment. *Urgh*. I had about 17 times more food than him and I only needed it until halfway through, when we'd get our food pickup off the dirt road from Old Man.

'I've got some you can have,' Kate and I chorused. We glanced at each other and grinned, then waterfalled all manner of Haribo, soup packets, oatmeal and granola bars on this man we hadn't known for more than 30 minutes. He willingly took what we offered and set about flapping his little pieces of fabric out and magicking them into his shelter, almost right on the path. I looked at it, weighing up exposing myself as a novice (and a tit) by asking him about his set-up, or just nodding towards it and making that face that men use when they look inside each other's car bonnets. Like 'Yeah, I see what you've done there' and all that. Considering my bulging pack, legs full of scratches and the fact he knew we'd done a *huge* 12 miles that day, I figured I wasn't fooling anyone.

'How do you sleep under… ? Err, what happens when it… um? What's that?' I gestured at the sheet pegged 2 feet off the ground, with his shortened hiking poles supporting each end.

'That's ma tarp.' He grinned, wriggling underneath it, feet first, and then expertly pulling in all his belongings as his arms darted out at different angles to gather them all. 'See?' he said, muffled by a quilt and all his things now in the tarp-burrow. 'Super light, keeps me dry and easy to put up anywhere.'

I had lots of thoughts about this. What about when it rained – didn't the water just run over his body because the tarp sides didn't touch the ground? And the wind – didn't that just blow right through? And bears. BEARS COULD REACH IN FOR SNACKS. On that, I realised that Kate and I hadn't gone about our nightly ritual.

'Bear bags, Kate,' I said. Not a question. A statement. Bear bags were a Kate job. One of the things she'd worked hard on before coming with me was how to tie the knots and hang the bags. I didn't do this. I'm afraid of knots. I can't understand the many different planes that the rope has to go through on all those stupid diagrams and it just makes me mad that I don't get it, so I had decided to not think about it. Luckily, she had. She dragged herself up and moved towards her food sack, and then to mine, which I'd snapped at the top and slung out of my tent. I heard a snort of laughter from under the tarp.

'Bearrrr bags? Fuckin' *bear bags*?' Our new friend clearly found this very amusing. 'You don't need those.' He poked his head out of the tarp, until his whole head, aside from his big beard, was clear. 'Ain't no bears around here that're brave enough to come get food from us. Maine hunts bears, and they ain't stupid. You don't need to hang yer food. Sling it in yer tent.'

Our new friend had a point. When settlers first arrived in Maine, the black bear population was so large that they caused myriad problems for people. In an effort to nip this in the bud, the state put its first bounty on bears in 1770. Since then, bear hunting has been a popular pastime in Maine and other states, with cash rewards for hunting bears only disappearing in 1957. Although well regulated, popular, and in keeping with our friend's laissez-faire attitude to bear bags, hunting of bears has actually *decreased* in the state, meaning that the number of bears has doubled in the last 35 years because hunters aren't shooting enough of them. I love this statistic for the bears, but not for being careless with my food. As the saying goes (I didn't know the saying yet but I would soon enough), a fed bear is a dead bear, so I was keen to get that food into those trees.

'Well, you know, we just want to,' I said to his tarp, as I gestured at Kate that we should go hang the bags. She nodded and we scoped the clearing around the trail where we had pitched up.

94

Nothing obvious. You've got to find a branch at the right height, that's the right distance from the trunk so a bear can't shimmy up and lean out to grab it. Smart little ursines. We eventually found something that could work and tried to get it up. Kate was the knot-tying logistical one, and I was the jumping, throwing one. After a couple of tries, it was clear I was too short to get it over, and we looked like a pair of idiots. As I crouched to take another leap, I realised that all 6 feet 4 of our friendly hiker was standing right behind us, grinning from ear to ear.

'You want some help?' he asked.

I nodded, furious that I had to let a man step in to help but so exhausted that I didn't really care anymore. He put out a giant paw, took the bag from me and extended his long arm up, casually hooking the bags onto a long bough. 'That'll do it,' he said, and loped back.

Kate had already gone to pass out in her sleeping bag, so I padded back to my tent in time to see Buckshot's head and shoulders disappear under his tarp. Done for the day. It was silent as I walked by, but as I unzipped my tent fly I heard, 'G'night, Appalachian Gail. Glad to have met ya.'

'You too, Buckshot.' And I slept more soundly that night than before.

*

The next morning I stirred awake to the sounds of low voices close to my tent.

'So, I'll lead this morning's stretch, and you guys think of a stretch of your own, and somewhere you've always wanted to visit in the world. Then when I've done mine I'll point to a person and you can show us your stretch and talk to us as we copy. Everyone good?'

I wriggled outside in all my layers. 'MORNING,' I honked with a grin at the group of nine or so people in a circle across the path. 'How are you all? What's going on?'

'Stretching circle,' said a familiar face from the trail crew the night before.

'Cool.' I thought for a beat. 'Um, can I join in?'

They looked at each other and one or two shrugged. 'Sure, OK.'

So I gave Kate's tent a little nudge with my foot as I heaved myself up and went to join them. She emerged and with her happy-sullen face I knew she was begrudgingly pleased to be involved. We stretched, bent, hopped and steadied ourselves for the next 10 minutes, listening to people show all manner of body movements (of which some were more like someone had turned the music off in musical statues than stretching), and listened to stories and dreams about visits to Italy, Japan and Canada. Buckshot didn't stir.

After the crew had hoicked their tools and bags up and dispersed into the woods, we set about packing up. Kate went to get water from the spring (no bears) and I chatted with a recently emerged Buckshot. I finished squashing a million things down into my pack and fisting the tendrils back inside – a constant battle for someone who bought an ultra-lite pack and then stuffed it with enough shit to sink a ship.

'I'm gonna head down a couple blue blazes today to see the waterfalls at Gulf Hagas. Wanna come?'

Looking up at him through my 4-day-old hair-nest, I thought this sounded like a fantastic idea. Adventure! He was so confident and I was so buoyed up by his enthusiasm after my days of slog that this was like a little electric jolt. Kate though. I couldn't leave Kate.

'Do it, mate! Do it.' She ambled up behind us, arms filled with slithery slick water pouches that wouldn't stay put. 'Fuck me, it'll be great. You can go the longer way on a blue blaze, and I'll follow the AT. By the time you get back on the path, then I'll have made it to about the same place as you but at my own pace! Perfect.' She looked hard at me. She meant it.

'I don't know. I feel bad. What if you get lost or something happens? You don't have the GPS and the phones don't work. What if we miss meeting? How will we ever find each other again?'

'Jeesus.' Buckshot grinned. 'Just relax. It's one path. Choose a shelter. We'll go there and so will she, and no one leaves until the others get there. Easy.'

I wasn't sure. A blue blaze is a spur trail leading off the main trail and can lead to all kinds of things: a shelter, view, campground or some beautiful natural feature like… waterfalls. Gulf Hagas, I was told by Buckshot, was well worth the visit. A long, tumbling gorge with rushing snow-melt waters foisting themselves through narrow gaps and long drops. Dammit. It did sound exciting and I *was* here to experience things.

'OK! I'm in. You *promise* you will be OK, Kate?'

'Yes, yes. Fuck off and go. See you later.' She grinned and gestured down the path, where Buckshot was already steadily wandering ahead.

'Fuck!' OK. OK, fuck it. Right. See you soon. Don't go off path. Keep safe! I'll see you at the shelter.' And I was gone, hop-skipping after the long-legged sturdy mystery who had vanished between the trees.

*

'Hey-heyyy, Appalachian Gail,' he drawled as he sensed me coming up behind him. So we walked, a few miles still following the white blazes before we turned off into the unknown. I balanced on rocks over swollen streams as he moved his huge frame nimbly between trees and under overhangs. I asked him what he 'did', a question I was later to become aware was not OK with many hikers on trail, but at this stage I was still happily blundering into trail faux pas and having the time of my life.

He had been a cook (or 'a chef' as he first presented it, later to be a cook at a college canteen) and was now a 'full-time hiker'. To my amazement, this was his third stint on the Appalachian Trail, and his first time Sobo. He'd hiked northbound a few years before – his first long hike – then almost completed another Nobo before deciding to hike the Continental Divide Trail last year, a much longer and more remote trail stretching 3,100 miles from where the Mexican border meets the USA in New Mexico, to the northern border of Alberta, Canada. It was a distant dream of mine to hike it, and I was under no illusion that it was easy. Not so much a simple trail but a journey through an immensely diverse landscape, it is described by the Continental Divide Trail org as a 'living museum of the American West'. I enjoyed hearing him describe the water-carries and animals, but then he tired of talking and peppered me with questions instead.

The flurry of our excited chat petered out into companionable silence. The only thing slowing my roll was my unwieldy pack catching on branches and my feet slipping sideways from slick rocks into the mud. Then a blue blaze. It was time to turn off trail.

We had been walking a little while. I wasn't paying much attention to the trail because we were deep in conversation again. I was in awe of his ease and comfort in the surroundings. We discussed childhood, the UK, language, and then the conversation turned to Netflix, TV shows and podcasts. It was a little while into our chattering about *My Favourite Murder* and other unsolved abduction shows that I began to feel a tickling unease.

'And how do these women just not even second-guess when the dude is clearly psycho?' he said from ahead of me, pushing back branches as he shouldered through.

A cold wash spread from my lower back around to my tummy, making my guts clench and my jaw tighten before I had any idea why. I started sweating and began to feel nauseous. What was it? Buckshot was four paces ahead, his huge legs stepping over blowdowns and pulling greenery out of the pathway – this pathway where no one else had been for a very long time. My hindbrain grabbed me and shook me into understanding. Danger.

DANGER.

I swooned at my idiocy. What was I doing? How could I have prepared for 10 months for this trip and considered every conceivable aspect of it, and then found myself following a huge man I didn't know for over a mile down track in the deepest forest imaginable to a 'waterfall' with no signal, service or way of contacting my friend.

Is this how it happens? So blithely and easily we are lured into vulnerability and then it's too late.

I've lived an adult lifetime of trying to balance my deep fear and lived experience with the usual gut warnings that we all get and should listen to. 'Listen to your gut, ladies' is the usual mantra. 'If something feels wrong then it usually is!' Well. Is it? What if you have already, like me, been assaulted in your life? Then perhaps on some level you're insecure about your judgement and ability to make decisions, because once you made some and they were deeply wrong.

'So, anyway, I've been hearing that there are some great *new* podcasts about true crime. Apparently there's one where these people talk about folks who go missing, and they're tryna figure out where they went. Kinda cool but weird too, y'know?' He looked back at me with what I saw as a sinister smile.

This is where we were at. I flipped back into focus. *Fuck.* I've come out here with a murderer. One who's not even trying to be secretive. I watched him ahead, clearing the way for me and not looking backwards. I jumped as a returning branch flipped itself out of the bush next to me and brushed my shoulder. I knew I was going to die. Only choice – keep him talking.

'So, Buckshot. Ha. Um. Well, do you have friends out here? Didn't you say you were hiking with some other people too? A guy?'

'Oh, yeah, Lazybean and Dozer. She's kinda new to hiking. He was waitin' on her and they were takin' ages, so I just carried on walking. They're behind. I'll see 'em.'

I wondered then if the friends were a lie to make him seem more approachable. My mind was spiralling. What if there was someone waiting for us ahead, in a place already laid out with where they come and take women? We were *deep* in the woods. I hadn't seen or heard a soul for a long time, and it was clear people didn't take this path. I could feel my body moving forwards whilst at the same time not wanting to move forwards.

Don't. Give. Myself. Away.

I was wet with sweat, my skin pulsing with a thousand heart-beats. I wanted to make a joke, to make light of my fear. I wanted to not feel so caught in the gossamer strings of deliberation: between feeling like I was afraid and wanting to run; between the risk of embarrassing myself into utter mortification and the dreadful instilled coding that was telling me not to be rude or disrespectful. I didn't want to make a fuss. I was too afraid I'd be mocked – or even worse – actually incite the violence I feared would come.

Stupid. Stupid. *Stupid.*

I remained mute as I walked towards what I was convinced was now my fate. My death would be my reward for trying to achieve something so far outside of my comfort zone. *Of course* this was it for me. My *Final Destination* moment. Always here, waiting for me.

With slippery hands riven with red mosquito bites, I tried to unzip my bumbag without changing the cadence of my walk, lest he hear and turn around. Wedging one finger and my thumb through the tiny gap, I managed to winkle out my knife – a gift from my father before I left home. I flicked the blade open and held it behind my back, all the while still walking deeper into the woods with this man. Mortified, terrified and choked by my blinding fear. But then I stopped. My grey matter was tallying up options and suddenly triaged them down to a course of action. I said clearly, 'Buckshot.'

He stopped. 'Yeah?'

My voice was trembling. 'I need to ask. I mean, I've been thinking. I'm just going to ask. Look, if you were going to do it, it wouldn't matter anyway that I've asked, but I just can't bear it.' So direct. Now cut to the *chase*.

'What the heck's the matter?' His bushy beard corralled a concerned line where previously a big smile had sat. 'Sure, ask anything you want.' He leaned slightly forwards towards me on his stick and obviously noted my pasty skin and wide eyes.

'Gail, what is it?' Such a long pause. Such suffocating silence except the tick of greenery unfolding behind us to cover the scene. Complicit. Nature more his friend than mine.

I took a deep breath.

'Are you going to kill me?'

He paused and squinted at me for a brief moment, serious and sinister, before throwing his head backwards and laughing so loudly it made me jump out of my skin.

Such embarrassment. It consumed me in an instantaneous roar. A Roman Candle of shame. *Of course* my gut was wrong. My compass broke when I was 18. It's just set up for hyper-vigilance now.

'Well I just need to *know*. I can't *bear* it. I've been thinking about it for the last 10 minutes and we've been talking all about murder podcasts and I'm miles away and don't know the way back and…' He was grinning and proffered a hand in my direction, patting the air and still lazed louchely on his stick. Unfazed.

'It's OK. It's OK, Appalachian Gail,' he said, drawling out my name like a cowboy. 'Listen. I'm not gonna kill you. I just really wanna see these waterfalls. Damn hikers always miss the blue blazes because they don't wanna walk an extra mile or two. Well, fuck it. I decided this time I was gonna see the good stuff and thought you might want to see it too. Sooooo, I am not gonna kill you and I'm sorry you've been... Wait. What're you holding?'

'Nothing.' Fuck.

'What you got there?'

'Honestly, nothing, just fixing my straps,' I managed to stuff the knife into a side pocket on my pack. His stillness, surety and comfort with being so off trail, so deep in the woods with no fear of being alone out here were amazing and so soothing to me. I so desperately wanted to be like him and not feel so scared. I wanted to go on with him, but I knew I couldn't. I was still so afraid. This stirring in me – the memory of before the fear – I knew going through the process to get my courage would bring physical pain with it too. My mental trauma always loved some physical company.

Later, I'd look back, tell this story and laugh. But not now. I felt sick, ashamed, embarrassed, and angry at my gut for giving me warnings too late in my life, and me being wrong about them – ruining yet more chances at fun. 'Hmm,' I said, looking at my feet.

'What you wanna do?' he asked, looking busy swigging water from his pack and giving me space. I was too embarrassed to speak, a deep red.

'I'm going to go.'

'OK.' Pause.

'I don't know how to get back and not double hike all those miles though.' I wanted to bark hysterically at the lunacy of asking my imagined captor for directions home.

'OK. No problem.' And he explained the route kindly and patiently, then: 'It's OK you know, G. No judgement. Here in the woods it all comes out. No hiding from nature. She knows.'

I nodded, turned and walked. Looking over my shoulder until he'd gone and then running. Racing through the path and crying. Hot tears of shame. Memories of hands on me in the dark; fear I couldn't contain. The hounds of hell were coming for me and I ran for what seemed like forever in the lonely forest, looking for my friend. It wouldn't be the last time.

CHAPTER SIX

The Real Beginning

After I'd caught up with Kate and gathered my tears back in, we ploughed on, both slowing as the elevation increased. Buckshot passed me later in the afternoon on strong legs and, with a cheery smile, hollered hello, checking in on me as I cringed in embarrassment. It was as though he'd just forgotten, which suited me just fine.

The days blended together as we became dirtier and more exhausted. I became more short-tempered with Kate the further we fell behind. Finally we met Lazybean and Dozer, wearing tunics and reading paperbacks by the fire on the night our paths crossed, ripping pages read and tossing them into the flames to keep their pack weight as low as possible.

It seemed an interminable amount of time to still be in the 100 Mile Wilderness, but we had only a day or two to go. We were filthy – a level of grime I never felt possible. Falling in streams, down mudbanks and being rained on for over 40 hours at one point meant that every item we had was damp, cold or putrid and our food was nearly gone. There was only the shit stuff left. Oh, what a bad decision – leaving the grossest food until last when we felt the worst. We had no choices though. We had to keep going, imagine the beer at the end, and mentally remove ourselves from the discomfort.

Most other hikers were suffering, so we took solace in each other. Some trail friends passed us fast and went on in a final

GAIL MULLER

burst of energy to get to the end of this stretch. Others caught up
and joined us, staying close. Our legs took us down from mountaintops into bogs and swamps where whatever was left of our
skin was feasted upon by the bugs. Tiredness made us less alert,
brought home to me by a foolish misstep on a slimy rock which
made me skid forwards towards a steep edge. In an effort to not
topple over, I pulled my body back into a swerve and a few rapid
steps in the other direction – down trail again, teetering over the
edge of another slimy, slick descent and not finding balance in
time, momentum pushing me off the little precipice I had tried
to stabilise on. Any split-second relief I felt from avoiding a more
fateful fall disappeared as I landed on the side of the trail over the
sharp spikes of some lower tree branches. I could feel one of them
had ripped through my top, and I gasped at the sharp sting of
slightly broken skin between my lower ribs. In that brief moment
of slowed time I realised that my heavy pack hadn't quite yet
caught up with me. Mere microseconds later it arrived, slamming
into my back and wedging the sharp stick through the scratch it
had made and deeper in between my ribs. Such pain!

I lay unmoving for a few more moments, gathering my wits.
Then I gently and slowly extricated my arms from my pack straps
and unbuckled the belt. As the pack rolled and fell into the mud
beside me, I braced my hand on the floor and pushed off the stick I
was impaled on, gasping at the pain and looking gingerly down for
damage. A rip through my top, a precise rip through my double-
layered sports bra and a genuine dark bloody hole in my side where
the stick had pushed in. Nothing too bad, just a little painful to
move, but I was aware of how close I had come to a more signifi-

106

cant injury. It was clear that I really needed the rest and respite that was only days away.

And then, the end was tantalisingly within sight. We had aimed to emerge from the forest late that final evening, but it became clear that it just wasn't possible. We were slowing and frustrated that we had to spend another night in the woods a mere 2 hours from the exit point, but it was what it was.

The next morning our shelter friends had organised a shuttle with Shaw's, the legendary hostel at this side of the 100 Mile, for 6:30 a.m. at the trailhead, and asked us if we'd like in. Shaw's sits in the town of Monson, the first town that any southbound hiker comes to after days (ten for Kate and me) of privation, filth and exhaustion. For many hikers, the 100 Mile Wilderness is truly like nothing they've ever experienced and puts the body through some semblance of shock and awe. The idea of a shower, warm bed and home-cooked food becomes a fixation the closer to town you hike. Shaw's looms large in the imagination.

In the late '70s, the Shaws started welcoming in hungry, tired hikers and cooking up huge breakfasts to feed them. Since then, the hostel has retained their name but moved through different ownerships, still keeping the traditions of excellent breakfasts and a warm welcome alive, or so we had been repeatedly told. Now owned by Poet and Hippie Chick, thru hikers themselves, it was raved about more than ever. I was so thoroughly ready to wash and eat that I didn't have much patience for a slow 4:30 a.m. start, foot-dragging hiking and the clear likelihood of missing the shuttle.

But then we were out. Emerging into the light to a hard-top road and civilisation! Swept up by the shuttle, we were handed a welcome beer at 6:30 a.m. – a classic Shaw's tradition, whatever time you arrive. No sleep for us!

Showering off 10 days of grime was a biblical experience, and the hot water baptism brought new vigour. I stood in a dreamlike state in the wooden hall next to the bathroom door I had chosen, slathered in dirt and high on hunger and exhaustion. It was 7:30 a.m. and I would have been swaying from my one beer if a hiker I'd come to know as 'Rock Naps' hadn't swiped it to drink the moment I put it down to find clean loaner clothes. '*Oh*, my *bad*!' he exclaimed. 'Shit, dude, I'll get you another later.' Well, anyone who wanted a beer at 7:30 in the morning needed it more than me, and he was clearly a nice guy.

The bathroom door opened and I walked into a cloud of hot steam. There was nothing 'clinical' about this hostel. Each of the many bathrooms was a warm family space with an abundance of warm towels, toiletries to choose from and the essentials that we hikers didn't have: nail clippers, scrubbing brushes and wash cloths. In the stingingly hot water, I stood watching rivers of the darkest brown stream down my bruised and battered legs into the tub. I had never been so grateful. Over a never-ending breakfast with a pancake avalanche to eat, we met and chatted to our first northbound hikers, the friendly and helpful Resident Daddy and his crew. Hikers who had travelled over 2,000 miles – battle weary and lean – breaking bread with fresh, plump, new hikers 100 miles in, eager to glean info. It was hard for them to know what to say to us – we were too green to hear how hard it would become, and too far in to be fobbed off with pleasantries – but we shared tales and they gave much great, kind advice before we left the table.

After breakfast, full and finding my bearings, I called home to talk to my parents. It had only been 2 weeks since we'd done more than send brief messages through my GPS tracker to assure them of my safety and for them to assure me of theirs, but it seemed already that there was a gulf between what they knew I was doing 'on paper' and how I could explain the reality of it to them. I just didn't have a way to accurately explain the privation, pain and joy of the wilderness, but they were happy to listen to my attempts and be excited by my telling of it. After leaving them with assurances that I'd make contact again when I could, I enjoyed spending the rest of the day navigating laundry, beers and sunshine on the lawn.

The next morning, I peeled the covers off my face in the old wooden bedroom and contemplated the incessant thumping of my head. I make poor decisions after drinking, even after only a couple of beers, so I ran through the tally of events the night before to figure out where I was at. OK, not too bad. Kissing, no more. Lots of kissing and maybe some pressing of bodies together, but I was extremely glad I didn't give in to the impulse to take it further. Buckshot had been keen, but I'd stood firm (and scurried to my room when it got too steamy) and replied to his texts from up there whilst he stood in the kitchen in the main house, texting to assure me that no one was awake if I wanted to come back over.

When I said no, I also explained that one-night stands were not my thing. I mean, I'd had them, but I knew how awful they made me feel; and with Kate about to leave and a new adventure in the woods about to begin alone, I didn't need the emotional or mental self-flagellation of getting humped and dumped by a hiker as I set out alone. Also, perhaps he and his crew might be great trail buddies for a while, and I didn't want to spoil it, though there was no chance I'd be able to keep up with them. Two guys who'd already hiked the AT *and* the CDT? A girlfriend who had just completed a 100+-mile hike with them as a warm-up? Unlikely. I didn't really have a clue what I was doing and it was only now becoming clear in reality that Kate was going and I was just going to keep walking by myself.

I felt the desperate schoolgirl yearning to be included, to not be left behind, but I squashed it with a reminder that I was a grown-ass woman and I didn't need to be included by anyone, that it would all work out. I grabbed for my phone on the nightstand, finally now working on Wi-Fi. Time: 8:30. Fuck!

Up and dressed in moments, I decided not to waste my precious prescribed painkillers on something as self-inflicted as a hangover, so I necked a couple of ibuprofen and staggered down the stairs. I didn't want to miss breakfast or chatting to folks to see what people's plans were, and another breakfast at Shaws was not to be missed.

I was a little bit late into the main dining area and felt immediately panicked. People were coming out, chatting in groups and putting stuff in packs. Kate was there, milling around and organising her things. 'Hey, mate! How long until you go?' I asked. I suddenly didn't want her to go at all. I needed the yin to my yang; her friendship and stoic logic felt so necessary.

'About an hour,' she said, 'Are you going to be OK, Muller? It feels super strange to leave you.' She looked at me closely. 'I'm so excited to see my babies though.'

'I'm really going to miss you. I can't quite believe you're actually going.' I also felt really bad that I'd been so short with her in the days towards the end of the 100 Mile. I'm not sure whether this is indicative of who I really am under that much exhaustion and privation, or if it was just a reflection of the moods we had both been in.

I left Kate to figure out her final packing and taxi order – she had a long and multi-part journey back, to get out of the USA.

As I wandered around the side of the large, white clapboard hostel to the back garden, I saw Buckshot, Lazybean and Dozer standing with Rock Naps and some others, smoking pipes and chatting, the heavy and delicious smell of weed hanging in clouds. Rock Naps was smoking something called 'Dabs', which I'd never seen before. He had a little tray like a paint palette, with six or so different types of high-purity cannabis resin. These he heated and inhaled on a regular basis. He was so chatty and merry, I couldn't quite understand how he was 'stoned', because it didn't at all equate with the stoned I'd seen at home when I was younger, or even nowadays. I guess that might be the difference between legal marijuana and illegal – maybe you get better stuff when it's more regulated, and fewer people indoors just watching cartoons all day? At least, that's what it seemed like out here.

'Heyyyyy, Appalachian Gail, all packed up?' Buckshot said and grinned at me as he took a hit off his pipe. The others were putting final snacks into the sides of their packs but not looking as though any departure was imminent, lolling on the side of the house.

'Um, kind of,' I said. 'Pretty much done.' I was thinking about my pack explosion in the bedroom, and that I needed to collect laundry and that I had a bunch of crap I needed to give Kate to take back home with her. Fuuuck it! 'Shouldn't take me long.' I tried my best to sound nonchalant as I asked, 'What are you guys doing? Staying around today?' although I could clearly see they probably weren't. They'd had 2 days off now, resting and chilling. It was me who wasn't rested, what with 10 days in the deep woods, utter shock and exhaustion, and then arriving here at dawn the previous day to drink and whoop it up all day in celebration. I definitely needed a break, some vegetables and a good sleep with no booze. I didn't think I was going to get it.

'Nah, we're heading out in an hour or two. Kit's probably gonna come too, and Rock Naps maybe.' He looked over the grass at where Rock Naps had crawled into the tent he'd pitched on the lawn the night before, feet poking out the end. 'Not sure about him though.' Buckshot looked down at me again from his height and stature. Not just his pure size; he also inhabited a mile-wide confidence and assuredness, like he knew anything and everything that could happen next out here, and none of it would faze him in the slightest. The corners of his big mouth twitched up as he let the pause and gaze linger. 'And you?'

'What?' I said, with a throwaway cackle. 'Hahaha, you must be kidding, me? I can't keep up with you guys – I haven't even had a zero yet. You're all experienced and, shit, I'm just learning this stuff.'

Lazybean turned and smiled at me and then at Buckshot.

'Shit Buck, she's right,' he drawled. We're going to pull out of here around 11 a.m. and drop a 30-miler, I reckon.' He squinted at me, his face kind and joking. 'Reckon you can do 30 miles before dark tonight, G? Come on, I know you can.'

I had no fucking idea what was going on. Were they joking entirely? Were they looking for me to start with them, then laugh at me as they went on and left me 10 miles in, scratched, dirty and bawling? Or did they honestly mistake me as someone who could keep up? I didn't quite know what to say, so laughed and nodded. 'Sure, sure, I could keep up, y'know.' And I told them I was going to pack up.

I wandered across the yard casually, opened the back door to the steps up to my room and, as soon as the door closed behind me, rocketed up to get my stuff together in a wild, panicked flurry. As I packed, my brain carried on a solid narrative – you know, really helpful like brains are. I despaired that I felt such urgency to be part of a group. Surely the whole reason to try this incredible feat was to complete it without help, without support. I *had* to show that my body could thrive. That all the times I'd had to stop or give up in the past and needed help were behind me. I was a new person; I was *brave* now. I didn't need help or support. I was *well*. I didn't need help. But, my God, the urge to be accepted into a circle, to not do it alone, was overwhelming – physically as well as mentally – shown by the speed of the very hands I was looking at as they shoved everything and anything haphazardly into my bag so I could get outside in time.

I stopped to take a breath. More haste, less speed. Just be present in myself and what will be will be. I packed slowly and carefully, and then took my things down to the yard, not knowing who or what would be there, but knowing for sure that saying goodbye to Kate was my first priority.

We hugged and I slipped her my GoPro and Kindle, some chargers and various bits of memorabilia I'd picked up in the last 2 weeks – all to take home, and the first of many shakedowns.

Thanking her, I explained with swimming eyes what she had meant to me in coming to see me through the beginning of this journey. Only now, in the losing of her, realising how much I had needed her. Kate isn't one for emotion, but she hugged me hard in return. 'Sorry,' I said again, 'for losing my temper and being short sometimes. I didn't really know myself.'

'It's OK.' She raised a tired smile. 'No more than I deserved in the bigger picture.' Always with the logic. She hoisted her bag and we walked to the waiting taxi, with her waving at Buckshot and his friends and giving Rock Naps a hard hug before she opened the door and moved to sling herself in after her pack.

I hustled up to the window. 'Please stay,' I blurted out, wiping unexpected tears with the back of my hand so she didn't see. She stopped and reversed direction, lifting herself back out.

'Poppet,' she said, looking hard at me, 'you don't need me to stay. You're going to be alright. This is it – your journey. It starts now.' My face crumpled and she put her hand on my shoulder. 'Muller, you can do this. I love you.'

'Love you too,' I said and pulled her, the hug-hater, into another big squeeze. I closed the door on her and leaned to wave through the glass. The taxi, in no way as emotionally connected to the moment as I was, reversed neatly away from me out of the driveway, paused and then pulled forwards again, Kate's little face pressed to the glass and her fingertips waving over the headrest until she was gone from sight.

I felt so naked, caught in this moment. Blankets whipped off. The thought through my body like a flush of cold water that I'd made the wrong choice and wasn't strong enough for this, that I was a fraud. Too old, too fat, my body too weak and unreliable. I'd tap out with pain again; it's always been that way.

Ahh, my pain. It always turned up in the end when I had something fun planned, some adventure or event to look forward to. Sometimes it let me really get close and my excitement to truly build, but it would always appear, slipping into the scene with a dark nod to tell me that my time was up. It wasn't unassuming and small either – it eventually came to inhabit the entire right side of my body, snaking through my pelvis and up my spine, through the back of my ribs and down my arm. Pain that was amorphous, that had no sides or shape or 'point to where it hurts' clarity. It was a pain that felt like a swelling; that one side of my body had died and was bloating whilst attached to me, but also electrified and awake. Not phantom pain; zombie pain.

It changed everything about me in my life – even having a say in how I dressed, like a controlling partner. I wore no tight trousers, no stylish clothes with interesting cuts. I wore frumpy, elasticated-waist trousers to work rather than tailored styles, because I couldn't stand any fabric or pressure on my skin. I dragged my right foot but hid it by pausing and leaning on walls at school. I had to lift my right leg in and out of the car and would inwardly scream when jostled at a supermarket. I would drive into town to buy clothes or to Sainsburys to buy food, and then would drive around the car park and out again when I saw how many people there were as I didn't know how I could navigate my way through without the agony that came with moving the trolley left and right to avoid people. I cancelled drinks with friends, dodged birthday parties, bailed on weekends away, swerved happy social gatherings and sports events, and even let my rowing team down without a proper explanation. How do you convincingly explain what's wrong when you don't know, the doctors don't know and no one, not even you, can see it? It's easier to shrink away, hide and just save your spoons of effort for working and bringing in money to pay the bills and the modicum of dignity this provides. And now I was here, my body so far having showed itself to be worth this most recent mustering of self-belief in its ability to get through the last 10 days.

But what if this was another trick? What if, with Kate leaving, the pain would slide in and take her spot and shame me for ever having thought I could get any further that it had allowed? I could feel my fear of continuing – I would be the one left behind, with people catching up and overtaking me until I gave up, too demoralised to continue and ready to face the ridicule; or worse, the kind, knowing commiseration of those who believed I'd never make it but didn't want to say so as they waved me off, unsurprised to see me back.

No. I couldn't give in to this anymore. I was going to push it, see how far I *could* get, and take the consequences that came. I studied the dusty road, unclenched my fists, put one hand on my chest and breathed deeply once, then turned, smiled, and walked towards the house.

'Y'OK?' Buckshot asked casually, standing apart from the others, but they were already milling closer. I'd already noticed this about him. He was the electric current in a group, the light bulb that people gravitated around, but he didn't always like it, swinging between enjoying holding court and wanting to strike off into his own world. Never totally gone, never quite arrived. Peripheral – that was, until he decided to turn it on full beam.

Once I had nodded mutely that I was OK and was going to finish packing some food, he wandered off, getting up to walk on the slackline he'd played around on the day before – agile for a man of his stature on the tightrope-like band.

I took a moment to speak to Dozer. Twenty years old, yet a wise hiker of at *least* 100 miles – experienced in my eyes.

'So, I might come with you guys,' I said, hating the need I could hear in my own voice and hoping it wasn't clear to her.

'Of course,' she said, smiling. 'Those assholes are just messin'' with you. It's like that. We want you to come, you're fun, we like you. And we're not doing a damn 30-mile day. They're just bein' big shots. AIN'T YOU, LB?' She laughed over at Lazybean, whose long hair poked out the back of his faded hat, and he turned and shot me a big grin.

'Sure as shit, Appalachian Gail; course you're coming with us. Now get rid of some of that heavy crap in your pack into the hiker box and let's get goin'. You don't need that much food. We're stopping in a few days at Caratunk – there's a little resupply there.'

I smiled towards Lazybean and watched him pull his socks over his stick-and-poke 'Tits and Bass' tattoo that sat on the inside of his foot. I felt overcome with gratitude to them, for their inclusion and kindness, and that their thousands of miles of trail experience – especially Lazybean's and Buckshot's – hadn't made them gatekeepers or made them look down their noses at beginners like me. Even old beginners, although at this stage I wondered how old they thought I was, because they were treating me like I wasn't *that* much older than them.

I shoved a huge jar of Nutella and some bars I'd just bought at Shaw's hostel shop straight into the hiker box, cursing myself for wasting money, as someone instantaneously came up behind me and leaned over with a '*Hey*, check it out! Someone binned a new Nutella in here, dude!', scooping it up over my shoulder even before I let it go. Hiker boxes are an incredible repository of things hikers don't want or need. Most every town or hostel has one, and they range from a tatty shoe box to a range of plastic tubs labelled 'food', 'shoes', 'clothes' and 'gear'. This one was pretty full and when I later asked why, I understood that Sobo hikers coming out of the 100 Mile realised they'd brought too much for their thru and dumped stuff before they carried on. Then people going *into* the 100 Mile – Nobos – realised they were on the last stretch so didn't want to carry anything unnecessary in order to make way for food instead. No Nobos had really come through yet – it was too early in the season – so the food box was laden with the extra food that overpacked Sobos didn't need. Some people had even packed themselves up a resupply box and sent it to Shaw's before they started the trail, just like they sent their boxes to other post offices to resupply themselves along the way, but they also came out of the 100 mile with extra food, so it all got dumped in the tubs.

I realised the gang was assembling, so I hot-footed it to them, grinning and excited. I was somehow expecting some kind of fanfare for us going as we'd made lots of new friends in the 24 hours I'd been at Shaw's, but it's clearly the way of it – people slide in and they slip out again, and the people you meet don't expect goodbyes. 'See you down trail' is the most you'll hear, whether it's this trail or the next. Nothing forced, no requests for a 'plan'.

Poet got into the driver's seat and we got shuttled back to the spot we were picked up at – only the morning before for me. I was so damn tired. I could feel it in my shaking legs, but I couldn't say anything now. If I'd have stopped another day then I could have had my first zero and rested, but I'd be left behind, and I could already feel that the vibe of this little crew was perfectly aligned with my own and could teach me a lot, so I pushed through on wobbly legs and a hungover head.

CHAPTER SEVEN

How Low Can You Go?

Starting the trail in Maine was the opposite of how I like to eat a good plate of food: we were starting with the best bits first, and I usually saved them 'til last. Who can know if I would have loved Maine the same if I had ended there; if, in fact, I ever made it that far. But for me this was Utopia; the wildest outdoors on the Appalachian Trail and by far the most remote. Unbridged stream crossings with just rope to grip to stop you being swept downstream. Moose, loon and coyote in abundance, and the rugged remoteness that made me unsure of which century I was in for days at a time. I had never felt so close to nature, so deeply pulled in and assessed by an entity that was wholly fundamental to me as a living being, but that I had alienated myself from so wilfully with my walls, highways and technology.

I experienced deep grief and ecstatic euphoria in Maine, purely from being reunited with the wild that I hadn't known I needed. But as much as I felt the electric beginnings of this glorious reconnection, at the same time this state was about as far out of my comfort zone as I could ever imagine. The 100 Mile Wilderness had been hyped so hard that I hadn't really considered what happened after it. I never went beyond those first huge hurdles in my mind to envisage how the rest of Maine might look, or really where the trail went next beyond a vague idea of the map. I was already beginning the stomach-lurching freefall of not being organised in advance and having no plan. No plan! Me, who organised my days in and around work, social life and adventure with barely a sparrow's fart in between, with a wall planner compulsively filled a year in advance. No plan meant panic, loneliness, noisy thoughts and the fear of missing out. But now I'd been born out of the end of the 100 Mile Wilderness into a blank agenda which had nothing to fill it bar walking and whatever and whomever each day might deliver. How exquisitely terrifying. I hoped my body wouldn't let me down.

What came next was more than I could appreciate at the time. Like an ecstasy-pill high, the Maine section of the AT was rammed with nature's oxytocin and serotonin, blasting my senses with forest highs, the exhilaration of views ascended, the exhaustion and euphoria of making it down valleys and up peaks. The taste of well-earned food by a fire under a starry sky was the finest I've ever tasted. No light pollution made the night sky a movie screen, and the daytime was a feast of forest. And under these canopies, in these branched arms, sat folks like me, and strangers like them, a meeting and sharing of a journey from the start. The little group were bonding fast and were quite unlike the more uptight 100 Mile folks I'd met so far (of which I had been one). The thaw from real life to relaxed hiker trash must come over time in the woods, and this group were all liquid after their combined thousands of miles. They felt wild, delinquent even, but with kind-hearted humour under their rougher exteriors.

After the day's miles were done, we set up at East Carry Pond. I wandered around the site a little before deciding where to put my tent, kicking leaves and looking for a good flat spot, but all the while checking out where the others were putting theirs. I could see a group of people by the shelter having a nice time, cooking fish they'd caught in the lake and laughing by the fire. I wished we could all congregate, but the crew I really wanted to be with set themselves apart, further back from the main clearing in a little side space. I saw Buckshot's tarp go up and knew I wanted to be closer to him, so when Lazybean waved and beckoned me over, I grinned and went.

The dirt was soft and loamy, as it had been throughout Maine so far. Pine needles deeply layered and dried out beneath us; a fire hazard like no other. Once a fire caught, even if you were to put it out on the surface, the burning pine needles transferred their flame and heat below to their deeper comrades, and soon little wires of fire would spread like roots underground, dipping below tree trunks and under paths to reach, gasping for air, in another spot, looking for all the world like a spontaneous combustion from nowhere if anyone was there to see it, which they often weren't, so the blaze would take hold. For this reason, we didn't make fires anywhere other than in the designated firepits, which weren't where we had settled. So, fireless – but my heart warmed nevertheless, I heated my water on the stove and cooked up a meal. Packet rice with some dehydrated veg and cheese.

Buckshot didn't say much that evening. I felt a yearning for him to flirt with me again, to show some of the lustful interest he had at Shaw's not two nights before. But he was focused on hiking, smoking weed and sleeping, pulling back from me in front of his friends and only locking deep eye contact and lingering smiles when we were alone. I didn't understand but I scolded myself for giving a shit. This trail was *not* going to end up being about a man. It was about me.

I had spent the tail end of the 100 Mile and the whole of my time at Shaw's telling myself (and Kate) that I didn't know why I was thinking about Buckshot, that he wasn't my type; that I thought he was flirting with me, but I wasn't interested. And now something had changed. We had some connection I couldn't explain that had zinged into life the moment he'd skidded into our camp below Whitecap, and then after days in the wild he'd kissed me. Now he'd retreated. Best not to get further involved, I told myself, as he smiled at me across the dirt and leaves, said goodnight to all and slipped under his tarp.

I looked at the tarp for a moment longer. I spent a lot of my time in awe of everything at the moment. Of how light people packed, of how comfortable they were in the deep woods, that this amount of forest existed and that it didn't panic people with its oppressive green weight masquerading as 'nature lite'. On its fringes it was safe, but further inside was a labyrinthine universe for which I had no skills and was in awe of those that did.

I looked over at Lazybean and Dozer. They had put their large bright-green tarp up higher than Buckshot's and it covered their camp well. They were pulling in for the night and drawing their belongings around them under the canopy, Dozer pulling out the tattered paperback book I'd seen her with in the 100 Mile and settling in to read softly to Lazybean before they slept. I nodded my goodnight and walked back to my tent. It was closing in on hiker midnight, a term I'd only recently learned, which really meant

9 p.m. and an unspoken code to be quiet, which was wonderful because I was feeling shattered. Thirteen days so far without a zero on fresh legs. My gaze lingered over Buckshot's tarp as I moved past, feeling buzzed thinking of him beneath it but knowing that was a hornet's nest I didn't need to nudge. I turned towards my tent by the lake.

Behind me I heard him drawl, 'If it starts rainin', I'm gonna have to come shelter in that little tent with you.'

I turned to look. I couldn't see him, the dusky darkness covering us all. A small flame, sharp inhalation and glowing buds in his pipe gave him away, his bearded head sticking out of the tarp's far end, eyes gleaming. 'You might have to move over a touch,' he murmured. I coughed a sharp laugh, then cringed at the volume of it.

'You'll be lucky, Buckshot,' I shot back, like an embarrassed schoolgirl, and then, 'Night, sleep well,' turning to my tent feeling exposed in a way that seemed impossible when cloaked in forest and night. Excited in a way I hadn't been for a long time. *Everything* was exciting, and my every sense was alive. This was where I was supposed to be, and this was the right tribe to be with. I knew that to keep up with these people I needed to get ahead of them.

*

My alarm went off at 5 a.m. and I crept outside, stretching, packing all my belongings and eschewing food or coffee until later. I felt panicked that my slow and shaky legs were going to let me down. Therefore it was vital that I get out ahead of these experienced hikers so that by the time they caught up and overtook me, I would have covered so much ground it would still be feasible to catch up with them by nightfall and camp with them again. I could feel that, although they enjoyed my company, they wouldn't be waiting for me. That was the way out here though; it wasn't about being special enough or good enough; people just didn't wait. If you slowed down then you hiked alone until you met the next folks dropping into trail, or the ones coming up behind who started after you but who would overtake you. For someone like me who thrived on getting out front and leading, hiking had set me right on my ass on the bench. It didn't matter how quick my mind was, if my legs weren't fast enough, I was going to fall back. I imagined my mindset about it would change, but at the moment it just gave me rising panic. I'd always been so reliant on my mind, but now I needed to have faith in my body too. The body that had let me down so often in the past.

The day was tough. The narrow dirt path through high-sided, slick grey boulders in the heat made me think of *Picnic at Hanging Rock*, a movie that haunted me in my teens. I scrambled and scraped my way up, imagining the younger and more vital crew behind me, packing up, snapping close on my heels. The anxiety and dread of my own ineptitude spurred me on. Perhaps it wasn't the fear of losing 'them' particularly, but the confirmation that even though I'd now reached a stage where I could push my body hard into physicality, it was all for nothing and too late because I'd passed out of any youthful demographic into an 'old lady' category where people were polite and nodded as they passed, commenting to each other how lovely it was that all ages were in the outdoors. Fuck. Perhaps that was why I found Buckshot so strangely appealing, as he was definitely at least seven or eight years younger than me – he was perhaps 35? I don't know, but I was clearly hankering to relive some of the years I'd lost, and I felt instinctively that here, where the rules of real life didn't apply, was the place to do it.

I hiked hard that day, pushed myself far and enjoyed the feeling of limbs burning and shuddering. I passed few souls and no day hikers, but I did speak briefly to two skeletal Nobo thru hikers, a couple hours apart. They were together, which I realised when the second asked me if I'd seen the first, and how far ahead he was. Long beards, gaunt faces with concave cheeks, the men reeked not only of dirt and grime but also of ammonia and desperation. I left them behind – they didn't want to speak for long, their focus easily mistaken for aloofness. I continued, wondering whether I'd ever get that skinny by the end and hoping I would. I then wondered why I still cared, having already understood my body as being so much more than I appraised it for before: a tool, a friend and a piece of machinery for my own ends, rather than conforming it to fit into the agendas and preferences of others.

After summiting two sister peaks, I romped down the descent back into the woods, with my headphones in and a steady stride. It must have been some hours later that I swayed and lost my balance, propping myself up on a knobbled trunk that grazed my soft palm. The sharp pain shook me from the constant cadence of my swinging arms and legs and I crumpled onto the dirt, realising I hadn't eaten in a long time. It was here that I heard voices behind me for the first time that day. My chest gripped; they'd caught up with me! I swivelled on my butt and looked, still a little hunger high. No, not the crew. It was Flowers and his son.

'Hey! I was hoping I'd finally meet you!' He was an online avatar made real and I was happy to see him. I'd been in touch with him on Instagram in the months leading up to the hike, with him also set for a Sobo. He had offered to receive US packages for me when I was still home in the UK, which was my first inkling of how kind trail folks were. 'Heck you're *movin'*!' he said. 'We've just had a little break in the shelter.' He pointed down a little blue blaze side trail that I'd missed. 'Not doing that many miles today but heading to Caratunk to the B&B. What about you?'

'Yes, me too! Hope I see you there. Anyone else around today?'

'Smudge, Pinecone, some others, I think. Not sure where, maybe they pulled off already to make camp and chill. They were havin' a lot of fun. You gonna be OK? You look kind of spaced out.' He peered at me in a paternal way, his son quiet and smiling behind him.

'Oh yeah, yes, I'm fine. I'm with the others but they'll catch up soon,' I said. Well, so I hoped. I was just now realising that it had got late and I wasn't going to reach Caratunk until it was almost dusk. I knew from Guthook that the B&B didn't like to accept people when it got late, but I was tired. Now though, I had no idea where the crew was, and yet I'd been sure they'd have caught up with me.

'Hmm. Well, OK then. You make sure you're drinking enough too. There's a nicely flowing stream back in there if you need it, before you go too far along. I don't know where the next water is.' He smiled and straightened, putting his hand on my shoulder as he passed. 'Take care now, AG. See you down the road tonight for a beer.' They waved me off and I felt their leaving hard upon

me as the silence of the woods enveloped me again. OK. Up. *Up*.
I was so tired.

It was 8 p.m. when I dragged myself to the door of the Caratunk B&B, staggering onto the hardtop street from the woods and
under the lone humming streetlight. The crew had never caught
up with me and I felt flat when I should have felt elated. Nineteen
miles. I had walked over mountains in Maine for 19 miles alone,
not even 2 weeks into my thru hike, and I felt shit.

The owner of the small B&B opened the door with a suspicious
scowl, making clear his intolerance for anything verging on fun or
loud, and telling me finally that I could come in but he wasn't sure
about it, impressing on me the importance of not speaking above
a whisper as it was after 8 p.m. 'There are other guests to think of.'

Really? Who are silent at 8 p.m.? What is this? A convent in the
1860s? I could barely focus on him and just asked for a bed, some
water for noodles and a cup of tea. He began to warm slightly and
led me to the kitchen where he gestured to a stool and put water on
the stove. He explained where I'd find my room and then left me
for his bed, taking my laundry with him for the washer on the way.

The stairs creaked underfoot, the still air seeming to magnify
sounds. I passed through a multitude of doors in a tiny maze to
reach my bed for the night. The room was stifling, with dark
brown drapes, furniture and floorboards, and two beds but no
occupants. Religious paraphernalia on the walls gazed down at me
and prayed over my inert form delirious with exhaustion as sleep
swiftly pulled me under.

Waking was excruciating. Every piece of me hurt. I stared at
my feet in abject horror. Never ever before had I seen them like

this: sets of five sausages stuck on two watermelons. How could I walk? Or get them into my shoes? I felt done for. Everything was throbbing and hot and perhaps I was dying. I definitely wanted my mum and her reassuring knowledge of whether I was OK or not. Sometimes when I just couldn't gauge my own real state, she'd be able to tell and let me know if I was just freaking out, or if I was a real mess that needed a rest. But there was no chance of that – my phone had refused to connect to any internet for days now and I looked at it hopelessly, jabbing the airplane mode on and off to try to make it find a signal. Nope. No service, no Mama, no way to reach my new trail friends, no way to know if those I'd hiked with before had already risen earlier than me and hiked past this town, over the river and away, and I'd never catch up with them again. Perhaps they thought I was still ahead, or perhaps they had forgotten about me already. Urgh, I couldn't handle it.

I stabbed at the phone some more. I wanted to phone home, but no dice. Instead, I opened my ziplock stash of pills and potions and pulled out two of the co-codamol I was trying to ration. These, swilled down with some Vitamin I, should see me through the morning.

These sharp new aches and pains from hiking were almost an agonising pleasure because it was no *mystery* to me what was causing them. I had pushed my body and now it made sense that it hurt and was repairing. If I rested a few days, it wouldn't hurt at all anymore. Brilliant. Not like chronic pain, which pipes up and chips in all the time without any provocation. It starts small, niggling, and then sits in the background, slowly mushrooming until it fills the room and pushes your face up against the wall.

Like a lobster in a pot of gently heating water, you don't always realise you're cooking until you're nearly cooked and then it's too late to reverse it.

It's a long road to Chronic, and all the time that I was struggling with my pain, I was also struggling with metacognition that told me it was silly, stupid and shameful to be ill; that no one could see it and no one really believed me. The doctors definitely didn't at first. My hardworking teaching colleagues were kind but sceptical. 'Why didn't I think of that?' may have been a theme for some of them when they looked at me limping and grimacing over 'nothing' and having to take rare days off. The management of my school just wanted my efficient ass to be at work and not make further staffing issues for them. I had always been so reliable, so stalwart. I couldn't allow myself to be this thundering let-down and 'rest' when I looked absolutely fine… so I listened to *that* voice instead of my body and 'soldiered on'. Too ashamed to stop and be long-term sick. Such a clever trick of our society to gaslight us into believing we can and should keep going just a little more. And then when the wheels start to come off with panic attacks, opiate addictions, drinking too much to cope and some chronic fatigue, it becomes 'performance management' or 'you're not cut out for this; everyone else is cOpInG.'

My doctor's appointments became predictable.

Me: 'Bad back.'

Them: 'Oh?'

Me: 'Hmmm. It's really sore.'

Doctor: *Feels about a bit*

Them: 'Bend over for me. Touch your toes.'

Me: 'Ow.'

Them: 'Everyone has back pain. We can't do much. You'll be OK. Take ibuprofen.'

Me: *Embarrassed* 'OK.'

And off I would go, knowing it was worse than that, feeling the pain growing hot and threatening, but not having any way to explain it to them. Pulled underwater. Not waving but drowning.

This cycle of medical attention/inattention repeated semi-regularly over a number of years. My general heath was slowly declining, and the ibuprofen didn't help anymore. I was compensating in my movement patterns to work around the pain: changing how I walked and sat, limiting my flexibility. I drank more because it helped me fall asleep through the pain. I exercised less and put on weight, beginning to hate the outside *as well as* the inside of myself. I became ashamed of going to the doctor's again because I wasn't able to get better. No improvement – obviously a failure on my part because no one else seemed to think I was unwell. Me, not improving? Unthinkable. So, slowly and silently, I started thinking that something was truly 'wrong' with me. I was either going crazy or was valued so little by the system that 'they' were going to let me fade away and die in front of their very eyes.

The pills upgraded to amitriptyline, which made my mouth dry and left me with slurred speech but no difference in my pain levels. I refused to continue taking them. Back to the over-the-counter meds, tears and sleepless nights. MRIs were done but nothing remarkable was found to explain my spreading pain and twisting body. There were days when I felt suddenly better for

GAIL MULLER

no reason. How glorious to be better, but how distressing to not understand how or why. And still, no one could explain.

It wasn't just dull pain. It was muscle spasms and tightening of fascia in imperceptible ways – a slow-motion wrenching of my hip out of alignment to the point that I couldn't lie flat on a bed without one pelvic bone visibly raised and feeling as though it was 3 inches off the bed. My brain eventually stopped telling the right side of my body what to do properly. My leg didn't lift when I wanted it to. My arm didn't grip a pen like it should. My head kept locking off-centre and my right shoulder was pulled almost an inch out of place by my muscles twisting and twisting. Sometimes there was an inch between the height of each of my hipbones.

It was casual and arbitrary; for example, after a few reasonable days where I thought things might be OK, my body would pull itself out of whack whilst walking to the car with schoolbooks after breakfast and a new wave of awful would begin. The only person I could ever really rely on to put my body back into its functional order was my chiropractor. The practice is sniffed at by some but is a healing modality that has remained a constant in my life for the last 20 years. But there was nothing like that out here along the trail in Maine. No one to trundle along to in the afternoon who would assess my posture and guide me back to neutral alignment with a few prods and clicks, so I was darn glad that at the moment the pain I was experiencing was just the same as anyone else's who'd done what I'd done in the last few weeks. I was going to embrace the normality of my aches and enjoy the respite I was clearly getting from my old friend Chronic.

A loud shout made me start.

'BREAKFAST IS NOW!' a stern patrician voice thundered through the floorboards.

Shit! Oh yes, that was right. He'd impressed on me the importance of not being late for an 8 a.m. breakfast so as not to keep the other guests waiting. No flexibility here.

'Yes, coming!' I shouted, feeling horrible, like a naughty child being berated.

Getting downstairs was slow and hard. In the austere dining room there was an eclectic mix of quiet, severe and slightly uptight people, who were all solo visitors but seemed united by awkwardness. All were hikers but in different guises: day hikers and section hikers but no other thru hikers like me. I was appraised by all in the doorway and then encouraged to sit. Silently.

A tall, slight older man entered with baskets of rolls and muffins. When asked how he came to be here, he quietly murmured that he'd stumbled in 2 weeks ago after losing too much weight at the beginning of his thru hike and was too weak to carry on. His terse tone and stern manner with himself and us seemed to come from his realisation of how close he'd come to some form of madness in his hunger but had been saved – like a born-again religious man, atoning and feeling safe.

Just then his saviour entered to tell me my laundry would be ready for collection when I left, and to urge us to take more muffins and leftover waffles for the day ahead. It was a sombre start to what felt like the start of a new iteration of this thru. There had been so many of these already, it was always impossible to know what the next day would hold, and my organised nature was finding it very stressful.

Out of the corner of my eye I saw a flash of pink and yellow through the heavily netted curtains. More hikers! I grabbed the muffins and shoved them in a ziplock as I made my excuses and fled through the corridor to the main door. Dozer! Lazybean! I flung the door open to see Lazybean's head deep inside the big hiker box on the porch.

'Hell, there's some good shit right here, Dozer! Ohhhhh.' He lifted his head and grinned laconically at me. 'Here she is! Shit, Gail, where the hell did you get to?'

'Well, I—' And then I was cut off by a booming voice.

'YOU WENT ALL THE WAAAAAAY!' I snapped my head around. 'I'm so proud of you. Haha, hell fire, DAMN. I am PROUD.' There he stood, like the Viking of the woods, beaming.

'Yeah, thanks, Buckshot. It was nothing though. Just kept thinking you guys were gonna catch me up any minute. Where'd you go?'

'Ahh, we stopped about 7 miles back and pulled up for the night. Smoked some and slept good. That was a hard day. You did real good.'

God, I wanted to hug him, but he wasn't for the hugging, that I could tell.

'You tried these milkshakes here? He does 'em good. That's why everyone's showing up.' He gestured behind him to a straggling line of hikers, perhaps making us ten or so in all. Everyone stopping here in the bottleneck of Caratunk River, shallow enough to wade but uncrossable without risk of sudden death from the flooding that happened with no warning from a hydroelectric plant further upstream. A hiker had died the year before trying the crossing, and people were taking the town's pleas seriously. Instead, there was a river boatman, rowing two at a time over the wide expanse. Everyone was here to wait for him to show up and get the day's hiking underway on the other side.

We moseyed down to the river in dribs and drabs. I was feeling pretty damn good at the dawning realisation that I could hike 19 miles, feel such pain but still carry on. I was used to pain taking me out totally. But here I stood, in awe of my ability to carry on. My brain was cycling in loop, questioning whether I was maybe *always* able to do such things, but my fear of previous pain had taken me, stopped me from pushing beyond my perceived limits. God, I hoped not. I wasn't sure though, because the hiking so far had been taxing every little muscle that I had – not just the steady limping lope of jogging or the single-plane movements of the gym.

Perhaps the magic was in the terrain and the pack on my back, forcing me to use my body as it should be used, in a multi-faceted animal survival mode. My days were showing up to being far from 'desk, desk, desk, desk, run, sofa, bed' and were more like 'bend, stretch, hike, climb, boulder, fall, balance, scramble, hike, collapse'. I wasn't fooling myself though. I had failed and fallen at enough simple hurdles to never believe in much anymore. Every hour could be the last, and every ascent and descent could be the one to put out my hip or flare my SI joint.

It was hard not to be jealous – such a terrible feeling – of the vital hikers all around me. I was trying to keep up not just to have friends I liked but because now, in my stubborn mind, any falling behind was failure, loss and defeat of a magnitude far greater than just sitting out a day and finding a new crew. This was sink or swim, and if I had to go home with injury or pain then I knew it would be hard to ever recover.

'Hey, you wanna row with me?' Buckshot snapped me out of my reverie, sitting on a sunny tree stump by the river's edge. It was fun, the lapping of the water, the life jackets and friendly river man. We bumped up onto the far shore where the Steinbecks, as I'd taken to calling Lazybean and Dozer for their love of reading paperbacks to each other at night, were sitting waiting. We all walked steadily for the rest of the day, weaving in and out of each other's company. Buck and I split off regularly as he would take me to see creeks and bridges along the way, and we would hide from rain squalls under bushy, tickly pines or in shelters that we raced to, laughing like lunatics as we were pelted, our wet hair plastered over our grins.

Over the long afternoon, even Buckshot and I strung out apart from each other. I was learning the cadence of the thru hike. The concertina of squishing hikers together at water sources, towns and night-times, then pulling them apart again over the terrain of the day. I was enjoying the pre-sunset glow of the path along another huge Maine lake when I ambled onto a small beach. There he was, in only his pants and his socks, with his T-shirt and other clothes dried on rocks around him. I ignored him, walking past and kicking my shoes off to paddle to my knees. I turned after a few moments, feeling his gaze.

'Got some whiskey?' I asked.

'You'll have to come get it,' he replied, eyes twinkling.

I waded back to shore, knowing I was asking for trouble. I reached out to take the proffered bottle and he held on just a moment, before releasing it to me and watching me drink. He stood to take it back, so many feet taller and broader than me, then placed his huge hand around the small of my back and pulled me closer to taste his hot whiskey breath.

*

I didn't see as much of him as the next few days unfolded, but it didn't matter. It was to be an exhilarating time. I hiked intermittently with a solo hiker called Kat – who, like me, didn't have a trail name yet – and most regularly with the Steinbecks. I tackled big climbs where the air was colder, feeling the temperature drop on my inhalations as my skin sweated hot with exertion. I scrambled up mudslides, gripping overhead branches, swinging out and back in again to the trail proper. These were the Bigelows, the highest and hardest yet in my short journey. Occasionally, I stopped to let people pass me going down. Although etiquette dictated that the ascender has the way, I was regularly delighted to pause and let people pass. I chatted to a fellow Brit – a northbounder called Togs who was on her way to the finish with the boyfriend she'd met here on trail. I asked, as was becoming the norm when passing northbounders, what it was like where I was heading, and she asked the same from whence I'd come. We swapped intel, our personal fears becoming clear as we probed different aspects. Is there water? How steep will my descent be? My knees are so painful. Are the crossings deep? And then we moved along.

I dug water from a cold stone trough at the top of Avery Peak, pitching my tent in the cold wind on one of the wooden platforms provided in this area of rocky surfaces and alpine flowers we were trying to protect. Cooking supper on the ledge, I heard whoops and animal calls from the Steinbecks arriving in camp behind me. I whooped back, they replied, and then I guessed they set their tent up somewhere else in the col, knowing I was here too. My first 4,000-footer done, I lay back on my noisy air mat, its irritating crinkles outdone by the howl of the wind, and scudded through sleep inside flapping fabric and whipping lines.

More days of hiking alone, more nights of finding stealth spots with the Steinbecks. We were a threesome for this period and it worked. I suddenly felt that I loved them in some quick and sharp way – a way that might not last but was deep – for their youthful sageness, the anachronism of their stoic wisdom in bodies so young and untravelled. And their deep kindness. I loved them for that. I felt I was falling in love with everything at that moment. I could feel myself peeling back to my bones, such a transformation already within 14 days. I was becoming naked, shedding layers of protection, grief and anger that were too heavy to carry on the trail. And I was grateful in a way I have never been. It only took someone to offer their extra hot water when my hands were cold, or to snap off part of a Snickers and hold it out to me to make me feel humbled and close to tears. Out here we could and must rely on each other. I have long hated dependency – my dependency on others and the risk of theirs on me. But then I embraced it, even as it gently took me apart. Each kindness an undoing.

*

Buckshot had been gone for days. I yearned to ask the Steinbecks where they thought we might catch up with him, considering they were supposed to be hiking together, but I knew my question would be seen through in a moment and they'd be on to me. I was damned if I was going to be picked out as a pink blazer, or the reverse of it, early on. I'm sure they realised there was something between us. It wasn't hard to spot it at Shaw's or over the subsequent nights on trail, but there was something unspoken about it. Not enough to trouble me yet, but enough to make me not want to talk about it. I had asked him at the lake if we were keeping our little connection quiet, and he said no, that it was all fine by him whoever knew. I wasn't sure I believed him, and anyway I didn't want to be the one to out it first. I wanted him to. But he was far ahead, Lazybean saying that perhaps it would be tens of miles that he'd covered by now.

'He'll stop. At some point,' he said, when the subject came up naturally. 'He did this on the CDT. Much wilder out there though, and a heap of different routes you could take, so it made sense that we'd lose each other from time to time, but he'd be gone for hundreds of miles sometimes. Just out there, alone. Happy as can be with the mountain lions and the grizzlies.' He paused, seeing my face. 'But he'll wait for us down the line. He always does.'

We hitched into Stratton to the base of Sugarloaf Mountain, and a gas-station sandwich has never tasted so good, sitting in the dirt at the door of the store, feeling entitled to sit there and bask in the joy of hard-earned food. Realising there was a new hostel nearby, we started to walk down to it, considering charging our phones and picking up a beer or two.

As we walked the road, a guy in a big truck heading the other way pulled a huge U-turn in the middle of the road and pulled up, asking if we were hikers. He pulled open the back flap and we sat inside, the wind blowing my hair and me gripping the sides in a flurry of ecstasy as visuals of American movies from my youth and my real life all came together in a whirl of pickup trucks and the open road. Dozer and I climbed out in the hostel car park as the man clanged down the hatch. Lazybean had sat up front. I was learning the rules: Buckshot had already told me that if it's a woman driving, the girl goes in the front to chat, and if it's a man, the guy hikers go in the front. I liked the arrangement, and I liked it even more when I realised that this guy was a bona fide creep. As the Steinbecks picked up their gear and made their way to the main doors, he strutted over and bent forwards towards me.

'Hmmm, yup.' And he looked me up and down with a leery smile. 'You're one a' them girl hikers ain't you? Nice strong young woman. Like that Dixie from the YouTube.' He paused and looked wistfully off into the distance, probably imagining Dixie sitting on a log smiling and walking him through the contents of her pack in her underwear. 'Tell you what, young lady. I've got a cabin up there in the woods. No snow right now. It's the off season o' course, but you can come right on up – bring your friends if you like – you can spend a couple nights there with me and just, y'know, take a load off. Uhhh hummm. There's a....' He paused and stroked his chin, perhaps considering if he was going too far. 'There's a jacuzzi.'

I had to stop my eyeballs from rolling back so far I'd be staring at my brain for the rest of the day. This fucking dream snatcher. There I was enjoying my American idyll of truck-riding and free-wheeling good souls, and he just wanted to pat my ass and tell me to come on over. Ahh well.

'Thanks, that's kind, but we've got a long way to go still so we can't stop yet!' I smiled and turned, waving goodbye before he could gather up a protest and get it out of his mouth.

Although this was my first encounter with a sleazebag on trail, I was sure it wouldn't be my last. I'd been so anxious about being part of what's traditionally been such a male-dominated space that I think I expected more sexual innuendo and some scorn, incredulity or a fiery brand of paternal patronising from the men I met. It hadn't been the case. In fact, I had mostly witnessed great respect. For example, at shelters and campsites, men routinely turned away whenever a female hiker looked as though they were going to change clothes, without making a big deal of it. They discussed gear and mileage with us in the same ways they would with male hikers. It seemed that the *actual* male hikers who were out here hiking were pretty chivalrous. It was the ones who were bashing their keyboards in the online groups that were the problem.

In my preparation for the trail I had spent time following hikers on social media who were doing the hike northbound, so I could learn from them and be inspired for when I began southbound in June. This usually worked well for me learning and feeling part of the community, and the online forums on Facebook were awash with help and support... until one day, when I was sent a variety of shocking, aggressive videos and photographs of a man masturbating.

There they were, right in my inbox, from a hiker I had thought seemed nice. He had previously been posting public photos of the trail and was raising money for a charity as he went. I was so stunned, and after years of thinking in the abstract that wouldn't a dick pic be horrible, I was now aware of how violating it felt to receive one in real life. Especially as I was idly scrolling my messages and opened them whilst having a wee at the time. Somehow it was extra violating to see gross photos whilst un-knickered.

Although women are in many ways more vulnerable in the outdoors than men, this wasn't a daily theme for me out on trail. Backpacking and long-distance hiking were clearly great equalisers in many respects. It didn't matter what car you drove, the money you made or the education you had out here. You were all equal and unified in your grit, determination and love of the outdoors. It appeared to be the same with gender, and things would generally only get creepy when you made contact with men like the one above, and now the man I had just had the distinct lack of pleasure of talking to in the parking lot of the hostel. He who perused 'female hikers' on the internet as though they were fantasy for his imagination to play out on. Giving all those other good men a bad name. I walked back over to my friends on the veranda of the hostel.

'What took you so long?' Lazybean enquired with a louchely raised brow.

'Oh, you know.' I looked at Dozer, then back at where the truck was, and returned my gaze to her, letting my eyeballs roll.

'Ohhhh.' She smirked. 'Fucking creeps, that's what,' she said, laughing as she watched the truck pull out of the lot. 'Fucking men.' And she flipped the bird at the air as she lay back on the deck in the sunshine.

'Heyyy, come on now.'

I turned, thinking Lazybean was talking to me, but realised he was shrugging at a sign on the door that said he couldn't come in without paying for a shower and wearing some loaner clothes. He and Dozer elected to sit on the porch, but as for me: well, hell, I'd have paid $100 for a 5-minute shower at this point. I bought them a beer as they waited for me before we hitched on back to the trailhead.

*

Why was Maine so conflicting? So beautiful but so brutal. It took me what felt like all day to ascend 4 miles. Sugarloaf was brutal, and the Crockers were steep, needing plenty of stops. Stops were all the better for listening out for moose though, which I was just so desperate to see. There were so many moose droppings on trail, some still steaming in the cool air, that I was sure they'd be around any corner, but no joy yet.

We crossed paths with section hikers and Nobos at various shelters, sometimes stopping to talk. At one spot I spoke to a quiet German girl whose name was 'No Plans'. She was very pale and thin, and explained she didn't have nearly enough food at the beginning but didn't want to tell anyone, losing so much weight she couldn't keep up with her previous trail family and let them drift away. She was back on trail properly with more plans than she had before, and hopefully eating enough to survive. I was amazed by these people I was meeting who had shed so much weight. I was physically working harder than I ever had but didn't feel too much different. Hmmm, it had only been just over 2 weeks, but I felt certain my body was going to hang on to its chub into eternity.

It was the 3rd July when we staggered a final dark 3 miles to a waterfall Lazybean knew from his last Nobo hike. He made a fire for us while Dozer and I set up our sleeping gear. A tent for me and a tarp for them, on soft bouncy moss and in a pretty clearing off the disused logging road we'd come to.

We sat by the fire and held our bruised feet in the freezing water of the pool at the base of the falls, before the torrent careened off the next ledge by our fire and down into the darkness below. It felt like the soles of my feet had been beaten with sticks, and I couldn't decide whether the freezing water made them feel better or worse. To my horror, I'd run out of food and my gas canister was too low to light. How the fuck could my pack be so damn heavy but carry so little useful stuff? I was an idiot.

Lazybean and Dozer boiled water for me and I ate my ramen, feeling very happy they didn't mind helping me and glad that I was making mistakes in such patient company.

CHAPTER EIGHT

I'll Never Learn

Getting up before others became a ritual for me in real life. If I didn't beat the household or the sun to rising, then somehow there would be guilt and a day playing catch-up, struggling behind where I should be. Perhaps it was a hangover from those days when I really *was* behind – literally – watching others make strides of progress with relationships, sports and daily life whilst I hobbled. Nevertheless, it was ingrained in me. So hearing the Steinbecks up and moving about as I was just waking gave me a cold feeling in my tummy. I was alert in moments, stuffing my pack and feeling like I needed to get out ahead. This was ridiculous, because there is no 'ahead' on the trail. It's a long line of people doing their own thing, or 'hiking their own hike' as it's commonly known. Take a day off, take a week off, race for 3 days or just sit by a river all morning – anything goes, but I still hadn't quite grasped it.

My body ached as I limped around the camp, packing my things. But then I stopped to stare – absolutely elated to watch the sun rise over the forest, knowing that a town was coming today. A town! The day would surely be easier – just an amble down a hill. No? No. Today was the Horns and Saddleback. Two peaks, junior and senior, and then along a wide expanse of flat ridge with gently sloping sides.

Wide-eyed and desperate at only halfway through, I nearly couldn't make it up and over the last horn, my legs quivering like a newborn foal and tears in my eyes the whole way. I repeatedly had to take off my pack and throw it up onto ledges or atop boulders with my poles so I could shimmy up heights, palms prickling and chest beating. I knew my stupidly heavy pack and extra bodyweight were slowing me down, but I could also begin to feel the old familiar pain creeping through my hips and right leg each time I pushed off to climb higher. More pain, less range. I couldn't say anything to anyone, couldn't admit it to myself, so I paused regularly to absorb the views and breathe the crisp air deeply. One step at a time, and I'd get there. Always my mantra. This was how I usually felt when my body was at its limits, but it dawned on me that perhaps these *weren't* its limits after all. My own false summit. How deep is the well?

The journey into testing limits is a strange one, and with chronic pain you don't always know what those limits are until you 'wake up' to yourself one day and realise that you're living a smaller life than the one you thought. When I was first in pain, I would keep pushing through and suffer extraordinarily just to feel my kind of normal. But as with any period of attrition, the energy needed to push through and fight the pain wore thin. In order to do just the basics of dressing, filling the cupboards and keeping myself ticking over with an income and a safe home, I would often pull back from the 'extra-curricular' enjoyable things that make a life worth living before I *had* to stop, because I had learned that on the other side of my limits would be a punishing echo of that effort in the shape of increasing pain for weeks to come: a swelling body-scream to intimidate me back into physical stasis.

Once I pushed my body past a certain point, it would be a long road back. I was always faced with choosing either to quietly reverse when standing right on the crumbling edge, or to throw myself over and then have to find a long way back right to the top where I started. So, although I'm a limit-pusher and felt like I had been living recent life so close to the edge of my abilities, I now realised that perhaps these boundaries that had fenced me in for so long had been in the wrong place and there was so much further I could go; that I had been conditioned to not look up and beyond them after so many years of being handed my ass and suffering for doing just that.

Why hadn't I revisited these limits in recent years? Why did I let the first twinges or stabs of pain take me out of the gym and my training regime and out of the pool or off the trail-running schedule? Perhaps because I'd come so far and was terrified of being thrown back to the very beginning. But out here I didn't have a choice. I was going to have to push right past my limits and fears to keep up and stay with friends and finish this trail. Two sets of personal fears opposing each other, and I knew which one would win: I'd grind my body back into the dust to not feel the shame of failure again.

Hauling myself off the rock edge I was seated on with both grimy, bleeding hands, I swivelled myself and my pack around in the tight space between boulders and thorns and set my mind. One pole down, spike into the dirt. One hand-haul up to the next ledge and I was on my way, slow and inexorable as an encroaching tide.

The sweeping views of lakes and forest at the top made the grind worth it. I sat on a cairn, grimy forehead to the top of my pole, and cried with pure joy and exhaustion. This was my 18th day without a day off. On my Bambi legs I had hiked, and I had not given up. My body had let me push it far further than it had been before. I think it was beginning to thrive on the exertion, and I was high on the feeling.

The rest of the day was long and beautiful. Once up on the summit of Saddleback, the views were wide and sweeping, with the open, flat ridge of the mountain ahead of me. I imagine it's called Saddleback because it looks exactly that – a gentle ridgeline across the centre, sloping evenly down the sides of the mountain, the same way a saddle sits around the belly of a fat pony. It was a blessed relief to be up in the open air, and I slowed my pace further to breathe in the open skies and to stop and eat handfuls of the wild blueberries that grew along the trail. Careful to not step off onto the preserved and protected areas, I made my way across the saddle. This part of the day was only eventful for my gazing at the sweet alpine flowers scattered along the way, and subsequently falling over my own two feet, gouging a deep chunk of flesh from my knee on a bare rock corner. A few more tears and a huge strip of gaffer tape later, I was on my way again, noting but ignoring long, deep-red rivulets of blood drying around my ankle, clotting in my sock.

As the flat ridge turned into a descent, I glimpsed civilisation in the distance in the form of buildings twinkling in the afternoon sunshine around one of the many lakes I'd seen from the very top. Reinvigorated, my speed increased and the pathway beneath me fluttered like a ribbon in the wind as I raced down as best I could with my many bumps and bruises. I eventually hobbled off trail and onto a hardtop highway, joining my friends to walk on surprisingly painful flat ground to Sam's Hiker Hut, a peaceful, welcoming green space with little electricity, some huts and a river running alongside. It wasn't the town I'd seen, but it *was* the first stage of finding a ride to get me there. Buckshot was sitting holding court on a long picnic table, and we scooped him up with us as we hitched a long ride to the closest town, Rangeley, where I had booked myself a room for the night in anticipation of a double zero. Come hell, high water, or other folks leaving to hike out… I was going to sit my ass down.

The sunset was breathtaking purples and pinks as we entered the town, a small conurbation set along a road next to a large lake. I was finding it hard to get used to these American towns – their lack of a 'centre' or a town square equivalent to what I was used to in Europe, and especially at home in Cornwall, where each seaside town had a harbour *and* a centre. A little hug of humanity in a semi-circular space. So far in the USA, each town seemed to have grown from someone scattering the seeds for buildings out of the window when driving through; shops and houses were sprinkled on the left and right of the road but there was no significant depth or central point.

The boys were lazy and slow off trail, the opposite to their on-trail focus and effort. Lolloping and thinking only of beer, soporific with heavy limbs and glassy eyes. Stoned and in recharging mode. I booked into my room behind a biker who mentioned he'd seen fourteen moose along the roads riding into town. Goddammit, that's where all the moose were – watching bikers.

As I wrote my details down in the '50s reception area, I realised that the Steinbecks had their own room too, so only Buckshot didn't. I mean, who am I kidding? I grinned to myself. I totally

149

knew that he didn't and that he would probably stay with me. Isn't it funny that you can simultaneously think something is a brilliant but also a terrible idea, and look forward to it but also dread the aftermath? I guess whichever's pull is the strongest wins out, and after 18 days of physical exhaustion, a few cold ciders and a big man's arm around me on the walk back to the motel in the moonlight, I knew what was pulling me. So I let it pull my clothes off, pull me down onto the bed and into the embrace of something more welcoming than the rocks and boulders of the last 2 weeks.

*

We spent the next day canoeing on the lake, drinking beer in the sun and speaking to the guests at the lakeside motel, some of whom brought us beer whilst others brought fresh trout they'd caught for us to grill on the barbecue we'd lit. We hikers were a locus of interest because we'd walked in and we'd walk out again. Where were we from? Where were we going? Modern nomads and raconteurs. It was fun while the sun was as high as my trail family with their huge bags of weed, but the sun set and they peaked early, eyes and words lazy with the long evening shadows.

It's not a surprise to me that men sometimes act half their age. They walk around the room naked, leaving a trail of messy destruction behind them that they have no care to clean up. 'Leave it,' they say, 'that's what the cleaners are for.' Hmm, no. And so it was that amongst the fun and frolics of my first zero with this little trail family, I also found myself cleaning, tidying and seeing the men from the woods with different eyes now they had emerged into civilisation, their *lack* of it being shown in sharp relief. I wasn't going to be associated with leaving a filthy room behind me, so it fell to me to keep it nice.

It was extremely frustrating to find that this role exists everywhere; this slipping into gender stereotypes that I didn't think had such a defined grip on those in generations younger than mine. Perhaps women are conditioned to *notice* things that men don't, to be more aware of how things smell and how tidy rooms are left. It's not that I want to live in splendour or luxury – far from it – but just that I can't conscionably leave something in a terrible mess just because I've paid to stay and someone else will clean. Taking advantage of this system means that someone on a low wage has an even tougher day than they needed to, just because we were selfish and lazy. But I don't know why that would be a female consideration. Perhaps it never gets to be many men's consideration because by the time they might need to think about it, it's already been taken care of.

On trail, life had seemed very balanced and equal between the genders so far. I hadn't come across any patronising looks or comments from male hikers that I'd met. No one had sneered at my vulnerability or tried to help me with my pack because it looked 'heavy'. Everyone kind of assumed that if you're out there hiking, then you could carry your own load and look after yourself unless you asked or said otherwise. And if you did ask, it wasn't put down to you being a 'girl', but just that you're clearly a person who needed to ask for a hand. Once on trail, hikers mostly seemed to be… hikers. Almost sexless for all intents and purposes when it came to the usual men versus women debates. We were all in it together. That's why I was so taken aback that these men who felt so passionate about the wilderness would be so lax in transferring this care and respect to civilisation.

Mind you, seeing an experienced hiker having pooped on the *surface* of a side trail – and merely top it off with some toilet paper on top and leave it there – had already made me think that perhaps these people didn't respect the wild as much as they said they did. Pooping on trail is fine and dandy as long as it's in a cathole dug 6–8 inches deep and filled back in and over with earth so animals can't get to it. And not in dry, arid soil where it can't decompose of course... but that didn't apply here on the loamy, rain-soaked terrain of the AT.

So, shocked at my code-switch into the matriarchal role, I cleaned up filthy towels from all over the motel-room floor and swept empty chip packets with empty beer cans into binbags before going back outside on the veranda to relax. The biggest shock, however, came the next day when talking to Dozer in our amble to have some lunch in town. I was intent on helping her celebrate her 21st birthday by buying the fanciest legal alcoholic drink she desired. This turned out to be a delicious margarita or two.

'*How old?*' I gasped, stopping mid-lick of the salt around the rim of the glass. 'Are you fucking joking?'

She threw her head back and cackled. She wasn't.

'Don't worry, G, they think you're close to our age. Men are so dumb sometimes. Big dicks, small brains those guys. Well, not small brains, but you know, they don't use them all the time. Lazybean asked me how old I thought you were. I said I had no clue but just nodded when he said like, maybe 29 or tops 30?'

'Jesus,' I gasped, 'I'm 41.'

'Yeah. I figured mid- to late 30s at least. No offence, but I'm not dumb. You look young but you've done a lot of stuff, so it kinda makes sense you'd be older.'

'But Buckshot can't be 25. He *can't* be. He looks like he's mid-30s at *least*, and I thought that was kinda young, but what the hell, it's the trail.'

'Yeah, he does look old as hell. It's the big beard and the hair, I think. But look, it doesn't matter. No one cares out here on trail. It's no big deal, and even if he knew, he wouldn't give a shit. I wouldn't worry about it.'

I wasn't sure, but we left that topic behind and chatted about life, her having experienced a lot in her short years.

After drinks, we both ordered sandwiches for our 'men' back at the motel. Mildly buzzed and feeling like some kind of good wife, I arrived back at the room and presented the food, which Buckshot snatched up with a laconic peer in the box and a brief 'Yeah, cheers', and ate it like a starving animal.

In the bright light of civilisation, in town, he was different. My regular old brain was waking back up after the weeks in the woods, seeing what used to matter to me – things like manners, respect and equity rather than survival, food, shelter and safety. With those scales fallen from my eyes, I could now see more clearly what I had seemingly hitched my cart to in the woods. I couldn't quite make sense of how I was feeling. Definitely some disgust about his behaviour here in town. Crudely sexual, messy, inconsiderate and loutish. But this disgust also tugged something deeper in me that had woken up out there in the trees. Some appreciation for a more animalistic man, with the ability to navigate the wild, to be strong and fearless, knowledgeable in an environment that I was lost in, as he might be just as lost in settings I felt at home in. I was attracted to and repulsed by him in some equal measure, but mostly I wanted him, this man of the woods, to see me as worthy: like this would be the thing that could validate my strength; that despite my age and my previously unreliable body, now I could keep up and finally be part of a team; be one of those who had run past and before me for so many years whilst I had been only able to exercise my brain.

I woke in the night and went to the bathroom, seeing on my return that Buckshot had fallen asleep with food on his chest and whiskey in his hand. In the morning I was amazed at myself when he began to talk about the hiking ahead, feeling my annoyance swivel back to admiration. I was clearly a groupie – a Grom who had fallen for their surfing instructor or some such, with him now as my coach and the hiking leader, heading back into an environment where I was out of my depth. Urgh, how predictable of me.

I needed to feel like I was doing something to contribute to my own independence, so I left him packing the coffee machine with his huge paws and grabbed my filthy clothes, taking the long walk to the launderette where I met 'Trailblazer', a friendly man who had hiked the AT in the '90s and, like many others who have hiked it before, was keen to support the new cohort. After he had helped me buy powder and start the washer, he set me up with Wi-Fi and the hiker box to rummage through and asked where I was going.

'To the supermarket next!' I smiled, thinking it was around the corner. Everything *is* around the corner in the UK.

'Hooo, that'll take you 20 minutes or some to walk up the highway.' He rubbed his chin and broke into a big smile. 'Say, would you like to use my car?'

I loved the idea, but after discussing my lack of US permit and insurance we shelved it and I resigned myself to the walk. I pocketed a couple of items from the hiker box on my lap that had been made by Trailblazer himself; the contents clearly bearing the hallmarks of a previous hiker. A couple of Band-Aids, a Q-tip and some Vitamin I. I thanked him, picked up my empty pack for the groceries and stepped out into the bright morning.

It was a trudge, and I berated myself with a grin about walking unnecessarily when I had so much bloody walking still to do. Ruminating over my night with Buckshot, I was slightly dreamy, when in the distance on the quiet misty road ahead I saw a deer step out of the trees onto the hardtop. It was huge, even at this distance. *What a massive deer*, I thought, like a moron. How unusual. Then a truck came over the ridge of the hill and slowly cruised down towards me. The deer wasn't the slightest bit perturbed by the vehicle, but I certainly was, because even at a distance this 'deer' was much larger than the truck. What a weird thing. My perspective must be off.

I squinted, shook my head, and refocused as though the view was one of those magic paintings you would squint at and eventually see shapes in the pattern. Then the penny dropped. *Moose*. It was a bloody *moose*! Wow.

I broke into a hobbling run on my bruised feet, muttering an entreaty for the animal to stay right where it was until I could get there. It was so far away from me that I knew it was hopeless. The

155

truck swooshed close past me and my clothes flapped in the dirty breeze. I stopped and stood instead, enjoying the last moment of watching the majestic creature step delicately hoof over hoof across the road, turn its giant, serene head towards me once, and then gracefully slip into the woods on the other side. My mouth was open. Did I really see that? It was a giant! I hustled as fast as I could to the spot it had vanished into and peered into the dimness between the pines. Gone. Dammit.

I resupplied at the mart with more than I needed, as ever, and bumped into the others coming in as I left. I hung by the door to wait for them and we all piled back into the launderette without seeing any more moose. There was something I didn't like about how Buckshot riffled through the hiker box and discarded it. I knew he liked to travel light and there may have been nothing of any value in there for him, but I had seen Trailblazer look pleased when I picked up one of his little bundles, and I knew he had bought more of the things that were in there for people coming through. Perhaps I'm soft, but with Buckshot it felt like watching a child ripping boxes open at Christmas and walking away to the next thing, disinterested. It was already clear to me how much wonder and joy on this trail came from the network of people surrounding it, so I could see that hikers needed to give gratitude as well as take gestures of kindness.

Sam came and drove us all back to the Hiker Hut for our final night before we hit trail again, squeezed into his car amongst the bags of shopping that I already knew I wouldn't be able to fit into my pack. Every time I leave a place, I leave a bulging hiker box, but I kinda like that. I felt good right now. Great even. There was a warm glow in my chest because I was with a little group that I liked, I was feeling more confident on the trails, I had rested a little, and now that I had some kind of attraction in the mix too, things felt even more exciting.

There were more people at Sam's than when we had left. An entirely different set, which made me marvel that we're all having the most exciting and challenging time and it feels like we're the centre of the universe, but half a day or a day behind us is another group of people for whom the same things are happening, and so on and so forth behind them. You could hike the whole trail and never meet the people a day behind you or a couple of days ahead.

I was introduced to some of the folk who sat engaged in various tasks. Abbi, an illustrator, was finishing a beautiful watercolour of a wooden plank bridge she'd crossed. She told me she was taking the trail slowly because she wanted to stop and draw along the way. Bonsai was also there, goofing around and telling stories of how he was a coastguard in real life. I watched Buckshot's eyes roll at his stories of bravery and derring-do, looking to tamp down any rival showboating like a duelling peacock.

'Fuckin' coastguard? That's the most stupid of all of them. Just sits in a little room watching the sea, never really goes anywhere. Ha, he ain't gonna make it.'

I ignored him and asked if anyone had nail clippers. My nails seemed to have grown more in the last 2 weeks than in the last 2 months, and they were cutting into my toes. Perhaps walking for 10 hours a day might be the cause.

Jeannie brought some over and I started clipping, gathering cuttings in my hand to throw away, which made my friends laugh at me. Jeannie didn't laugh though. In her early 60s and from Alaska, she was a serious woman who always seemed very focused on whatever she was doing, and now she was looking at my can of beer next to me. Her gaze scanned the others and their beers; Buckshot was on his third or fourth. Her mouth pursed into a little line. I didn't like to feel judged, but the gang were getting louder and I didn't want to seem ill-mannered, so semi-successfully I engaged her in conversation about her hike so far, then returned the clippers. Oh, my poor feet. Bruised and battered already, some blisters and blackening toes. I gingerly stepped over in the darkness to the cooler by the picnic table to get a Sprite, meeting a couple bent over, the woman immersing her feet in an ice bucket. I dipped to scoop a can out of the slush and asked how she was.

'She's OK,' her partner answered. She looked at me, her expression so sad. I glimpsed her feet in the bucket, swollen like melons with puffy ankles and calves.

'Oh, no, what happened?' I couldn't imagine it was a sprain, not on both legs.

'Leukotape. It was the Leukotape,' she said. Leukotape is the special zinc tape that hikers use to plaster up their feet on hotspots to prevent blisters. I didn't own any but probably should. Her eyes welled up. 'I think I'm allergic to it. I've been here for 2 days now and the swelling isn't going down. I think I have to stop.'

Her partner put his arm around her as she started to cry, crushed disappointment on her face. To be out of this so soon, after planning so long. I could imagine how she felt as it was my own fear writ large on another person. I nodded and murmured some support as Sam came by and swept me back towards the bunkhouse under his skinny arm. On the way he gave me a hug and whispered in my ear.

'I have been watching you. I can see what's happening.'

I stopped. He stopped alongside me and grinned, eyes twinkling in the light of candles and solars. Sam was a nice guy, but what was this?

'What do you mean?' I looked at him, smiling politely but resigning myself to it being something annoyingly smutty.

'Buckshot. Those guys. They're great fun, Gail, and you're having a ball, but they're not going to be good for you. I can see how you look at him, and I've been looking out for hikers for enough years to have seen all sorts come through here. They'll keep you partying and whooping it up, but they can carry on and you'll run out of steam and then it'll go sour. Have some fun but be careful. He's a taker, not a giver, and for all the excitement he brings, he's only going to think of himself.'

I wasn't sure how to respond, because after our days in the Rangeley motel I could only agree on some sensible level, but I was going back into the forest and that's when this crew became my teachers. I needed them and, besides, I liked them.

The night grew quieter, with only Bonsai still singing to himself and drinking by the fire. The rest of us hunkered down in the bunkhouse, Buck in the bunk above mine, kissing me before bed, holding my hand over the wooden rail and saying, 'Is this what you mean by affection?' then grinning down at me in the gap between the bunk and the wall before he rolled back and slept. I stayed awake for a while, considering how I was going to manage to blend my real-life self and my wild-life self. Being sensible and making good, responsible decisions seemed to fit only in the past. Wasn't I out here to achieve something different? I had the urge to be reckless, do questionable things with wild and free people. Sam was right, but I wasn't for turning. I'd managed to stumble upon some wild ones and I was sticking with them.

*

We started out as a group the next day and strung out into a line as was becoming the norm. I kept my eyes peeled for beaver in the lakes and swamps on either side of me and enjoyed fireflies in my tent at night. A couple of days later I had my first experience of Trail Magic proper as I ascended a climb set back over a deserted highway. There in the dirt sat a white cooler with 'AT Hikers' written on the lid in sharpie. I flipped it up and inside sat all manner of treats: sodas, freshly made sandwiches labelled with marker 'PB&J' or 'Nutella'. Snack bars, chips and a spiral-bound notebook sealed up inside a ziplock. I wrestled it open and read.

'We, Geri and Simon, love to provide magic for the hikers who come through here. Please take whatever you need but leave some for those behind. We also love to know where you come from! Please write your name and hometown in the book.'

I flicked back, reading names from all over. A mix of trail names and real ones, with the locations mostly in the USA but some further afield, like the Israeli man I'd met on some boulder or other, face all smashed up from falling over, full of stitches but only a week or so left before he had to join up in the Israeli army, so he wasn't stopping for anything. I grabbed some crackers and stuffed them in my mouth, delighted to sit and stop.

Just then, Smudge came up from behind me – fit, young, sweet and everything you'd want in a trail buddy. We chatted, and then behind him came Geri and Simon themselves, excited to be replenishing the cooler while there were actual hikers eating from it! Like fishermen checking their nets, but only to feed us and see us go free. They told us they'd seen an otter and a bald eagle on the short drive from their house and I then listened to other gathering hikers tell tales of all the beavers and moose they'd seen too. I was clearly making too much noise stomping up and down to see the wildlife!

Trail Magic was the perfect flytrap for north and south hikers alike, and we stopped to chat as a tiny bubble for 10 minutes before I filled in the logbooks for our magic couple and then started out, always keen to get out a little ahead because I always expected to be overtaken. I didn't know where we were going to stop that night and I really didn't want to camp alone yet – I wasn't ready for it, so I needed to be far enough ahead to keep up when I was overtaken, but not so far ahead to be a far outpost when everyone else stopped for the night.

It was Lazybean's birthday, and the four of us had started out that morning together. Buckshot pulled away ahead, and while I waited for my favourite couple a few times, it was clear they wanted to take the day slowly, smoking plenty of weed and enjoying the views. That was fine – I'd catch Buckshot and they'd catch us later. Lunch was spent on a warm, sunny log with another panoramic view, lazily munching peanut M&Ms and making peanut-butter tortillas. I moseyed on, happy to be with my thoughts and stopping to pick pine needles out of my socks every 20 minutes. Oh for some gaiters!

*

Hours later and still no Buckshot. It wasn't until balmy late afternoon that I found him sitting at a viewpoint. I had begun to feel anxious that I was caught in the middle – Buckshot thinking I was back with the others, and they believing I was up ahead with Buckshot – neither needing to give me much thought, so I was very glad to find him.

'Theeeeere you are! I was wondering where y'all had gotten to!'

It wasn't that Buckshot was a super-fast hiker; he was just tall and had enormous endurance. He could hike for 15 hours a day without feeling any ill effects. A steady pace and consistency was all he seemed to need. 'No, they're miles behind,' I said to him.

'Well I don't think they're coming if it's his birthday and they're not here already. Probably just smokin' bowls and making love in the great outdoors.' He grinned and gestured around at the beauty.

'And you, Appalachian Gail? How are you doing?'

We talked about my worry of being between people, of getting lost in the cracks, of not feeling safe. He listened carefully and asked why. I tried to explain but I didn't quite have the right words. The story of my being attacked in the past wasn't fluid enough to articulate, and the highlights of it (or lowlights if you like) seemed trite to blurt out like a staccato headline. So instead I burst into tears. From nowhere really. I just said I had been assaulted before, and that being out here in the woods with no one knowing where I was or how to get to me *and* in a foreign land had me all kinds of anxious.

'Right. Welllll. Let's get you a gun.' A fine response, but not the one I needed.

'Very kind, Buckshot, but not necessary.'

'I can teach you to shoot it? Or maybe pepper spray? Y'all want that? I'll get you some of those.'

I nodded, wiping tears from my face and deeply grateful that he wasn't minimising my fears or making me feel weak or broken.

'Y'all be OK. You can do this. You stick with me – I'll hike with you for a good while yet. It's another month or so until I need to go off and pick up my speed. I can hang back with you and I'll keep you safe.' He didn't try to hug or kiss me but leaned over to touch my leg. 'We like you. You're with us. We won't let anything happen to you.' And with that holding of space for me to be afraid *and* accepted, I felt my heart expand and my connection to him deepen.

'Think you can do a few more miles as it grows dark? It's a helluva descent, but I know a place by a river.'

'Sure.' I nodded and followed him on wobbly legs for another 6 miles to a place of beauty and solitude. We made love under the pines and stars, cooked a hearty meal in the darkness and cowboy camped by a roaring river, miles from anyone.

NEW HAMPSHIRE

160.9 miles

CHAPTER NINE

These Mountains
Have Serious Range

Maine released us into New Hampshire, a state filled with beauty, high mountains and fancy tourists. Buckshot and I piled into Gorham to take a zero before tackling the famed Presidential Range in the White Mountains. We hit town within hours of each other, him before me, and I called to see where he was before I went to the hotel I'd booked for us.

No reply – strange.

I settled in and showered off the filth, hanging out all my clothes and sleep gear to try to dry it after having been pelted by rainstorms for the past 24 hours. I tried him again. Nothing. Perhaps he'd hit a bar or was with trail friends somewhere in this small town? He often knew people along the way from his previous hikes, so I wasn't going to worry too much.

However, when I finally got hold of him he didn't sound quite right and had, mysteriously, booked himself his own cheap motel room up the road.

'But we had arranged to stay here!' I exclaimed. 'I don't understand. Are you OK?' I couldn't quite place his tone; in a mood I wasn't familiar with.

'Yeah. Well. I forgot.' He was hostile for some reason. 'I got so wet I needed somewhere to be and dry out. Didn't know how long you were gonna take.' He tailed off into a mumble and I told him where I was, and to come on over when he was ready.

A few hours later, there was a knock at the door. I'd had a bath and was lying on one of the two double beds in a daze, staring at the ceiling and breathing in and out with the throbbing of my feet, knowing I was ravenous but not sure where to go for the biggest feed or if I had the energy to get there. I opened up and let him in, the smell of spirits wafting in before he followed behind – drunk. Drunk by mid-afternoon and in a strange mood. I wondered what was going on, sat back down and gave him space to roam the room.

'What's wrong?' I asked after a while. He'd opened a beer from the fridge that I'd stocked up for him and was tapping his foot looking into space.

He glanced up. 'Nothing. I'm just tired.'

Lies, I was sure. He was a man who clearly enjoyed his own space and I wasn't surprised that he'd wanted his own room, but I was surprised that after our intense time together in the last weeks that he couldn't tell me what was troubling him. Eventually he put the beer down and came over, pulled me off the bed and into an embrace. It felt off.

'No, wait, Buckshot. This doesn't feel right,' I said, pushing him back.

He stopped and stood looking at me. 'Can't we just, you know, hit the bed and not worry about it?' he asked, averting my eyes.

'Well no, not really. Something feels strange and I need to know what it is. If you can't tell me, then OK, but jumping right into bed feels like I'm being used as a distraction more than any-thing. So no.'

He looked annoyed and sat down again. Instead of his beer, he pulled a half-empty quart bottle of vodka from his pocket and swigged from it, nearly draining it completely. He lifted his head again after a moment and said, 'I can't do this anymore.'

My heart dropped. What did he *mean*? The friendship? The sex? The clearly emerging relationship we were in?

'What?' I asked, keeping it simple so as not to give him any ideas for any extra things he 'couldn't do'.

He stood up again and put his back to the wall, between the thin plywood door with the feeble chain and the small circular side table covered in rows of Nuun hydration tablets that I'd ordered in bulk for everyone to have. There was a hollow knock as the almost empty bottle of vodka hit the wall through his coat pocket. He pulled it out, slightly frowned at the contents, then polished it off.

'I can't *do* this, Gail. It wasn't my plan. None of this was. I had set myself a goal, a target, to do this damn trail in 100 days. I was gonna start with Lazybean and Dozer and then just go ahead when I needed to. My folks need me back home to cut trees before winter, and I just… I *can't*.' He hung his head, breaking the earnest eye contact he'd just held.

I wasn't new to this. These conversations of people saying they can't and then giving reasons why. Sometimes it would be me and sometimes them, but either way I could kind of tell when the words or the gestures were genuine or not. It was clear to me that although his reasons might not be the full picture, he was absolutely a torn man. He was sad, and I could see it.

'I understand, Buck,' I said. 'I know what you wanted to achieve and I'm so *glad* we had this time together, but it makes me sad that you have to be unkind about how you're telling me. I don't understand why we can't do this *nicely*. What are you so... irritated and upset about?'

'I just can't have a girlfriend on trail, Gail. I can't.' He stared at me, then away, frustrated.

I was surprised at this. I hadn't thought he had considered it that way or was even beginning to. I certainly had wondered how we might go about shaping our lovely connection, considering his pace and mine didn't truly match, which wasn't going to be sustainable, but I didn't realise he'd been stewing. His moods had ebbed and flowed over the past weeks, that was true. Sometimes he would make me go off before him in the morning, saying he wanted time to smoke and that I should get miles under my belt because he'd catch up so quickly, but then when he'd catch me a couple of hours later he would be a different man; offish and cold. Seemingly cross with me for reasons I couldn't fathom. If I asked him about it or probed at all, it would make everything worse, so eventually I stopped asking and waited for the dark clouds to pass. I just figured he was mercurial. Now it appeared there was more.

'I get it. Don't worry. We have something lovely, you and me. We don't need to worry about it. I'm sad, though, that you want it to end like this. Really sad.'

I could feel myself starting to rip a little inside. The reality that this might be *it* was just hitting me. He could just *go*. Out of the door, back to his hotel and then hike out the next day, or that night, and I could feasibly never see or hear from him again. We were in an unreal world, and I was in a foreign land, and he had become the lynchpin to my experience. My root system, feeding me friendship and security up through the soil of our connection. What the fuck was I going to do? But also, dammit, I was hopelessly attracted to him. How had this happened? He wasn't my 'type'. He chewed tobacco, tucked dip in his lip, carried bags of weed in his pack to sell to hikers, didn't brush his teeth that regularly and was pretty single-minded and obtuse – but, my gosh, it somehow worked. Pheromones – is that the thing? The thing where he didn't smell bad or look bad to me? That made me overlook all the signs that we might not be suited in real life? The thing that made my head swim when I was close to him, that made us unable to stay away from each other? I didn't know, but I did know that I was watching it disappear from me across the room, and I wasn't sure I believed or understood entirely why.

'I didn't mean to get attached to you,' he said mournfully. 'I was just *hiking*, man, and then there you were, and now I just want to hike *with you* and it's fucked everything *up*. I can't. I can't talk about it. I don't want to. I just gotta go. I don't want to leave you, and if I could carry on hiking this whole damn trail with you to the very end, I would, but I can't. So I've gotta make myself *not* care about you anymore. I'm leaving. And that's it.' He put the empty vodka bottle down on the table as I felt a wash of deep sadness sweep up and over me.

'OK,' I said. 'I don't want you to go but I understand. You don't have to be so *hostile* though, Buckshot. I don't understand why it all has to be so sudden.' But he had turned already and was partway out the door. Without a further goodbye, he was gone, slamming the door behind him.

I cried all night under the flickering TV playing a biopic of JFK Junior. I was there, working on Cape Cod during the summer his plane crashed into the sea. Day after day, people came to search the shorelines for him. Lost. Pulled under. It was sad and fitted my mood. Eventually I slept, letting go of the wondering what was next.

In the morning I decided that all there was to do was carry on as usual, and so I met up with a very special father and son duo, Diesel (dad – slow and steady pulling up hills) and Pony Express (tall, fast and light-footed), who had hit town at the same time as me. It was a zero day, so after a full breakfast I wandered the strip of road that formed the town, diving into pawn shops and wishing I had a suitcase to take home treasures. Looking at guns and knives of the like I'd never seen in real life before. I meandered to the post office to mail some postcards, and on the way back, dulled and tired, I heard Buckshot yell my name. How? He was gone!

But he wasn't.

'Hey,' he said when he got closer, pack on his back and pole in hand. 'Wondered if I could come chat to you for a minute?'

'Sure,' I said, completely *unsure* of what to expect. Did he just want to get some Nuun tabs? Some beer from the fridge I'd bought him the night before in preparation for a good time? He loved to take things I offered, and sometimes things I didn't.

Tucked into the fusty dimness of the motel bedroom with sunlight winking through pulled curtains, he explained that he'd tried to leave town but couldn't do it. He didn't want to leave me. His realisation, he said, was that he'd rather be with me and not finish the trail in 100 days, than not be with me and be miserable.

'I'm sorry,' he said earnestly and clearly. 'My behaviour last night, it wasn't OK. I don't know how to talk about my feelings, all that stuff. Y'know. I just…' He tailed off and looked at the floor.

'I get it,' I said, so relieved and shocked at this expression of his care for me.

'There are things you don't understand, Gail. Things I can't talk about or explain. But I don't want to talk anymore. Can we just carry on? Can it be like last night didn't happen? Please?'

'Sure,' I said, not knowing quite how I *wasn't* going to probe deeper about the things I wasn't allowed to know about. I mean, that was now *alll* the stuff I wanted to know. But I was wise enough to realise that for right now it was best left to settle. We spent the rest of the zero day as usual: a little resupply, a little drinking and sex, some laundry and TV. Then, later that day, Lazybean and Dozer rolled into town and called us. We welcomed them into the room and I offered the second double bed.

The day stretched on. Buckshot's father had flown into the area on business and arrived to take him to a bigger town for a few hours to get some new pieces of gear and hang out. When he returned, he brought with him a pair of trail shoes he'd found that were in my size on sale. He knew mine were falling apart and proffered them to me as a gift. I was again surprised but happy. Very happy. More laundry, chatting and beers followed, and then bed, but not before packing to leave. The next morning Buckshot and I rose long before dawn, leaving the Steinbecks for their zero and rest as we headed together up into the intimidating Whites. I wasn't to see Lazybean and Dozer again.

The White Mountains are a slice of the Appalachians. They are high and hard, containing the highest elevations of the north-eastern USA. Our first port of call was the Presidential range, and we *went* for it. Traversing across more mounts than I could remember to count. Perhaps eleven? Madison, Adams, Jefferson… It became a blur of huge boulders and elevation that took your breath away. It was steep, difficult and felt endless, despite taking just over a day. I would have done less if I had been alone, would have stopped in one of the overpriced and exclusive huts on the way to beg a bed, but with Buckshot's encouragement I kept going, hiking well into dusk on the descent out of the range, my legs shaking like Bambi and my aching feet making me wince with each step.

It had been a dangerous day. Mt Washington has some of the worst weather in the USA, and if bad weather is predicted, then the advice, starkly painted on signs at many access trailheads, is to abandon all pride and plans, back down immediately and return another day. Luckily for us, we had clear weather, but people often die up there. I didn't die but I did fall very badly. It might have been my worst fall yet. Head down and marching forwards over uneven rocks, the wind buffeting me and blinding me with my hair… I was walking and then I was falling, forwards, at speed. Wrestling with the straps that attached my poles to my wrists, I got tangled. I couldn't get my arms out in front of me to protect myself from falling face forwards onto the moonscape rocks that were rushing up to meet me.

Resignation to incoming pain hit me before the ground did, then a jagged edge met my chest hard. I was winded, squirming face down, pain racing through my front like a defibrillator must feel like. But still in that briefest of moments I was glad my chest had broken my fall. There'd been only centimetres to go before my face would have met the next rock down and then things would have been much worse.

I couldn't get up though. My heavy pack pinned me to the ground and Buckshot had already hiked far ahead. But then, mid-wondering what would happen to me, I felt a hand on my back and my pack was lifted up from behind, taking me up with it. Once on my feet, I turned to thank my saviour and took her in with a gasp. She was a girl in her 20s with blood under her nose, a cut on her eye and black swelling on one side of her face.

'You OK?' she asked me. Me! She was clearly hurting.

'Yes. Just.' I couldn't seem to take a full breath to be able to speak. I was clearly not quite OK yet and was also beginning to feel embarrassed, which she could see.

'Don't worry,' she said. 'It's easy to do.'

I couldn't stop looking at her face. 'What happened to you?' I asked bluntly. She looked blankly at me, as though she wasn't quite... in there.

'I fell over earlier today, just the same as you. Only, when I did it, it was so shocking and painful that I wet myself.' She paused and watched my eyes widen. 'Did you?'

Dumbstruck, I shook my head, staring at her and imagining how much it must hurt. Knowing, like her, that there's no way down this mountain range that's easy and you just have to get through whatever happens. Observe, detach and keep moving.

'Well,' she said, 'you're doing OK then. Have a good hike and take care.' And with that, she walked past me and steadily away, as

I touched my body to reorient myself and check for injury. My rib. Oh, my rib. It hurt to breathe in, to breathe out and to buckle my front chest strap. It also hurt to swing my arm with my pole. Oh well. I knew if it was bruised or cracked, there was nothing to be done but keep going. So on I went, stunned by the hardship of this range and simultaneously annoyed and glad that Buckshot hadn't been here to see me go down. But mostly I was thinking about the girl with the smashed face who had stopped to help me while deep in her own misery. Kindness was riven through this dirt ribbon.

On the way down that night I experienced my second 'cowboy camp' with Buckshot. The Appalachian Mountain Club managed the huts in the Whites and they charged a lot of money for people to stay in packed rooms of small bunks. If you arrived late but not too late (but also not too early), then the crew of young folks who were working in each hut might let you help them out with the washing-up or cleaning that night, then let you sleep on the dining-room floor once the paying guests had gone to bed. I didn't mind the idea, but Buckshot wasn't having any of it, preferring to spend the night out under the stars in the cold elevation than give in to the rule of the AMC and clean their dishes. We would, however, be heading to one of the final huts the next morning on our way out of the Presidentials, purely because there was often cold leftover breakfasts being given away for free on account of the crews not wanting to carry out any more waste than they needed to. But that would have to wait until morning.

As the sun set that night, Buckshot pushed through bushes and undergrowth to a secret spot he remembered from a previous year, where trail crews stashed their tools. We picked over axes and rebar to spread out our mats on the dirt. He didn't even cook or eat, too exhausted to bother. I set about heating up Stove Top stuffing mix with a half stick of butter, and then lay back, full. Glad that I'd carried on. Glad Buckshot had agreed to sleep across the entrance way to the small clearing so wolves would get him instead of me (the only wolves were in my imagination), and blissfully happy to be under huge dark skies and eschewing a tent to count stars and feel the wind on my face.

*

The next morning, happily uneaten by wolves or bears, I decided I liked cowboy camping. Buckshot woke in a good mood and, after I'd brewed a coffee, urged me to hike ahead to get whatever cold pancakes and sausage might be waiting for us at the hut on the way down. He was happy to sit and smoke, taking some time to pack up camp slowly, he said. Pack up camp? He had the least possessions of anyone I knew out here. Off I went though, on to coffee and to fill my tummy at Mizpah Hut. Then it was the long, difficult descent down Mt Webster cliffs to the road at the bottom.

Legs like jelly from the previous day's exertion, I stumbled and fell often, tired and feeling a little flat. Buckshot had passed me after breakfast, as expected, but his mood was now sullen and dark. As though something had occurred in the time between my leaving him and his arriving to join me. Like I had made him mad, but I hadn't been there to have done so. I couldn't worry too much about it as survival was my focus. It wasn't beyond me to trip over my own two feet, and on the crumbling, shale ridge edges I'd pay for it with more than simple embarrassment.

On the other side of the fast highway at the bottom, Buckshot was waiting, visibly angry. He'd broken his new pole, there was no cell-phone service to call his dad, who had some of his gear, to resupply, and it was beginning to rain. His dad had also taken some of my non-essentials for the last few days in order to lighten my load a little, and that included a heap of my meds. I felt panicked, thinking I wouldn't get them immediately, but knew when not to speak to Buckshot, so I sat silently by the road while a plan formed in his head.

'I'm going up the road to try to get service,' he muttered, and disappeared up a small hardtop road leading off the main highway. He wasn't gone too long before he came bounding back down with a huge grin on his face. 'You get two guesses!' he shouted.

'Cell service?'

'Nope!'

'A store?'

'Nope! *Trail Magic*! A whole damn set-up with tables and chairs and a tarp for the rain. Woohoo! Come on, let's go.'

We hustled up to the top of the road, which was part of the AT connecting back into the next set of White Mountains, including Franconia Ridge. There, in the parking lot, was the spread as Buckshot had described. Everything an exhausted hiker could wish for, from hand-sanitiser refills and toilet paper bundles to chips, cookies and a whole BBQ grill set-up for hot dogs and onions.

Our kind host was a man called Whispers, who enjoyed setting up in different places on trail to pay back the magic he himself had received as a hiker some years before. A slight man in his early 40s, with long dark hair cascading around his shoulders, he smoked a traditional pipe and talked of his other loves in the 'real world', such as the tech field he worked in.

We filled up and he exhorted us to take more for our packs for later. Then we whiled away a good few hours resting and chatting, with northbound hikers coming from the other direction to join us, staying to swap stories of what was ahead for each of us.

In the latter part of our time there I heard Whispers and Buckshot speaking in hushed tones and picked up that our host was a fervent lover of New Hampshire and all the off-the-AT trails that meant you saw *more*, felt wilder and didn't have to stick to the formulaic path that was white blazed. Purists didn't get to experience these, they agreed. I joined them as Whispers described a wild and remote route that looped through the Pemigewasset Wilderness along the next stretch. Taking this off-trail route meant that we wouldn't go up and over the ridge lines with the storms that were coming. Whispers described the things we'd see en route: old logging camps from the late 1800s, washed-out bridges and deserted settlements left to the elements. Buckshot's eyes lit up and I knew we were heading for an adventure in the following days as he accepted the paper map with instructions and sketches that Whispers proffered to him.

We didn't make it far that night into the trail before we pulled over and slept out in a hollow next to the path on a bed of leaves and bark. It was a terrible place to sleep – mosquitoes and bugs trampled our skin all night – but we were exhausted. I was now taking more of my meds than ever to stave off the agony in my chest from my fall, slightly worrying that they were never going to last me the length of the trail and that I'd need to find a way to replenish them or risk seeing what life was like in withdrawal and without them. After 14 years of a steady low opiate dosage, I had a fairly good idea that running out wouldn't be pleasant and that ibuprofen and paracetamol were not going to cut it.

The next day we followed the AT until we came close to a rushing river swollen with snow melt and took a moment to orient ourselves. The AT continued on and up into the storms that were brewing overhead and already peppering us with rain. The paper map showed that if we *crossed* this river then we would begin the Pemi Wilderness loop, which would eventually deliver us back onto the AT just before the ascent onto Franconia. Buckshot looked at me, clearly giving me a choice. He was going to explore and I was welcome to go with him – but if I wanted to stick to the tried-and-true AT, to not deviate from the white blazes, then I was welcome to go and *perhaps* see him down trail – phone service was sketchy and rare here.

After listening to the two men talk the night before about the benefits of stepping off trail to see different routes and sights, I was sorely tempted. I didn't like to do what I was supposed to do, even if I was the one that had decided I was *supposed* to do it – for example, hike the AT – and so, with a wash of cold fear in my tummy, I let go of my attachment to the blazes and the marked, safe trail I had been following, nodded at Buckshot and stepped onto the wide flat river rocks marking the top of a waterfall, moving onto the wild, less travelled road behind him. He was gone in an instant, and I quick-stepped after his pack that was already disappearing into the thick green undergrowth. This marked the start of 2 days of off-route wandering that changed how I looked at the maps and altered my adherence to the fixed trail from then on.

We forded wide rivers where century-old bridges had been lost and were now mere lumps and bumps midstream. We scrambled over downed railway tracks, explored abandoned tools and cauldrons left from 100 years before and joined flat, overgrown tram routes that led us where we needed to go. Silence under the canopy. No waiting for other AT hikers to come up from behind or passing northbounders from ahead. I was still tired from the Presidentials, so we camped a night in a scouting campground we found after making it to a more well-trodden route, then re-joined the AT at the base of Franconia ridge the next day. I was very glad for the experience and happy to have missed the socked-in storms and wild rain atop the last set of ridge lines that AT hikers I met were talking about. Non-purist hiking definitely had its benefits.

Franconia Ridge was long and hot once the rains had gone and the sun came out. I had run out of water, not realising the distance under sun that I would need to traverse before I hit the next source, so I was glad to see day hikers coming up the side trails to enjoy the views and the summit. It took a little asking, but eventually one group gave me some of their spare water, eyeing my bleeding legs, scratched arms and filthy face with no small consternation. 'Hell, miss, you can't even breathe properly. What happened to you? You need me to call someone?'

'No, that's OK,' I replied. 'I just busted a rib falling on Mt Washington a few days ago. I'm a thru hiker.' And I smiled at them reassuringly, which I'm sure looked deranged and manic. Perhaps the very reason they gave me their water was because I looked like saying no might not be an option.

Delirious with heat and thirst, I came skidding down from Franconia Ridge on a side trail – clinging on and swinging off of branches like a kid to hasten my descent. Arriving in the car park, I could see in desperation there was no easy way into town – no buses or shuttles. Buckshot was long gone and I couldn't give a shit where at this point. He'd be somewhere around, but I was focusing on the fact that I was going to have to attempt my first Yogi ride. I began a tentative approach to a group of folks who were clearly walking towards some cars, but just then a nice girl named Katie whom I'd met on the ridge came over to ask if I was OK and offered me a lift. Thank goodness. I was delighted to accept and learned all about her passions for the outdoors and her study of forestry at Perdue as she chatted merrily to me on the ride.

She dropped me along the road in the usual strip-style town I was getting used to seeing, and I made my way to a Dunkin' for a cup of tea. Of course it would be 'tea' when I was feeling out of sorts – soothing and familiar.

Smelly and tired, I got chatting with a lovely couple at the next table who were visiting the area. During the back and forth, Buckshot messaged to tell me he was at the fabled 'Chet's' and I should come. I looked at my maps – from where I was sitting, Chet's was about a 45-minute walk through some suburbs. Why do American towns need to be so… long? I just couldn't face it. Maybe I'd just live here in Dunkin' now. My legs were not going to move.

My lovely new Dunkin' friends asked me what was wrong, and as soon as I explained, they offered me a lift and dropped me at Chet's door, stinking to high heaven I'm sure. People along this trail continually make me want to be a better person.

'Chet's Place' was the stuff of lore, and I'd have found it hard to find without Buckshot's help. Chet himself had been an avid outdoorsman who suffered catastrophically when his stove exploded whilst camping, a number of years ago. He was left with life-altering injuries – blind and confined to a wheelchair – but this hadn't dampened his passion for hiking and hikers. Living right in the middle of the beautiful New Hampshire mountains, he had taken the money awarded him in his court case against the manufacturer and poured it into providing a place for hikers to stay, rest, eat and recover in the garage and carport next to his home. People paid if they could, or helped out with chores if they couldn't, but most did a little of both. His garage was filled with bunks and armchairs, and the basement was a kitchen wonderland filled with boxes and packets for hikers to take. I was grateful and happy to be there, especially as it wasn't an advertised or official spot.

We ended up staying at Chet's for the night and decided on a zero the next day which would mean a second night. I loved the feeling of the night before a zero. There was no need to go to sleep early, no need to gather your energies. You could sit and talk until late, drinking and having fun, which is exactly what we did. I walked back to town and picked up some IPA for Chet and cider for us, and we sat on his veranda putting the world to rights. Little did I know that my world was going to take a shake back into 'wrong' the very next day.

The zero started lazy. There was no one else in the bunkhouse that night, and in my single bunk I wasn't stirred awake by Buckshot's snoring. We'd resupplied, wandered around doing our own thing in the morning and then reconvened back at Chet's around midday, lolling about, reading or meandering around the internet, downloading music for the next stretch and catching up with news from home.

My fingernail caught across my screen mid-scroll and I sighed, deciding that with its patchwork of cracks, my phone screen protector had finally reached the end of its life. I had a spare from the two-pack that I'd picked up in Maine and had been saving it until this one had got really tired. I decided that after dropping the phone multiple times up and down mountains, it was time to let it go and change up. As I began to peel off the cracked and shattered protector, I could see Buckshot looking over. 'That thing still holding together?' he asked, watching it come off my screen in one piece.

'Yeah, but it's pretty trashed though.' I looked at it in my hand. It might last another couple of weeks maybe, all the spiderweb parts held together by the top coating.

'I'll take it,' he said.

'Sure!' I replied. 'Pass me over your phone and I'll see if it's the right size for your screen with my new sealed one before you slap it on – the sticky is already pretty rubbish.'

He stood up and padded over, pulling his phone from his pocket. I took it from him and held up my new protector over it. 'Yes! Perfect. A little wrong for the side edges but it'll do for a while!'

I flipped his phone over to take it out of the case to see if the size looked any better without it. Oh wait. A phone case? I hadn't seen this before. I vaguely knew his phone had a case as I'd seen it when it was clipped to his pack for hiking, but I didn't remember it ever being in a case sitting around in motel rooms. I'd never really seen it up close, and as I looked down at the back of it, flipped over in my hand, I realised why.

It was a girl.

Buckshot and a girl.

Standing together at an overlook, arms around each other. Wearing hiking gear and smiling.

Together.

My skin goose fleshed and went cold. He hadn't yet clocked it – what he'd done. He'd clearly been hiding the case when we were together and clipping it back on for hiking. I looked up at him.

'What's this?' I asked.

'What?' He wasn't paying attention. 'Uh, my *phone*? Do you want me to put the protector on? Here let me…' And he looked back down at my hands properly and at the back of the phone case turned up towards us. At two sets of women's eyes looking at him.

Only one of the women could currently speak though, so I did the asking for us both.

'What the heck?' I asked. 'Who is this?' I said, gesturing at the case. He froze, like the deer in the woods we frequented.

'What do you mean?' He studiously looked *around* the case at me, at the floor, at anything except my hands. A naughty dog caught out next to a destroyed garbage bag in the kitchen.

'What do you mean, what do I mean? Who is this *girl*, Buckshot?'

He frowned. Rallied. Then a torrent rushed out. 'Oh, she's my friend. I don't know why she sent me that case.'

My heart was pounding in my mouth and I couldn't speak. I just raised my eyebrows above my welling eyes.

He shrugged maniacally. 'I don't know why. She just posted it over. We hiked sometime in the past. It's dumb. So dumb she sent it. She's just a friend. I don't know.'

I just stared at him.

'JESUS, GAIL,' he said. Exasperated with me. Annoyed. Caught. Exposed. He bowed his head, wiped his face with both hands like splashing it from a stream. Silence. We were racing towards the crossroads where everything was about to change and I wanted to stay frozen in this moment before. I didn't want to know this; what was coming.

'OK, FINE. I HAVE A FUCKING GIRLFRIEND.' He looked at me furiously.

I couldn't speak. I managed a 'But?' and then was quiet. We were both quiet, him kneeling up, me kneeling low, facing each other. The crossroad moment reached.

I had vaguely known he'd had a girlfriend in the past. In Maine I'd been told by Dozer that she lived overseas, that they hadn't seen each other in a long time and that he'd finished with her; nothing to do with me, so I hadn't raised it. But no, that wasn't right. I *had* raised it on our first night together in bed in the Rangeley motel. I had asked whether he was seeing anyone and he had replied no and was *offended* by the question. After that I had just leaned into it, to him. Fell forwards into it all, talked myself out of the differences, the difficulties, the disappearing, which I now guessed was for phone calls to her on mountaintops where there was a good signal. The inexplicable sullen moods and distance when he caught up to

185

me in the late mornings after he'd probably made contact with her and then felt a surge of guilt about me. But I had been so stupid and now I was deeply in it – I had opened my heart to this man and let myself *rely* on him. Trusted his words and felt safe with him. He was my partner, my trail family, my everything right now.

He had begun talking, but I wasn't really listening. I mentally shook myself, tuned out of my own mind and into his words.

'I feel bad. I keep feeling bad. I didn't mean to *do* this, but I couldn't seem to stay away from you. I *tried*. I tried to leave but I couldn't.'

'Where is she, Buckshot?'

'In Europe.'

'Right. Well. Does she know about *me*? Like, is she OK with it? Do you guys have an open relationship?' I looked down at the smiling girl on the phone case. She would not be OK with it.

'No, she doesn't know. And *no*, she wouldn't be OK. Look…' Angry now. 'Look, Gail, I don't want to talk about it, about her. I thought about breaking up with her but I'm not going to. It's complicated.' And with that, he turned away.

I moved myself outside onto the dusky terrace, started slapping stinging DEET onto my legs and arms, enjoying the pain of the noxious liquid seeping into wounds, hurting me. What a stupid, *stupid* woman I was. So embarrassed, so hurt. The humiliation surged through me. I had thought we had something special. Oh, you fool.

I sat, stared into the woods and let my analytical, overthinking brain spin uselessly through the Rubik's cube of ways this could still be OK and how I could still maintain any combination of ethical integrity, this trail family unit, our closeness, my safety and my heart. Why wasn't I angry? I should be angry. I wasn't. I was more worried about losing my partner out here. How could he really have a girlfriend? We'd been with each other since Day 5 on the trail – surely I'd have known if it were true? But there was a photo. He had admitted it.

Well. Maybe on trail it didn't matter. It was a different world, a different reality. We could still keep it how it was – at least the friendship element – until he had to go and join his family in a few weeks for a vacation. That's what would have to happen. I needed that to happen. Oh, but my heart. My heart hurt so much. I stared out into the dark garden and let the tears come, knowing that whatever came next, something had been irrevocably broken.

He came outside after some time had passed. I'd seen him looking, felt him coming closer, then leaving again. He was unsettled. He had nothing he could say to make it better – he was with her, but he also had done what he'd done. He cared about me; I think this much I knew.

'It's up to you what we do,' he said, standing behind me in the dark. 'I'll do it whatever way you want. But at some point I have to go, you know that. I've always known that. I don't want to go. If it means anything, I really like you.'

I didn't turn. Just spoke my need. 'I don't want to be without you right now.'

He was quiet as he absorbed this: my lack of anger, the chance to have his cake and eat it too, if he could swallow the guilt with it; my choice to sacrifice some ethical code to stay safe. I was grateful that this silent wrangling of trade-offs was happening in the darkness.

'Good, I'm glad,' he said eventually. 'I'm not a bad person, Gail.'

And with that, we went to our beds.

The next day we hiked into the Kinsmans, on the surface like nothing had happened. I was willing the knowledge I had to disappear, but I couldn't help but run our whole time together through a different lens, looking for things I'd missed, either honestly or being dishonestly blind with myself to live out the day-to-day that I was in. Thankfully the events of the hike that day were to overshadow our emotional circumstances. Buckshot's sandal breaking on a steep descent and an extreme red heat alert took me out of dwelling in my head and to problem-solving in the moment, which meant a double-back to the Days Inn hotel in Lincoln for our third night in the town, and a Chinese feast and beer to chase away any blues.

I slept deeply, desperate to put Lincoln and all that had been revealed there far behind me.

CHAPTER TEN

I Can't See the Wood
for the Trees

We'd finally left Lincoln for good, and the first mountain out, Moosilauke, was the biggest and baddest we'd have to hike for a while. Buckshot pulled ahead quickly and I fell further back, happy but tired and toting a full pack with a quart of whiskey tucked inside my front pouch for the summit. It took me a while to ascend, and I chatted to others coming down. I was quite happy with this, our cadence. He was ahead, I fell behind. I didn't have breaks in the whole day, but he did, and in those moments I'd catch up with him, always waiting for me by a stream or river, snacking or smoking. It was the norm and I liked it.

Just as I cleared the forest cover and hiked up some boulders over beyond the treeline, I passed a younger couple and asked if they'd seen Buckshot – my usual description of him being a huge man with a big beard. The usual reply: 'Yes, yes. About 20 or 30 minutes ahead.' Fantastic. He'd be at the summit waiting for me.

He wasn't at the summit. All that was at the summit were bitter winds cutting through my clothes and a series of confusing paths and signs. I waited a little, muddled, and looked a little way down the paths. I then started out, only to double back when I looked behind at a noise and noticed a sign pointing back the way I'd come, which wasn't a white blaze. I'd picked the wrong way down. How the hell did I manage that? Back I went, smiling ruefully at my near miss, and headed down the other side. It was a hectic descent, clambering down a cascade of huge rocks which had sat there for eons, each step down more than one and a half times deeper than my usual gait, each foot placement more likely to be the sharp edge of a boulder tipped sideways than a flat plane. My trusty poles took the burden that my wobbly legs were struggling with.

I was cross with myself really. I loved a plan, to know where I was going and where I was going to sleep; to aim for the end of the day and know when relaxation was in sight. Buckshot didn't want to make plans. He wanted to hike until dark, or beyond. See how far he could push it each day and then lie in the dirt, wherever that was. He seemed joyfully invincible and I wished I could be the same, so I tried to embrace this feeling of never knowing where he would be, or when I could stop for the day. I knew the alternative was being totally alone, because I'd let other chances at trail families slip by as I focused on the excitement and adventure that our bizarre on/ off connection could provide. But I knew it was losing its lustre and that I'd gambled too much and was now at risk of throwing good money after bad on my dedication to this union. Dammit, I hated facing my cowardice, but soon I figured I'd have to stop, regroup, let him go and set back off at my own pace and make my own plans. Surely that was why I had taken this on in the first place? Mastery of my fear, a challenge to my body and a goodbye to the physical limits that had been imposed on me by my pain.

For some reason, I have always felt deeply unsettled out in the deep woods when the early evening arrives. A gentle warning, when the fading light sends stretching shadows and the atmosphere shifts from being expansive to claustrophobic. I feel less welcome and have to press down hard on my rising panic. I had been canny at avoiding this uneasy feeling by ensuring I had someone who knew where I was, or that I was coming and they expected me to arrive, and I'd made peace with the fact that this made me a wimp. I didn't care because right now I had found someone who had helped build my confidence and knew I wasn't ready to take the leap alone yet. But on this day, as afternoon came, I hadn't seen him for many hours.

I knew he must be just ahead, so I sped up and began flying down the mountain at an increasing pace, looking round every bend and anticipating every spring, thinking he would be waiting for me.

He wasn't. I couldn't conceive that he'd just left me. Even though we both knew that his departure was inevitable soon, I thought we were closely enough joined that he would warn me. Or so I hoped. I couldn't understand where he was.

It wasn't until I dropped out of the bottom of the mountain proper and crossed a few dusty roads that I began to feel properly worried. We hadn't crossed many roads on trail at this point, and roads always felt strangely like someone shining a torch in my eyes. It was also where everyone sagely advises you not to be if you're a woman alone, because it's where you are most likely to encounter anyone with ill intentions, within a few miles of trailheads.

I blundered across the roads and through the trail to the next shelter, which was about 400 feet in. The dark was swallowing the path and I was convinced Buckshot would be there, even if only to tell me he was heading on and this was it – the moment he was leaving.

He wasn't. It was a forest-twilight-filled empty space surrounded by pines, containing exactly no one. It was here that I tipped over into the place that I think I'd always feared most. The place that had held me back from camping alone, from certain risks that engendered rising panic I always felt and put so many coping mechanisms in place to avoid bubbling over, even mechanisms that weren't healthy and caused me to share a bed with men that weren't good for me but that were less risky than letting the terror in.

But now terror had its foot in the door and I had nothing in my arsenal to stop it. No taxi to call, no hotel room to book into, no girlfriends to go and see, no excuses to make to get into my car – and no amount of good upbringing, career, money in the bank or achievements could protect me from how I was feeling. The walls were torn down and the fears were mixing. No antidote.

I started to sob. Terror sprang from nowhere and everywhere. I was seeing faces and shapes in the woods that weren't there.

*

It was the day of my A-level results. Sweaty fisted, holding the envelope which contained what I wanted – perhaps more than I deserved and less that I could have achieved. I put that down to the two years of college being the best and most sociable of my life thus far, deservedly so after the trials of secondary school. Warwick University! Archaeology and Ancient Classics! I was in. My boyfriend at the time had already moved close to Warwick ahead of me and got himself a job, and it was now just on me to head on up in September.

Late August – hot, sunny days and warm evenings. I had centred my social scene in the pubs that dotted the area and were only a 30 minute or so drive from my parents' house near Falmouth. I'd been happily folded into a group of girls who were much savvier than me, heading to parties in the countryside, deep down bumpy green lanes in big cowsheds or barns. DJs playing music that made your whole body thrum and the illicit thrill of seeing older people letting very loose, knowing that I was in a bigger pond than I was used to and loving the excitement. These big parties weren't every weekend but on special occasions. We found out about them from a friend who dated one of the 'cool' folks, men from well-to-do families and second-homers with land and space to host some debauchery. I didn't feel as cool as they were – not by a long way – so it felt great when I was with them and was nodded at with recognition or smiled at in the pub.

Yes, the pub, where most of the action happened in this bustling Cornish corner. I would often drive over there in between lectures in my little Toyota Starlet, with the girls crammed in beside me, singing our heads off to Alanis Morissette's *Jagged Little Pill* and chattering about who would be there, whether the 'hot ones' would turn up that night and how long we could feasibly expect to be away from lectures before we got a bollocking. We would push open the doors in daylight, feeling so naughty as we sank into faux Chesterfields in the dim interior with half a shandy over lunch, watching people with real jobs dip in and out like birds at a feeder.

Just before mobile phones existed, we rubbed along just fine. 'Tell so-and-so if you see them that I've gone into town' and the like. Friends were never far away from you, and the conversations always felt full and nourishing, even over a game of pool or when no one had that much to say. No heads bowed to the phone altar here, the closest thing being a brick-sized pager on someone's belt. But not us.

That night in August, we started in the pub. I drove over from Falmouth to meet the gang, already having agreed to stay at Ellie's house and buzzing with anticipation for a night of pure celebration. An adult! Heading to university with the world at my fingertips. A boyfriend who loved me, a family who were proud, and friends I would miss but be friends with forever. This night was where the seesaw should tip gently over into adulthood and independence, my feet creeping forwards along the beam, learning to trust my balance and embracing my future.

It was not to be.

We drank. Hyper and buoyant. Talking and not listening, shouting for the music to be turned up. Ferreting in each other's purses for lip gloss, Marlboro Lights, blusher, lighters. The summer dusk turned to dark outside and our eyes lit up with alcohol in place of the sun. Full beam forwards, nodding yes at both drinks and incoherent flirtations extended our way. The men came – older, sober, cruising like dead-eyed sharks that I wish I could have seen with my adult eyes and understanding of the world. In their late 20s, 30s… Men who doled kudos and cool out with their nods and smiles.

The staccato flashes of memory I have are tied up with the boozy high spirits of the evening. I have tried to never examine that night and all it changed in me, but my ignoring of it has cost me more than was stolen at the time, so in recent years I have worked to push it up to the surface like a splinter and heave it out of my body. It is heavy and has tangled itself to me as I've grown, so although I knew I could excise it, it has taken flesh from me that I believed was always my own but was not. The gaps left are like a tooth cavity. I know they will be filled with other, better things.

We tottered down the street, one friend stopping to pee in the road in an act so depraved to me at the time it stands out like a freeze-frame, her expression caught defiant and intoxicated. I should have known then that the night would bring more than mischief and innocent high jinks, but I was enjoying the wash of the exhilarating unknown and the feeling that I was going towards adulthood now, the naivety of my good humanity causing me to believe that all others might, when it came to the wire, be good humans too.

Piling through the doors of the club across the street and over a little footbridge, our hot fingers left smears through the condensation of the glass panels as we tottered in, one behind the other. We didn't have to pay. We were of age; bright and exciting. New meat herded in so easily, with our softly blurred vision and boozy bravado as substantial as our thin clothes. Welcome, welcome.

I can't recall the layout of the club in any detail. Not only because it was so long ago, but also because my fragmentary memory only gives me Polaroid shots. An industrial metal walkway above a sweaty dance floor, narrow corridors, a pressing of people. Hyped electric air around us, high fives and huge hellos. Why? We were nobodies, but it seemed our excitement gave us that 'aura' that parted groups as we walked, and made men turn around from the bar to watch.

Jess elbowed me as she saw them, the group that she dated and was held in such regard by: the men from the pub. As they beckoned us over, we grinned and swaggered. Hugs, long looks up and down our bodies, offers of drinks. I felt intoxicated beyond the alcohol, high on the admiration and the feeling of stepping into what I figured it must be like to be a real woman and worthy of real men's attention now. Oh, how I misunderstood what real men were, and have for most of my adult life, but in that moment, in this club and on my way to university, I felt sexy because this is what I thought sexy was. Approval and attention from men. This, despite having a boyfriend whom I dearly loved and had no inclination to stray from. I was flexing a confidence that I had never really felt before, and the joy of the taps of flirtation. On, off. On, off. I didn't ever imagine they would drown me.

He was there. This man who always flirted with me. Who knew I had a boyfriend. He was one of the 'cool' guys – older. He had dated a girl who had been a few years above me at school for a while – scandalous as he was 10 years older, but she had become hot property because of it. They had broken up, I was sure. He grinned at me. Long brown hair and huge eyes – chemically huger tonight. They loved their drugs, these folk. I grinned back, accepted a drink, then dived into the dance floor where I truly felt alive. Heat, a crowd, the pulsing beat and the wanton abandonment of moving my body however I needed to. I never imagined I was being watched so closely.

I had been transported by the music and lost my friends, and as I left the dance floor, I pushed through bodies along a dim corridor back to our bags. I was surprised to find *him* there. He laughed and said something I couldn't hear. 'What?' I yelled against the music. He said it again, but still too faintly. Why was he speaking so slowly? Was I so drunk? 'I CAN'T HEAR YOU,' I mouthed, which meant my mouth was wide as his fingers darted inside it, smearing powder all along my gum and cheek.

I slammed my mouth shut with force and pulled my head back. I couldn't compute what had happened, raising my own hand to my closed mouth but not sober enough to spit or decide quickly what to do, paralysed in that moment between looking a fool, looking not cool enough to handle whatever he'd done, and saving myself from oblivion. In the end I took my cue from him, foolish little girl. His wide, laughing eyes and hand on my arm spoke as if he'd done me a favour and that my fear was sweet and funny.

Pulling me into a hug whilst I swayed on heels too big and old for me, he pushed me towards Jess and my friends who were moving closer. 'You'll have fun now,' he whispered and grinned at me. I felt such terror and what I later knew to be violation, with no way to undo what had just been done either physically or emotionally.

I had been mocked and bullied at school so many times for standing up and speaking out, and now I was afraid of being the centre of the mockery in front of these people – these rich party people who seemed to like me. I told myself it would be OK, that Jess wouldn't know anyone who was *bad*, and nor would Ellie. He must be fine. I was overreacting. I didn't need to embarrass myself and make a scene, risk being laughed at. It was probably just a little bit of something fun. He didn't look scary. Just… hungry in some stomach-clenching way. Like a vulture. A hyena.

My drinks were stronger than I thought they should have been. I hadn't needed to buy one all night, which felt great in the beginning, but I knew through the fog of my brain that I was regretting enjoying the largesse. Hours passed, or it might have been moments. Unsteady, touching walls, clutching arms, a rictus smile and the seasickness of disassociation. Then it was cold on my skin and we were outside. The girls linking my arms and the movement of a group behind and around us.

'Such a lightweight…'

'Never seen her quite so hammered. Gail, you lameo, what's going on?'

'Come on, you can make it to the house for a party. Can't you? Everyone will be there.'

'I don't think I can,' I mumbled, trying desperately to remember where I was staying. Where were my clothes and things for the morning? Whose house had I taken them to? I wanted to go home, but it was so far away and I couldn't understand how to make it happen. My heart was everywhere under my skin, throbbing and pulsing. Why couldn't I focus properly? My legs were so slow, but my mind was so fast, alighting on idea and solution and skittering away again, leaving everything unsolved. Glimpses to orient myself: the bank, Topshop, Mounts Bay Trading. We were going along the road that the pub was on. Why? I felt myself slow to a stop and realised that Jess was trying to talk to me.

'Gail, Dan said he'll take you back to his house and keep an eye on you. He's not bothered about coming to the party up the hill. He offered. Come on, it might be best. He's really nice.'

'I don't want to go to the party.'

'No, exactly. You don't have to. Dan will take you home. Look, it's just along from the pub and down the road from the party. We'll come back in a bit to see if you feel better. I promise we really won't be long and we'll come back.'

'I don't know him. I don't want to. I want to go home. Please.' I was slurring and the tiny me sitting back inside my head was watching, horrified.

'It's OK, girls.' He took my arm with his big hand. 'I've got her. She'll be fine.'

'Honestly, Gail,' they chorused, eyes bright with booze and chems, desperate to go to their party. 'It'll be fine. We'll come back.' And in a series of strobes it seemed they had gone, first a metre away, turning back to look at me, then 10 metres, then gone. And all I could feel was his hand on my arm and the slow growing panic of my vulnerability.

House, door pushing open. Bare, bright lights in a front room that housed another man, a sofa and an armchair. I was placed in the armchair. I watched, glazed, as they smoked, talked and crushed white pills and powders together in the dip of the underside of a beer can. Snorting them, ignoring me. Mute. I was mute but screaming to get away, but my legs had given up and so had my belief that the girls were coming back.

'Do you want to go to bed?' Looking up at me from his floor through dark, dilated pupils. The echo of some laughter I had missed hanging in the air around my head. I nodded. Words gone. I wasn't anchored inside my body enough to know how to use the levers and pulleys of my mouth and tongue. A nod was all I had.

Stairs, hands on walls, staring at my fingernails pressing on the bannister as I moved upwards, crescent whites and pink flooding dark pink when I released to grip on again higher up. Another door opened. 'Here,' he said. A big bed. I lay down. The door closed and he was gone. I passed out in relief, giving in to the waves of nausea and disorientation.

I don't know how long I slept, but when I woke up, he was on me. Hands, fingers. Mouth. Clothes being pulled away and my mind floating above me looking down, paralysed through lack of connection with my drowsy, drug-addled body.

'No,' I whispered into the darkness, feebly slapping his hands away.

'Shhhh.'

'No, please.' I felt so stupid. 'No. Stop. Please stop.' Entreaties, with no confidence he would stop. It was as though I felt I deserved this, my chest tight with the naivety and hubris I'd shown that evening. A fawn swaying alluringly into the lion's den. My pleas fell away into dead air, missing their mark. His hand moved around my throat now to stop any more words and tightened enough to let me know he was committed. His body heavy on me, foul cigarette breath in my ear, face darting around mine in the dark. What was real? Where was he? My skin felt numb to touch and I couldn't feel myself, couldn't rouse myself to fight him off. I had backed myself into this corner and now I was paying.

'You're such a tease. Stop it.'

How could he have so many hands? I know his agility must have just been imagined against the torpor of my dulled senses, but my feeble bucking was no match and then he was inside. Hand still on my throat, my head pressed down in Lynx-smelling pillows and the tears in my eyes blurring the shape above me in the darkness. All I could think of was my boyfriend. My poor sweet boyfriend. I had betrayed him with my stupidity.

I think he rolled away after asking me why I was crying, and then he was asleep. I didn't know. I was too petrified to move, to clean myself up or to run. I had nowhere to go and I was unwell. The room moved around me and there I lay, ashamed, dirtied and used. And it was all my fault.

I don't remember leaving. I barely remembered any of this night until I decided to talk about it years later, once or twice to boyfriends to explain why I freaked out having sex drunk sometimes, when it was dark and I was too tipsy and I couldn't tell whose face it was in the dark; why I pushed them off and shouted. The embarrassed apologies afterwards, with men who felt emasculated and impotent hearing the damages done to their woman long before they could protect her, deflecting the information with defensive outrage rather than absorbing it to take some pain away from me. 'Why are you telling me that? What can I possibly do about it now?' or 'Jesus, that was years ago' or even 'Let's go find him – I'll fuck him up.' All useless attempts, just like my ability to process what had happened.

I know that at the time I tried to smooth it over myself, as if it hadn't happened. It seems lunacy now, but trying to be normal in the days afterwards was an attempt to make it a bad dream. To convince myself that I could still have my old life, that I could be my old me. She wasn't far away – only a few days on the other side of the 'event'. I needed her back. I blocked it out and returned to the pub to meet the girls two nights later, ready to embrace a fake memory. Pulse racing even as I parked my car. My shirt stuck to damp skin in the small of my back and my palms prickled with adrenaline. I pulled my stool to the bar and ordered half a lager next to Ellie. Panicked inside but desperate to brave it out, but then the door swung open and in he came with another of his cronies, swaggering up to the bar smiling as my heart tried to leap out of my mouth.

He sauntered over and I was again struck mute. I knew he could read the disgust in my face as his confident grin in my direction turned to annoyance. He tried an 'Alright?' and I ignored him entirely. Deer in the headlights, pouring sweat. His annoyance upgraded to anger and he paused, clocking that the situation made him look a little on the back foot, so he reasserted, picked up my half a lager and slowly raised it, tipping it over my head with a 'Don't say hello then, you little slag.'

My eyes went wide and Ellie said, 'Fuck! What the fuck did you do that for?' But I never really knew his response, or what any of them were ever told, because I fled out of the door of that pub and never returned – not to the pub nor to that friendship group. It would be years before I could even go into that town to the shops, and even then I would shake when I passed the pub or the café where he worked. He had not only violated me but he had humiliated me too.

202

It took me years to know that this was rape. The damage it did to me and to my life was many orders of magnitude larger than the time it took for it to occur. I could never understand how such a small thing could have such repercussions: make me so afraid of men, so sure I would be hurt or raped again, so convinced that any risks I took in future could so easily be rewarded with force and abuse. I compartmentalised it all for my entire adulthood up until I decided to hike this trail, which is when I knew that the walls between all my compartments would come down, and the fear, unmanaged, would join up together without the life-scaffolding I'd built to make me feel safe. Without seeking some therapy, I might give up before I even began. My goals were the woods, trusting strangers, sleeping alone, many days and nights far from a road on a well-travelled route for over half a year. I was afraid, and if anything bad was going to happen to me, I felt it would be there, and it would again be because I was naive and overconfident about my ability to control a situation.

Naive, stupid and without anyone looking out for me. Trusting the wrong people. Getting drawn in and abandoned. Just like right now, in the middle of the woods at dusk.

*

The clearing was so still and dim. Branches waved in the breeze in my periphery and I snapped my head left and right, seeing glimpses of things moving and people hiding. They weren't there, but I was still so afraid of them, I really wasn't ready to do this alone. I just couldn't be thrown into being alone unexpectedly in the night, miles from anywhere and anyone I knew, in a country that wasn't mine, with no phone service and no understanding of why I'd been abandoned. Writing this now, I feel so foolish, but the fear was real.

I wildly rotated my head and took in the dimming hostile space. I couldn't stay there – maybe he was at the next logging track a mile or so away? Yes, that was it.

I stumbled back to the path, palms scratched and bleeding as I grabbed rough branches and bark to keep upright. Crying so hard I fell over repeatedly; babbling and sobbing out loud through tears, snot and heaving breaths that sounded like I was drowning in air. I have *never* been so terrified. I've been afraid of being truly afraid, but this was it: true terror. What the hell was happening to me? I stumbled in a river in full panic, at this point ranting 'Get me out, get me out' on a repeated loop. I stumbled out onto the dusky road utterly wild-eyed and out of my mind. He wasn't there. I wailed across the hardtop; my breathing loud and laboured in the air.

With a start I saw on the other side of the road there were three Nobo hikers having a snack, deciding where to pull up and sleep. I was mortified but had no control over the desperate gasping and wailings coming from me. They looked shocked and stood, as one. I thought, *Christ, I'd better be normal and they won't worry then*, so I took in a ragged breath and shouted across the road: 'Have you seen' – huge, jagged intakes of crying breath – 'a really big, tall man?'

I understood in some abstract way that this wasn't helping.

'Very tall. *Tall*.' Gesturing with my arms. A sob broke out of me. '*A big man?*'

I gave up as they looked even more alarmed and beckoned me over to them, putting their gaze closely on me, looking for injury or evidence of harm.

One gently stated that when he wasn't hiking, he was an emergency medical technician. With extremely cautious kindness he asked me to sit and breathe while he checked me for concussion. I couldn't speak for a while because I couldn't breathe and was hyperventilating. When I could finally get words out through heaving sobs, I asked, 'What is happening to me?' I'd been trying to say this with my huge eyes when I couldn't speak. 'I am so sorry. I am so embarrassed. Thank you, thank you,' I mumbled repeatedly.

And they were incredible. Kind, patient and caring. They insisted on walking me along the road where there was a random hiker lodging (what luck!) and saw me into the door before they left.

Safely inside, I calmed down, set my tent up out back in the garden under the pines and sat around a large table listening to stories from the visiting hikers, laughing and smiling. They knew I'd had a 'situation', but this wasn't unusual for hikers along the way. Meltdowns, panic attacks, crying for days – all part of what the trails draw out of you, like sucking poison from a bite. Later, in my tent, with a heavy heart at Buckshot's abandonment of me, my mind turned to worry for him. Had he fallen between rocks? Become lost and disoriented? It didn't seem possible.

Fragmented sleep followed, and as I packed up early the next day with nothing else to do but keep going forwards, my phone pinged. The hikers from the night before! Checking in that I was OK.

Their last text added more:

We found your friend. The tall one you spoke of. He came into our camp after dark and asked if we'd seen a blonde British girl. He had taken the wrong path from the top of Moosilauke. We said you were fine and we thought you'd gone on to a hostel. We didn't tell him. Stay safe.

Angels. All over this trail.

PART THREE

Brave

VERMONT

150 miles

CHAPTER ELEVEN

Leaps of Faith

Later the next day, Buckshot caught up and, as we walked, we thrashed through the mix-up. It was apparently unusual for him to get lost and he didn't like to hear that I had been upset, although I didn't tell him exactly how bad it had been. After we had spoken and taken a break, he busied himself texting an old hiking buddy from his previous AT hike who lived in Hanover, New Hampshire – the location of the prestigious Ivy League university Dartmouth College, and the town we were going to cut through next. The friend was named 'Tall Boy' and was indeed damn tall when he stood with Buckshot waiting to greet me in the town's supermarket car park.

We spent a zero with Tall Boy, who couldn't have been kinder and more magnanimous, gifting us all the hiking accessories he had in his cache and feeding us with clear pleasure. The next day, whilst Buckshot lolled across the sofa shirtless and steadily drinking, I accepted Tall Boy's offer of a tour of the beautiful Dartmouth clock tower. He worked at the university in some area of site development management and had some impressive insider access. So I dressed in some loaner clothes and got an Uber into the town centre, enjoying the food stalls and music on the green before joining him for the adventure into bonging bells and clock faces hundreds of metres up, looking down upon fancy buildings and even fancier young folk. We polished our venture off with a few beers in the bar, gently flirting and enjoying discussion on topics ranging from politics to hiking lore. Such a kind, smart and decent man – I was sad to leave him the next day and thought about him on and off during the following weeks.

Buckshot began to behave a little strangely later on the day we left, arranging to meet me after our town errands to hike out but instead leaving me waiting for him outside a coffee shop. Like a gullible idiot, I stood holding a cup of joe for him for about 30 minutes before I called to find out if he was OK. When he eventually texted back 15 minutes later, it was to tell me he'd forgotten we were meeting and had gone on over the border into Vermont down trail – his tone defiant and irritated. It made me angry, but when I caught up with him a few miles later, he was so annoyed at the sight of the crossness on my face that my anger turned to sadness at his lack of care. I was finding him hard to read or judge: friend, lover, hiking buddy, teacher or trail family? All or none. He was mercurial and I was confused, so after asking why he thought it was good manners to stand someone up and getting 'You need to get used to people leaving' in response, I left it and remained silent as I hiked, not sure how to navigate this relationship and therefore unprepared to make a stand in any direction. Eventually though, by the time we had made it to the famous jumping bridge, he had thawed and was doing all he could to make it up to me.

The bridge jump was the stuff of legend, with a Trail Angel family in a house right next to it where you could sit on the porch and watch those jumping or return back to the porch after your jump for a soda, snack and to write in the hiker logbook they kept. We passed the house by at first, dumped our packs on the road and found the spot on the bridge where a marker had been discreetly painted to show where the deepest part of the river was in an attempt to stave off broken arms and legs.

There was already one man over the railing, gripping onto the metal struts behind him with his arms outstretched and a rictus grin on his face at me as I shimmied up and over to shuffle out next to him, heels pressed back against the tarmac between the rails and gripping on equally hard to the metal. Both of us looked down, then at each other.

'Hey,' I started, with a gentle opening. He looked terrified. 'Still thinking it over?'

'Yes,' he replied, scudding his eyes back and forth to me and to the depths below, in case something was going to shove him in. It clearly wasn't going to be himself. 'I've been here a little while. It's a long way down, isn't it?'

I looked. It was.

'Just take your time, friend.' I smiled at this fellow hiker, who I guessed was in his mid-50s, very fit, tan and muscular. 'It'll be OK whether you do it or not. Trying to give it a go is enough!'

He smiled at me.

'I might go first,' I said. 'What do you think? I can check it out for you, show you it's OK?'

'Really? You'd do that?'

'Sure!' But as soon as I'd said it, I saw a meaty fist grab the rail near my shoulder, and Buckshot propelled his hulking frame over the top, threw off his shirt and exclaimed, 'FILM MEEEEEEE!' Before I had time to properly get my camera out, he propelled himself off the ledge without looking back. A deep splash, white water and then nothing until he surfaced a short distance away, striking out for the shore.

'NUTHIN' TO IT!' he yelled up. 'C'MON, APPALACHIAN GAIIIILLLL!' So I looked at my new hiking friend clinging to the bridge, placed my phone through the railing behind me on the hardtop, straightened up and leaned as far forwards as my arms would let me. It was so... far... down. Looking back, I raised my eyebrows, looked up at the sky and let go.

We dried off with snacks and a soda as promised, chatting about those that jump and those who don't with the owners of the house. More came, from both directions, but no one else climbed the railing to take the plunge. All attention was off the bridge for now, so it was only me who saw the man who had stood gripping the rail for 30 minutes or more slowly give in, release his hands and climb back over to his pack on the road. Slipping his arms through his shirt, he shouldered his pack defeatedly and struck out away from us back to trail.

I felt for him. I knew all about trying and having to give it up – walking away, even when I desperately wanted to stay and *do* the *thing*. Not usually because of a lack of courage, but mostly because of pain. It was always there in some way or another. Pain ebbed and flowed in my life – sometimes greater and sometimes much lesser, which sounds good because it implies respite. However, even if these physical breathers were good, the mental anguish this doled out was worse. If my silent captor suddenly decided to free me for a few days or a week, what were my options? I could show up, arrange a dinner, see friends, dance, go running or jogging. But if I did that, looking just the same, wouldn't everyone just disbelieve me for the rest of the time that I was actually sick? So my options were to live bright and bold when I could but die a little inside, knowing I was misunderstood, or expire from loneliness even when I felt OK for those short periods. I didn't ever really know what to do. It was a lonely time.

As my condition worsened over those years, so did my hopelessness, and the doctor's raft of medications increased. I was shuffled from my GP to the pain clinic, where I was told to dose hard on gabapentin and pregabalin. I refused and was then told off for not trying hard enough to accept my fate and make the best of it. I wasn't being a biddable enough patient. But how could I be? They gave me no name of a condition to go with these drugs, no understandable explanation as to why I should take them. No sign to attach to my body to let people know that not only was I now unwell but also dulled.

It wasn't explained to me that sometimes the professionals just *don't know*. If we can all accept not knowing in life, then we have a right to be told that sometimes professionals don't know either. It would help us who suffer to know it's not our fault, or actually anyone's. But no – no clarity, no hope, no diagrams or explanations of how I might maintain some control of my condition; just plenty of dry mouth, night sweats and head-swimmingly bleary thought processing and attempts to push through and keep working. I refused to be a statistic.

So after one particularly shitty incident at the pain clinic and pretty swiftly after the heaviest drugs were placed in my hand, the meds were fucked right into the bin. I'm not anti-drugs, but I am anti-anything that wants to exchange my soul for pain relief without explanation. If I wanted to feel fucked up as well as totally fucked, then I'm sure I'd have found a more fun way. As it was, I was going to find my own route out of the mess I was in.

A checklist of things I tried to heal myself

Every therapy you can imagine, legal or otherwise:

☐ Fasting for 11 days, twice, in the Thai jungle
☐ Transcendental meditation
☐ Shamanic breathwork
☐ Returning to source
☐ Cacao ceremonies
☐ Chakra work
☐ Cranio-sacral therapy
☐ Acupuncture
☐ Chiropractic
☐ Osteopathy
☐ Chinese Medicine
☐ Massage – every kind
☐ Mindfulness
☐ Pilates
☐ Yoga
☐ Swimming
☐ Strength training
☐ Gratitude diary and journaling
☐ Cold water immersion
☐ Blue light glasses
☐ Ketogenic, amongst a myriad of other diets

This was the hotchpotch of solutions that kept me going. Sometimes things worked, sometimes they didn't. Sometimes I'd inexplicably get better and have what felt like a pain holiday, then I'd go back in the hurt locker for an extended period. I needed these little pockets of hope though – some momentum to feel as though I wasn't giving in. I couldn't just stop and surrender. I had no flag to wave to give people understanding. No broken leg, osteoarthritis, bone spur, permanent SI joint damage, scoliosis, cancer, or anything else that people might understand. It's a cliché because it's true: invisible pain is a cruel mistress.

As I watched the man I'd just met walk away from the bridge with his head hanging in disappointment at himself, I knew for certain that we all carry some sort of invisible pain – and amongst the hikers I'd met on trail so far, many of their packs were as full of it as my own.

*

Vermont was my favourite state after Maine, although I was aware it was only the third state I'd been in. People were so kind and welcoming after the slightly snooty and touristy world of New Hampshire that we'd seen in the Whites. We met plenty of weed-growing, pot-smoking hippies in Vermont who were keen to lend a hand, offer a ride or a joint, and smile us on our way. It felt safe and how I imagined the peace-and-love '60s might have felt. The state felt like somewhere I could have lived. The trail was pretty, and we explored a variety of off-trail variants including old ATV tracks and the old AT pathways, something we called 'retro-blazing'. The AT was always moving and shifting, sometimes to accommodate natural events and erosion, and at other times to allow regrowth, but at some point, the Appalachian Trail Conservancy had decided the trail wasn't *hard* enough, so took it out of some of the meandering and scenic routes and put it up and over more brutal ascents and descents, often deep in trees and away from the views. For variety, we'd look at our map apps and take side trails and old AT routes that we knew would reconnect with the AT proper. It was exciting.

It wasn't long before we rolled into Rutland, a Vermont town that was most famous for the 'Yellow Deli'. I'd been hearing about the Yellow Deli for weeks and was both fascinated and scared to see what it would be all about. Described as everything from a cult, a haven and a religious commune, it was actually a hostel run by the Twelve Tribes, an apocalyptic Christian sect started in 1972 by Elbert Eugene ('Gene') Spriggs. They made purportedly delicious food and drink in their deli, and above the shop they housed tired hikers and welcomed them in with love.

I wasn't sure what to expect. Buckshot had told me of a guy he knew from a previous thru who had been unravelling as they all moved north. He seemed to have few social skills, didn't understand cues, took advantage of others' generosity, and ultimately alienated almost everyone he hiked with. Buckshot, for all his hubris and arrogance, wasn't an unkind man, so I was surprised to hear genuine disdain in his voice when he explained how annoying this man was. Then his voice became quieter when he revealed that on their arrival at the Yellow Deli, the guy had been really losing it and no one knew what to do with him. He was emotional, lost and melting down.

Well the Yellow Deli did what they, apparently, are so good at. They welcomed him, assured him he could stay as long as he needed, gave him understanding, a warm bed, free food and some routine chores whilst he was there. And then, once he was comfortable, they asked him to stay, explaining that they really liked him and wanted him in their 'family'. So he did. He quit the trail and stayed at the Deli, which was why, one whole year later, Buckshot was determined to break the 'spell' they had over him and spring him out. Apparently, this wasn't an unusual tale. Many hikers had been taken off their well-beaten path by the Deli and then moved over time from the customer-facing shop to the farm miles away, not to be seen again by fellow hikers. I was curious about what I'd find and more than a little nervous.

Often folks who hike the trail seem to be looking for something or leaving something behind. The trail could act as a buffer between one way of life and the next, but sometimes people didn't realise this until it had already happened. It was clear from the stories of past thru hikers – who came to provide aid and Trail Magic and talked to us at length – that the effect of this great hike never left them – changing them beyond measure. It was therefore logical that some hikers every year would find new lives along the pathway of the AT. They would move into a new existence as though having opened a door along the great corridor of the trail into a different world, like at the top of the Magic Faraway Tree. It could take the shape of the Yellow Deli and a life of faith, or it might be that a temporary rest with a sprained ankle kept them in a tiny town they'd never previously heard of for a few days that turned into weeks, then months, then a life. It might be a new partner – I'd met folks going north who had got together on trail and would later post photos of their weddings and baby bumps, resettling in new towns. For some, it just might be a determined resolution to never return to the person and life they were when they set out to hike.

So I was curious to see what the Yellow Deli would be like. I thought it might feel *creepy* in some way, but in actual fact the experience was very pleasant. The Deli community didn't hide their religious affiliations and asked all hikers to strictly abide by their rules. Contribution for shelter, food and laundry was voluntary – we were asked to give only what we could afford. We were also asked to help with chores such as laundry and cooking the communal breakfasts down in the large back kitchens of the restaurant business, all of which to me seemed reasonable and fair. Curfews were strict, alcohol was forbidden and men were not allowed into the floor where the female hikers were – not even to say hello or to collect a girlfriend or wife. We women had to dress from head to toe in old-fashioned long skirts and high-necked shirts, as hiker clothes and swearing or any gratuitous cahoots at all seemed out of place. But all of this itself didn't seem to be *bad*. It was nice: calm, peaceful and reverent.

The women were, however, extremely conservatively dressed and silent. Shuffling around like in *The Handmaid's Tale*, making big eyes at the men who would tell them quietly what they should be doing at any given time. We were also under very close watch. Any down time was seen as a good opportunity to broach the subject of the Tribes with us and the benefit of their teachings. Fair enough; nothing manipulative that I could see, although I could definitely surmise that should you be a little adrift and emotionally exhausted, as so many hikers are at this stage, then you might be ripe for being folded into the mix. And once in, I imagined extraction would be tough.

Buckshot didn't manage to 'spring' his old trail buddy. In fact, upon glimpsing him across the dining room, he wasn't allowed contact with him – blocked at every request. Eventually, he conceded that the man looked happy and at peace, so perhaps he truly had found what he needed. Who are we to judge? But I do know that the welcome was hard to leave; one zero turned into a double, then 3 days off in total before we left. Buckshot and I had arrived as a duo, as we had been for nearly 2 months, but soon the hostel swelled with hikers from all directions. The longer we stayed, the more hikers we met, taking ourselves out to bars and restaurants in the town to socialise over beers before back to meet curfew at 9 p.m.

Wham (dressed in '80s neon), Chimney (smoked a lot), Granola (ate it), Moose (I have no idea), Wag (always happy, like a dog wagging its tail) and Captain (carried a handle of Captain Morgan in the side of his pack) were the main troops that were brought together here at the Deli. On walking into the third bar of the night, I was overjoyed to see Smudge again, seated at the bar and smiling with his usual calm, friendly demeanour. I hadn't seen him since earlier in Maine when we hiked with Dozer and Lazybean and couldn't understand how he had got *behind* us.

'Damn, Appalachian Gail, you've been CRUSHIN', man!' he said, grinning. 'I couldn't keep up with y'all! Buckshot and you are machines!'

Ha! I didn't know about that. I knew I was just trying to keep up with a 6 foot 4 experienced 25-year-old without reaching the point of total exhaustion. But it was clearly working, and my game had been raised in the process, so I was going to take it.

'Thanks, buddy! Just tryin' to keep up with the Buck!' I bought us a whiskey to celebrate catching up. So, including us three and the crew who had gathered, we created a force of hiking good times that would be known as 'The Vortex', pulling chaos, good folks and laughter into it as it moved forwards south down trail. What a place for such louche characters to coalesce – a strictly puritanical religious headquarters. Perfect.

So, rested and buddied up with a hugely larger tribe, we struck out and onwards to explore the rest of Vermont – and soon, I knew, to say goodbye to Buckshot as he left for his annual family vacation.

*

Vermont carried on being benevolent. We were out of the hardest mountains now and had more incessantly undulating terrain at a lower altitude to contend with. The days brought river swims, sunbathing and afternoon beers at dusty crossroads – everything a relaxing time could offer in the company of new and exciting companions. The highlight of these days was definitely the most spectacular Trail Magic that any of us had ever seen, flagged for us the day before by northbound hikers we passed in rain showers and mud.

'Duuuudes, whatever you do, don't miss the Trail Magic in the roadside pull-off – in about 15 miles.'

'Guys, guys. Sorry to stop you mid-stride, but in about 10 miles you're going to come to the most *insane* Trail Magic you've ever seen.'

'Hey, folks, you should get to the Trail Magic first thing tomorrow morning. It's only about 3 miles away! On the roadside. The dudes are camping there all week to provide, man! They have a charging station, they cook breakfasts, lunches and dinners all week, endless beer and whiskey and so much food you're going to pass out!'

We. Couldn't. Wait.

Early the next morning, we all trundled our way to the road, not sure what to expect but all hungry and keen for coffee and sustenance. We were not disappointed. We arrived at about 8 a.m. to the smell of sizzling bacon and sausage and were fed to bursting, with our coffee cups filled. We were bathed in the warmth and kindness of these two exceptional men, Chris and Steve. Every year they booked a week's vacation to come and provide Magic, having saved up for it every month until they could provide a spread like no other for anyone and everyone who turned up. Such generosity was humbling, and this particular pair of men made my heart sing.

We had arrived for breakfast, intending to leave by lunchtime, but we were tempted to stay for an afternoon snack and more whiskey shots, and we didn't manage to go anywhere at all. After being taught to 'engage targets' (shotgun tins of beer) as a finale, we finally left at 10:00 p.m. and staggered 1 mile to the next shelter, lighting a huge fire and whooping drunkenly into the night, singing songs and feeling on top of the world.

And then, before I knew it, we were in Manchester, and Buckshot was about to leave. I hadn't yet got used to the dynamic of Buckshot in a group setting – showing off, bro-ing down and being 'aloof' whilst still keen to ensure I was interested in him and available for more than what other hikers gave him. He reminded me of Danny Zuko in *Grease* when Sandy sees him at school after summer vacation, but this *trail* Danny Zuko seemed to give less of a hoot, and I was no Sandy. I didn't know what happened next – didn't really let myself feel the realisation that home for Buckshot meant breaking our spell: real life, family, phone service and calls to his girlfriend, which would irrevocably shift our dynamic. I should have known better. What was I doing? I should have finished the connection when I found out about her but I just *couldn't*, especially knowing this natural break was coming up. Plus, how could I? He was more than my lover out here. He was my *family* after 2 months side by side through thick and thin. My *friend*. It was what it was. And I'd get to see who *I* was once he had gone.

After the fun of hiking through a ski resort in the summer; enjoying the swinging lifts above my head and lying on the snow netting, we had straggled into Manchester over the course of a morning. Smudge and I were hiking together and enjoyed Magic at the trailhead car park from the father of a section hiker who had come up from New York to meet his daughter. He was *beaming* with pride at her achievement – Katahdin to here. He fed us from Mason jars of homemade pickles from his garden and we made firm friends with him before hitching into town proper. On arrival, there was pizza and beer, a few hours of Corn Hole, which involved throwing fabric bags stuffed with corn onto targets, a swim in the motel pool and a final night of togetherness before we all said goodbye.

There was no climactic 'moment', no lingering eye contact and clutching embrace. I'd rented Buckshot and me our own room, and The Vortex all rented a separate one, but we gathered together on the lawn the next morning to take our leave.

A quick smattering of fist bumps and 'Yooo's, and then it was my turn. A hug, unlike the others. A quick kiss and 'I'll see ya real soon. I'll catch up, I promise. Be safe.' This, an echo of the other conversations we'd had. He had offered me a gun, helped me buy pepper spray in Rutland, discussed how service would be patchy for his phone on the trip so I might not hear from him, and that he'd go at double speed to catch me up as soon as he got back. 'Take care of the crew,' he had said in our room that morning. 'I'll be back with you soon. Please take care.'

And then, in the squinting, sideways light of the morning, we were walking away from him and towards the road, thumbs extended for a hitch and me biting back the tears as I walked away from the one constant I'd had from the start.

*

I trailed the crew for a few hours, getting my head around the limbless feeling I had but knowing that it was inevitable, as were the fears and questions that were bubbling up in me about my capabilities. Not only to hike but to keep up. Not only to make friends but to fit in and make myself 'un-expendable' – someone that people didn't want to leave behind. Some of The Vortex were kind and funny, keen to be genuine and share stories, as well as take and offer support. Others were not so kind. The most experienced amongst us – a couple who had already hiked two long trails – firmly placed themselves as 'sages' and, though friendly enough, were happy to create cliques and pick 'favourites'. All was not equal on the trail, I was to learn, and the accepting devil-may-care attitude of Buckshot and his early crew wasn't always in evidence in others. I hadn't seen the hierarchies until my buffer was removed, but now I was seeing how the land really lay.

I wasn't interested in playground games. I was more keen to keep my head above water and build confidence in myself solo, so I focused my time and a friendship around Wag, Captain and Smudge, happy-go-lucky souls who radiated kindness above all else. Chimney had vanished for the time being, hiking ahead to meet his sister in New York with a tight deadline. But we were still a strong team and enjoyed the beauty of camping together next to Stratton Pond in the still sunset – and then after that, hiking through the famed and mysterious Bennington Triangle at dusk. It was without doubt a spooky spot, where many had disappeared over the years and UFOs and Bigfoot were seen on occasion. Getting lost was all too easy to do amidst thick trunks and tricksy signage, so we decided to subvert that risk in the dimming night and stealth camp together under the fire tower, hoping to see Bigfoot for ourselves.

It was in these Glastenbury mountains that we passed our last long trail hikers, who were just starting their journey north, using the AT for half the route, then breaking off to cut into upper Vermont to the border. Wild, overgrown and harsh, the trail after the AT was fabled to be very hard, and the hikers we met were either confident or terrified, but all as excited as you'd expect. Skipping past them and wishing them luck, we retro-blazed hard and descended into Bennington then on to North Adams and into our next and fourth state, Massachusetts.

I was used to feeling adrift like this, feeling that things might not work out. I had existed in those murky waters for years, fighting against the seemingly inevitable tide of incoming loss. I knew where I was in disappointment – without Buckshot, without Kate, without solid ground. And I didn't know how I'd do it, but I knew I'd pull through and make it to the next part of the story. I'd done it before when things were much worse.

Hope can drown so easily when weighted down with the realities of failure, one piled upon another. I knew from my battle to keep going, when the pain in my body and mind were against me, that for everything that didn't work, there would be something around the corner that would – something new. Naivety? Stubborn positivity? Who's to say? But there were times that I wanted to escape from this earth permanently, to shut down the torture of the pain and the effect it had on those who loved me and who were powerless to resolve it.

*

Back then, it wasn't until I reached my lowest ebb, far from home in a foreign land, high in the austere chill of Italian mountains and unfriendly locals, with a new, prestigious job and the loss of all my support systems, that I hit what I thought was to be my last wall. I had done it to myself with this move abroad, seeking accolades or self-assurance that I wasn't useless despite my condition. Yet merely weeks in, with friends hard to find and the winter closing in around my lonely home on Sacro Monte, the pain swelled to fill all the spaces that my moving here had created. Walking, breathing, dressing and moving my head to read or write made me sick with pain, and eventually even being utterly still was no respite.

At 3 a.m. one cold morning, I had pulled myself out onto my balcony, with no doctor yet to prescribe medication, and contemplated the unthinkable. I could just fall gently off into the snow and green trees below. It seemed such a sweet release for everyone. No more phone calls filled with tears and desperation to my loved ones of why and how I wasn't OK, no need for anyone to worry any more.

As I sat there on my Italian mountain, I idly worked a zipper in my pocket back and forth in increasing anxiety. I suddenly realised it was my purse and pulled it out. Opening the top, I extracted the contents and examined each photo, each card, each small thing, fat tears pooling on my fingers and hands. At the back of this handful of my life there was a business card from my chiropractor back home in Penryn, a magnificently talented man who had kept me stable for so long. On the back of the card was a number. I couldn't remember for a long moment what it was, but then it struck me. At our last appointment he had handed it to me, explaining he had remembered meeting a Belgian chiropractor at a course who was doing great and interesting things in the field, and that he was based in Como, by the lake and only 40 minutes from my town. 'If you get into trouble and it gets too much, Gail, give him a call. I think he might be what you need.'

In the dark and hovering on the line between going on and giving up, I shuffled backwards, leaned against the wall of the house and pulled my phone from my other pocket. In broken Italian and as close to the end as I'd ever been, I called the number and left a message. One last hope, and the call that saved my life.

I'd been alone facing enormous adversity before and come through, and I was going to do it again.

MASSACHUSETTS

90.2 miles

CHAPTER TWELVE

You Can't Have Your (Blueberry) Pancake and Eat It

The days bled together. We were out of the severe mountains and the constant risk of falling, death or exhaustion, and were now beginning the middle phase – the steady miles, the repetition, the summer heat rising and our cadence setting in. Our trail family was still gelling together behind Buckshot's departure. Many of the small group had known each other before the Yellow Deli, but the group had bonded anew in the journey from there to here.

Smudge and Captain flew the flag for hilarity and kindness – Smudge a quieter, more considered steady presence, and Captain the more unpredictable one with exuberant madcap energy. I loved them both dearly. Moose, Granola and Wag had known each other from early on and were close. Wag impressed me hugely with her wit, humour and warm friendship, but I felt a distance from the more experienced couple, Granola and Moose, who I felt enjoyed being revered for their knowledge and dirtbag 'wisdom'.

I felt part of the team but at times knew I was being mocked or eyes were rolling because of some of the things I said. I didn't really understand why, as in our group discussions I was answering questions from my life experience or sharing things I'd learned, but Granola made it clear at one point that it didn't matter *what* I or anyone did before hiking. Their take was that who you were and what you had achieved, seen or done in life off trail wasn't particularly valued here on trail – it was only how you survived and hiked that identified you and gave you value. I wasn't sure if I agreed with or understood this viewpoint as I was always interested in people, but I did fully understand the implicit message, which was 'Shut up'. So I did, but I didn't appreciate the hierarchy and gatekeeping of what being a 'real hiker' was.

As the days went by, I started feeling a little like we were at school again and although I was in a 'gang', there was a leader who didn't much like me and encouraged others to be *just* a little unkind. Regardless, I smiled and blithely moved with the flow. I organised a much-needed Airbnb in North Adams for all of us and was rewarded handsomely for my efforts in the meeting of our hosts – smart, cultured folks in their 50s, who took us to the Museum of Contemporary Art on our zero day, invited us into their *real* home just down the street where they grew weed on their back porch and shared their love of Cornwall with me. We relaxed, played cards and took them up on their offers of rides: to the supermarket to make a Vortex supper and – for the boys mainly – a trip to a weed dealer who provided excellent home-grown bud. We girls all dyed our hair pink, something I had *never* done before, and the boys cooked our supper. We rested again for the day and then we were taking our leave again. This time towards Mt Greylock.

Deep, ferocious storms chased us from the mountaintop to the town of Cheshire on the other side, where a change of church management meant we were no longer welcome to sleep inside, as had long been the case. Instead, we made do with the cold stone porch under a wooden portico, with Jesus sitting atop welcoming weary travellers into… the porch area only. We lasted a few hours on our mats and sleeping bags, leaning up against the church doors – enough time to draw the attention of a passer-by who stopped her car and ran over to give us all the snacks and food she had with her, explaining her father had hiked the AT in his youth and had a long, abiding love for it until he passed away.

Dinner eaten, the mosquitoes were biting relentlessly, so we stirred from our half-slumbers just before midnight to pitch our tents on the sodden, boggy lawns instead. Better damp than eaten alive.

*

The next adventures on our radar in Massachusetts were the Cookie Lady and Upper Goose Pond. Legend had it that en route to Upper Goose you were to first find and visit the Cookie Lady – an older woman who lived just off trail and loved to chat, welcoming hikers through the season every day to eat her freshly baked cookies and share stories. Then if you were lucky, you could pluck blueberries from her bushes and carry them with you until arriving, again slightly off trail, at Upper Goose Pond.

Here a cabin stands, owned and run by the National Park Service and managed by Appalachian Mountain Club volunteers through the season. They would lift the bag of blueberries from your proffered hands and welcome you to camp or bunk, joining others coming north or south. They would then use your travelling gift to provide you with delicious blueberry pancakes on your departure the next morning. And so it was that we arrived there with blue-stained fingers and a sopping bag of ripe fruit, pitched our tents and spent a blissful afternoon miles from anywhere, jumping off wooden docks into the still lake and borrowing kayaks to paddle around the central island. It couldn't have been more Swallows and Amazons if it tried.

I took my leave early the next morning, after the first pancakes but before the majority of the site had mobilised. I didn't want to speak to anyone, revelling in the freedom and independence I was feeling and needing to keep that vibe alive, walking off the need to check my phone for text messages or Instagram likes.

I realised that in the past weeks I had felt more distant from my previous *real* life, even though calls to family had been a little more frequent recently as I reoriented to life in a new group. Whenever I felt a little lost, I needed to dip back into the pool of those who knew and loved me as a yardstick for who I was outside of this experience. This recalibration seemed important. It was easy to drift from oneself out here. It was also easy to imagine that the people and places I left behind were in stasis – preserved in amber – whilst I lived out this long pilgrimage not only in a different country but what felt like a different dimension. Time was not marked out here by any more than the changes in the leaves. There was no news to follow, patchy service made any continuity on social media rare, and I was untethered to all the familiar trappings of my life. No gravity to me – adrift. It was impossible to imagine things happening at home, because out here every day felt fundamentally the same: find water, fuel the body, walk, sleep. Repeat ad infinitum.

I'd been walking now for over 2 months. My body was hurting but in a 'normal' way, the way that everyone's did at the end of a day. The more I was using my body across every plane of motion, the more it was giving me back in ease of movement. The more I trusted and leaned into its innate ability to know how to move and heal itself, the more it healed. All these years of believing my body had been doing me wrong, when really perhaps I'd been doing it wrong right back.

I hadn't known what to expect when I called the specialists on that fateful night, when I hated my body and pain the most – that initial period in Italy when I nearly shuffled myself off my balcony and this mortal coil. When I arrived at the clinic in Como, I was a broken woman, barely able to walk, holding walls for breaths and pain relief, so obviously unwell with deep, black eye bags and pallid, swollen skin. I didn't expect answers but still had some tiny piece of me that wouldn't give up.

In actuality, and to my eternal shock (and later gratitude), I was presented with head scans, diagnosis and possible resolution. When I was told that my teeth placement, the condylar head of my mandible on one side and my overall 'bite' was probably the root cause of my spiralling physical dysfunction, I initially wanted to scream. Another diagnosis. Another 'issue' that could be the problem. I'd heard so many as to believe that no one knew a damn thing, and everyone was a hustling charlatan. But on this occasion, I didn't really have any choices. When they described treatment – wearing a 'bite' for months, changing the placement of my teeth, wearing braces for over two years, teeth implants in the bone – and the *cost* of it all, I was faced with a decision. If I believed them and ran with the new treatments, I would be in debt and risked another cataclysmic disappointment, which, despite having run on a big tank of hope and optimism for 10 years, I didn't have the reserves to face. How much energy did I have left to believe in another process? I knew by this stage that treatment alone wasn't enough. I had to be invested in *recovery* too. My other option was, of course, ending it all.

I had broken down in the dentist's chair when the chiropractor and his dentist wife had presented all their findings. So I took my cue from the visible body-shaking relief I showed that there *might* be this other explanation for it all, that *this* might be the thing.

I wasn't done yet. Debt be damned, I was never giving up.

Over two and half years of rehabilitation and treatment followed. The process was slow and steady, and I regularly got worse before I improved. I soon moved from the care of the two leads at the ritzy clinic to work with the specialists in their team that I had been assigned to. These two incredibly kind men – another dentist and chiropractor pairing – became my friends. Over time they both decided to leave the Como clinic and I elected to go with them to their new base. They kept my progress going and showed me extremely humbling levels of compassion; coming to treat me in my own home when I couldn't move because of pain and assuring me that progress was not linear; that going backwards today didn't mean going backwards forever.

And so it was that, in a job and country that were not perfectly suited for me, after a near life-ending moment on a cold balcony far from home, at my lowest ebb, I found the men who saved my life. I had hope. I always had hope, and this hope – my parachute through the plummet of illness – had landed me in a foreign land and straight into the arms of my future via a card in my wallet and some talented folks who wanted to heal me. And now here I was: in that very future, leaning into my body and trusting that it knew how to heal and move forwards, because it had proven it could do so before.

But beyond the physical, my growing emotional independence on trail was highlighting how I had moved beyond my initial fears. This was reassuring, but I was proving to be like the proverbial onion: layer upon layer. One issue bubbled up after another, and all I had was time, forest and my thoughts. It was really the best therapy I could have imagined, and the trees were great listeners, but I hadn't had the faintest idea I still had so much to learn about myself.

I already knew I wouldn't be returning to life as it was before. I had no yearning for the 'busy' that meant nothing except noise and empty peacocking, all to convince myself I was needed, important and *going* somewhere. I could now see clearly that I had been going nowhere – not so much a peacock as a chicken with its head cut off. *Now* I was actually going somewhere. My actions were meaningful, and this was borne out physically in the miles I earned under my feet and the blissful exhaustion of my body in my sleeping bag. Back when life had seemed untethered, I had instinctively known that walking would ground me, bring me back down from my state of '*me*-mania', and it had. Now I would have to try to keep hold of that grounding as I moved past this initial excited euphoria of the first part of the trail and into the green tunnel grind that was coming up.

CONNECTICUT

51.6 miles

CHAPTER THIRTEEN

A Collision with Real Life

Massachusetts gave me my first legal weed shop and THC gummies before it gently nudged me over into Connecticut. I wasn't sure I liked this state. Ritzy and glitzy houses tucked back from the roadsides seemed to release regular drivers who would pass us with disdainful sneers as though we were vagrants or bums. Hiker facilities seemed rarer, and it was only when we arrived in my namesake town of Cornwall that things looked up, before they looked down again.

Smudge and Captain had attempted to hike the 'Connecticut Challenge' – 52 miles of the state in 1 day. They'd risen at 2 a.m. from our border camp at the edge of Massachusetts and set off with determination; Captain trying to resist the urge for a bucket bong before he left. Granola, Moose and I kept tabs on our buddies for this stretch, awaiting texts updating us of their progress.

Ping! *Ten miles done.*

Ping! *Fifteen in the bag.*

Ping! *Twenty-five! No problem, crushed 'em before lunchtime!!*

Then: disaster. A pulled muscle and the boys were holed up in a shelter down trail. We heard it from them and then from northbounders who kept us updated as they filed past.

'Your friends say hurry up!'

'They want you to get there soon. They want some beer.'

'Hey, are you friends with Cap and Smudge? They wanna change their Connecticut Challenge to the 24-hour challenge [24 miles and 24 beers in 24 hours]. They said they'll see you in town!'

And so we hustled to catch up with them. Granola and I were over CT and its ups and downs that looked so benign on maps, but in reality seemed unkind and pointlessly routed over every lump and bump by the ATC just to wear us out. So, tired, we hit the road to town whilst Moose soldiered on through the trail proper in the high heat. More fool us, needing the head nets we'd given away for the first time since Maine, for the swarms of black fly that followed us *so* thickly down the hardtop that we couldn't see any cars that came our way, let alone flag them down. Choking, coughing and smearing scores of dying flies into our hair with every swat of our hands, we rued our decision to come out of the thickets. Eventually, a kindly older lady in a headscarf scooped us up into her fancy vintage automobile as though we'd walked out from the forest and into the '50s, and deposited us graciously by the gas station in West Cornwall. A home from home.

The boys valiantly attempted the 24-hour challenge – but were thwarted by exhaustion. After our free beer each from Cornwall Packet Store for being hikers, we made our way to a state park by the river to camp together, the $7 fee a steal in order to have access to flat spots, showers, toilets and charging facilities. Moose had been vomiting after arriving, extremely dehydrated from his last exertions into town with no water filter (Granola had it and she was with me) and drinking litres of water too quickly. He had been in a terrible funk ever since.

Leaving him to his own devices, I joined Cap and Smudge with some beer shotguns, lining the 24 cans each for them along the picnic tables and wishing them well. After three or four, Smudge slowed down, switching to spirits from his pack instead. Captain wasn't to be deterred and soldiered on, almost reaching 24 but not quite. The next morning with the fog of aching muscles and hangover, he attempted to finish off the last three cans but no sooner had he shotgunned the first than it made an immediate reappearance directly onto the floor at his feet. 'Fuckin' goddamn.' He shook his head in faint disbelief that his youthful constitution had let him down. 'Guess that's not gonna work.' And so we packed up camp to hit the café in town for breakfast.

The tiny crossroads of a town greeted me with a coffee, some excellent breakfast bagels and a text message from my dad about the death of a family friend. I burst into tears in the middle of chatter over the breakfast table outside the little deli, and on processing and chatting to Dad on the phone, I decided I just couldn't face hiking that day. Relentlessly walking for day after day for so many months is exhausting, and psychic energy can be low at times. The news of the death at home had unsettled me, and I felt a wealth of other topics jostling up towards the crack in the surface it had caused, wanting to have their time in the sun too. Oppressed emotions surging for release. I wondered when my emotional well would finally run dry.

I tried to hike, I really did, but our hitch back to the trailhead involved a conversation with the driver where my friend's death came up, and the lady driving us said that she'd happily drive me the 20 miles to the next trail town of Kent so that I could meet my friends there that night. Perhaps I'd like to spend the day in the local library, she said, emailing family and taking my time to process things?

I considered her offer. I also had a new pair of Altras that had been sent to the Kent post office for me some weeks ago – judged for exactly when I predicted my current shoes would wear out. If I dilly-dallied on trail today with tears and tiredness, then I wouldn't get to Kent before the post office closed and I'd have to wait until after 9:00 the next morning when everyone else would have left camp for trail long before. Extremely inconvenient. I debated for a few more miles of hardtop and then, when Cap and Smudge got out of the car to gather their packs from the trunk, I said I wasn't coming with them. They were happy to see me taking some time out, as 20 miles with a heavy heart is hard. So I waved them off and got back into the passenger seat to have my new guardian angel take me to Kent.

It didn't take me long to realise that she was drunk.

I mean, beyond hammered. Chattering about life, love and hard times, this woman in her late 50s was struggling to keep her car on her side of the winding leafy road, one hand gesticulating about this and that whilst the other only cursorily kept us right side up by dancing over the wheel. I gripped both sides of the car seat, wondering if in my teary grief I was overreacting. I hadn't thought I could smell alcohol but occasionally I could – something sharp and spirity, mixed with cigarettes and my own hiker stink. Perhaps it was medication and I was poorly judging this kind lady, even after all she was doing to help me out. Who's to say, but most every muscle of my body was clenched tightly and

I uttered a few 'Oohs!' and 'Carefuls!' whilst waggling my hand, before we arrived safely in the next town some 45 minutes later. She hugged me tightly goodbye and wished me well, commiserating me for my loss. As I waved her off back the way she'd come, I was grateful to her but extremely annoyed with myself for staying in the car.

Shoes collected and the old, battered versions put into the bin, I shed my tears, called my parents and set about catching up with all my email admin from real life on the library computers. Then, my work done, I ventured into the street to sit on a bench under some pretty trees and watch the townsfolk go about their day. Later on, I joined forces with Mike and Mia, his beautiful dog, and we headed back up into the forest to join our team of friends.

NEW YORK

88.4 miles

CHAPTER FOURTEEN

Lions and Tigers
and Bears – Oh My...

The state of New York was a hot, dusty joy. Our abiding memories would be how parched we were and that a deep desperation for running water and dripping taps began to conjure up fantasies of cold fizzy pop and iced lollies in our dreams. Alas, there were none. Streams were mud, springs were dry and we were yet again relying on the kindnesses of strangers who would leave water caches at roadsides and behind walls and hedges for us to find. We were sparing, thinking of others, but it was hard not to gulp the cool liquid until you were a sloshing pool inside. But, no, it wasn't right.

On our way into Pawling, we were stopped by a kindly pair of photographers who made efforts each year to photograph passing thru hikers and collect snapshots not only of their faces but also of their lives and motivations. They were a delight to meet and we posed happily before immediately making for Tony's Deli, another famous trail-spot for hikers. Tony's New York Deli had everything you could imagine an Italian deli should contain – the selection of hoagies, bagels and wraps making my head spin. But more than this, Tony let hikers camp in the triangular patch of grass next to his store. It wasn't a haven of peace – the triangular patch was hemmed in by the store car park on one side, the highway along another and the final edge lined with train tracks for the regular New York line, which was to continue through the night, parping its horn from at least a mile away until it was at least a mile past. But we didn't care. Well we didn't care at the time, when we were desperate for a Philly cheese steak roll and four cans of cider in a heatwave, but we did care at 1 a.m. And 2 a.m. And 3:30 a.m., but we made it through. Tony's had provided taps and sockets outside for us to freely use. Such kindness. And it was an easy stroll inside in the morning to the bathroom and another delicious round of food with coffee.

Off we set again, this time Wag and I together. Within half a mile we were up in the hills again, the road far behind. I loved hiking with Wag for many reasons, but a big one was her pure honesty about sometimes hating the hills and the exhaustion. I didn't have to pretend to be anything other than what I was around her, nor she around me. We'd hoot at ourselves regularly as, after committing to powering up various huge slabs of elevation without distraction, we'd see each other stopping and sneaking out the Guthook app to see how far we'd come and how far there was to go. This was totally counter to our talk of just getting our heads down and pushing through like others seemed to do. Usually we'd only gone about 0.2 of a mile, which made us cackle. Eventually, we just decided to measure all hard things in 0.2 of a mile. 'We can do it!' she'd holler at me, grinning. 'We can do anything hard for 0.2 of a mile!' And so, through the rainstorms, skinned knees, droughts and endless ascents, we found no shame in bemoaning them together and then powering though – 0.2 miles at a time.

Smart, kind and accepting, she was a trail partner I was grateful to have. She'd recently graduated, and I soaked up her words and wisdom about how she had experienced life so far. I understood that the world she was stepping into was vastly different to when I had been her age. In fact, I had been exactly her age sitting on that train many moons ago, reading Bill Bryson and wondering how I'd one day step foot on this very trail. How would life be for her at my age, having experienced such radical freedom and awe in nature at the very beginning of her road? I could only imagine the benefits, but also difficulties, of approaching a 'traditional' working life for the first time after living in the wild this way. But perhaps there was no 'traditional' for this generation, and maybe that was no bad thing.

Close to the top of the steady climb, we smelled smoke and saw vague, billowy wisps in the air ahead where there were no people – a campfire that someone had set and left smouldering in a forest clearing. We poured some of the little water we had on it – hard to spare in drought – and both of us spoke angrily about the negligence of those not checking embers were out before they hiked away. Wag melted her pole basket, trying to ensure the coals were done, and swore heartily before we hiked along to find and hug the biggest and oldest oak on the whole trail. A truly majestic wonder to see.

The heat continued. We dipped in lakes that were *alleged* to be nuclear, took side trails to find rivers that weren't there, and guzzled more bottles left at roadsides for us. The draw to water was too much to bear, and before we crossed the Hudson we slipped down to Canopus Lake for a nero day of swimming, volleyball and drinking sodas with regular folks.

After that, onwards to one of the most incongruous points of the entire trail – the AT blue blaze that went straight through the centre of The Bear Mountain Zoo after crossing over the Hudson River. The zoo had begun as a bear den in the '20s and was now a place for rehabilitating animals of every stripe.

It was not only the zoo, which was interesting enough, that piqued our interest; on the far side of the pens before we started up Bear Mountain was an outside swimming pool which hikers had free access to. We duly lined up, a line of stink, and they let us descend to the poolside. Such crystal-clear water in the dappled sunlight, with the sound of the zoo animals baying and screeching in the trees around us. Such a travesty for regular folks enjoying their wholesome day at the pool, I'm sure, to watch us hikers peel off our filthy layers, pretend our pants and bras were 'bikinis' or 'trunks' and all jump in together to play and swim for a few hours. This trail was never not surprising.

Hot days gave rise to night hiking over the following week, along side trails to other lakes and stepping around tourist bins at national parks which had been broken open by confident bears seeking discarded burgers and fries. We homed in on park facilities in the early mornings or late at night, attracted by the glow of vending machines plugged in, desperate for a soda or an iced lolly. Wag and I took a few winding routes through this patch of trail, exploring and experimenting with different blazes and roads until we joined the Bottle Cap Trail, which delivered us, after stepping over hundreds of the tiny orange salamanders we had been seeing more and more of, to our matriarch, the AT, and the tightest rock alley of them all, The Lemon Squeezer.

My lemons squeezed (and pack held sideways over my head, despite my 16lb weight loss by this point), we were out and moving to the next border – New Jersey. A state no one was looking forward to because of all the images of suburbs and industry that it threw up in our minds, but which was to give us some of the most beautiful trails of all.

NEW JERSEY

72.2 miles

CHAPTER FIFTEEN

The Unbearable Pain of Shedding a Skin

The humidity was still crazy, but we were all buoyed up on our massive ice-cream sundaes from the famous Creamery the night before, and to top it off we'd called for delivery pizza to our tents pitched by the road. Slightly sugar-hungover, I left camp later than the others that morning.

The heat was still relentless.

'Hey, I'm dropping this here. Better get it before the bears.' My wake-up call was from Chimney dropping off cold slices for me before he peaced out of camp. Wag headed out next and then I was last. I never minded being last in but hated being last out. On the map the path looked straight, and flat in terms of elevation, but it was an unnecessarily rocky scramble – deliberately routed up and over every rocky outcrop in sight. I frightened the life out of a Nobo hiker who thought I was a bear coming and so had started singing and capering in the path to frighten me away, until I rounded the corner and we both collapsed into hoots of laughter. Ursines did make an appearance later as a baby bear fell out of a tree to my right and then, looking stunned and sheepish, scampered off into the brush. These baby bears aren't so good at balance just yet.

The crew caught up with and overtook each other in succession, each finding the others sprawled in the dirt at various junctures, desperate for water and squirting pure Mio electrolytes into our mouths with only the merest swig of precious water to see it down. Delirium was close, but so was the famed 'Drive-In' movie theatre in New Jersey which welcomed hikers and let them stay for free at the back of the movie field, with free speakers thrown in too.

A few of us scored a hitch into town and I hit the local chiropractor. My pain was acting up badly because of dehydration and the inflammation it was causing. My sleep was so poor in these hot and thirsty nights, the streams were barely brown trickles and no one was feeling good. I hitched back out to the movie field after resupplying with Wag and found some of The Vortex there, so pitched up and listened to a bubble of Nobos trash-talking us Sobos and warning us that we wouldn't be able to handle the trail in Pennsylvania. We listened and smiled as usual, knowing they had New Hampshire and Maine to tackle, so... whatever, fellas.

The lights of the ticker tape flashed all night long and interrupted what I had hoped would be a good rest. Few hikers had their rain fly on as the heat was so intense, and so walking to the bathrooms in the restless night afforded me a bird's-eye view into tents. Under the flickering neon they looked more like they belonged to festival-goers than to a group of hikers, with scattered beer and cider cans, pizza boxes and other junk. I didn't like the disrespect and was glad later in the day when the Nobos left and we cleaned around.

I knew there was another reason I wasn't sleeping well. Buckshot was closing in on us and I was hoping so hard that when he finally caught us up, things would be the same as they were before, but I knew deep down in the dread knot I carried in my gut that he was going to be different. His messages had thinned out; his replies were weak. There was no reason I could think of other than he was camping on a tiny island out of Maine with his family, but I had made enough excuses for shit men in my life to know when I was clutching at straws. A reckoning was coming, and I only hoped I was wrong about how it was going to pan out. He was too important to me to lose, and I felt like I'd been treading water until he returned. Silly girl.

'But why worry, G? He's just a guy. One who behaves pretty damn selfishly too.' Wag was good at advice. Wise for her 21 years.

'It's not just that. I know that.' I felt my cheeks flush. I was 41 damn years old. How could I be feeling like this about some 25-year-old wild man who was so undomesticated as to need to spend most of his life alone in the mountains and out under the stars. 'I think really he means so much to me because of how much he let me be me. How much he held space when I told him things, didn't judge me for struggling, taught me how to thrive out here when I would have given up. Made me feel so alive and excited through it all.'

She nodded. *He's like a portal*, I thought. *I walked through him with all my fear and I didn't die from it. I came through it to the other side and then was in some way cleansed of all the shame I had been carrying. And to keep up with him, to feel validated by someone so strong and bold; it put my sickness into a tiny corner of my identity instead of filling my whole nest like an interloping cuckoo. That's why. He is the tie tethering me to my new identity, and if he leaves then maybe that leaves too.*

Who are we anyway? A reflection of those around us? It was easy to feel like myself when I was surrounded by my own cocoon of books and artwork, clothes that spoke for me, plans and events that sculpted who I was, or wanted to become. But here on the trail these things don't matter. They are of no currency. Here the fierce, the famous, the rich or the impoverished all co-exist in anonymity, meaning there is no 'you' other than the one you are when stripped naked. I was waking up to the fact that I had been too scared to be naked, and as I stripped bare and gave away the place I'd carved in the world, I'd not had the courage to stay exposed. I kept myself shielded with people who reflected who I wanted to be, but without doing the work first – strong Buckshot, funny Dozer and Lazybean, kind Wag, experienced and confident Moose and Granola. Even when some of these people were unkind or unfriendly, I hadn't peeled myself away from them, and now I saw that it wasn't because I wanted *them* – it was that *I* was too afraid to see who I was and to be truly alone. The dread in my stomach over the past few days anticipating Buckshot's return told me it wasn't going to be long before I found out who I was.

That night, after our zero and a half, we barrelled into the cidery over the street from the Drive-In and were now seated in the hot, humid darkness. New friends from the Drive-In, Maple and Cruise, were now in our gang. We were chatting and laughing under fairy lights that hung around the bowers, drinking flights of cider and discussing their curious ingredients. Looking between the smiling faces of my friends, I saw him. On the road. Moving in the dim light from the field towards the supermarket.

He was here, and he hadn't let me know.

He knew I was here, and he didn't care.

My gut was right. It was over and this was how I was getting the news confirmed. I stood and forced a grin for the crew. 'Hey, guys, I'm just going to get something from the store before it closes.'

Feeling fevered and angry, I knew that walking over there was a bad idea but was unable to stop myself or the fury. He was a liar. He had used me. Used me for my ability to pay for food, book hotel rooms, sleep with him and make him laugh. I knew we weren't together, knew now he had a girlfriend, but I truly believed we were friends.

I felt grief-stricken – maybe the things I'd told him about myself had made him dislike me? Maybe he'd had time to think about my tears, my fear and my weakness and he didn't want to speak to me again. Maybe I was the girl I thought I was: weak. Lamed by my dark years. I had thought he had seen through the light and the dark to the real me inside, but I knew I was only angry at myself for not loving myself enough, not at him for not loving me. He had only ever been an exciting distraction and now it was being torn away in front of me and I knew I'd have to face myself at last.

I hustled over the road in the dark heat, knowing it was wrong, that I was erring into the space of losing control and wanting more than I had. I should have sat in my feelings and let them ebb, but instead I was propelled towards this man, hoping he could quiet the fears but knowing he would not. And, lo, I picked up some snacks and knew that I would somehow bump into him, that the universe would ping us together around a corner or by some food stand. I was so busy wondering how it would happen that when it actually did I was taken aback with a start.

'Appalachian Gail! How the hell are ya?' He stood back and appraised me, eyes taking off my clothes, grinning louche and large. 'Hell, you're lookin' good. Hope you've been well.' And he hoisted a twenty-four pack of beer onto his shoulder and turned slowly, going about his business. Crudely intimate but so deeply detached.

'Hey,' I managed. Grinning and trying for nonchalant. 'How was the trip? A while ago now, hey?' My fingers were gripping my sleeves with a pinching ferocity, but I kept my face relaxed.

'Yeah, you know, I been catching up with y'all, haven't I? Phew, I fuckin' walked so many miles so quick, and this heat is fuckin' terrible. Here with Cap and Cait. All good, gettin' the beer. Where are you staying?' He looked the question at me, faux innocently.

'Hmm. The same place as you, *Buckshot*.' I was getting pissed off. We knew each other too well and too intensely for this polite howdy bullshit. 'But you'd know that because I told you about this place like 2 days ago.'

'Yeah, yeah, that's true.' He was high and drunk already, but I was just noticing. He was good at hiding it until it got profound. 'OK, yeah, well maybe I'll see you up there later. Where you at now?'

'At the cidery over the street,' I said, gesturing. 'Wag too. Come over if you like?' Urgh. I was a fool. My mouth opened before my brain engaged gear way too often.

'Nah. Maybe later. Gotta get this crate back up to the *crew*.' Grinning again. So humiliated, so let down. We used to be a crew, he and I. We liked joining others for a while, but we were having great times. Not anymore it seemed, and it was unbuttoning my chest. I nodded and explained that I needed to pick up a few more things, moseying off down the aisle as if I didn't care a bit.

We ended up at the checkouts at the same time and spoke again, which is when he said, 'Oh, hey, Gail,' and gestured over to me. Thrilled but keeping my shit together, I slowly made my way over after I was done packing.

'Yep?' I said, knowing he was going to ask when I was leaving or what my plans were. He looked down at his still-open wallet from paying the cashier.

'Here. The 100 dollars you lent me.' And he tossed the money into the bottom of the checkout bin towards me and started to pack up. 'Cheers.' Not even looking up.

I didn't know how to process how that felt. Cheapened, paid off. A termination of our friendship by the swift closure of something owed. Done. Invoice paid. No comebacks.

'Great,' I snapped. My tone and face made it clear I was fucked off, and his then flashed with the irritation of a man who's realised he's been an asshole and doesn't want to be held accountable for it. We were walking together through the doors into the outside when I blurted, 'What the hell is going on?'

'What do you mean?'

'This. This isn't the same, it's... *weird*. It feels off. Like, what's happened?'

He rolled his eyes and stopped walking to look at me. 'Whaddya mean, man? Nothing's weird.' He fixed me with a hard stare. 'At least, it wasn't until *you* just made it weird. But yeah. It sure feels weird now, don't it.'

'But that's not fair, Buckshot. I thought we were friends. I don't understand why you can't treat me like a friend rather than someone you barely know. We don't need to be more than friends. I know you can't, but don't come back and be an asshole to me.'

'Fuck's sake, Gail. Everything's fine.' And he turned on his heel and walked up the road into the darkness, with only the white lettering from the pack of beer on his shoulder visible, bobbing up and down as he got further away. I was so angry with myself for losing control, and just made it back to the cidery before I dissolved. Maple, aghast, followed me to the bathroom, sure that someone had died or I was losing my marbles. I filled him in, he hugged me close, and Wag came to join us. The ridiculous cliché of it all was just making me feel more humiliated and I fought to control myself.

There was no sleep that night. I gave up on the group drinking and carousing around the tents. Buckshot was in the middle, rolling joints and smoking his pipe, egging on the others around him to shoot beers, crushing and throwing them to the ground all around the semi-sleeping hikers. I lay in my tent and listened, tears coursing down my cheeks into puddles in the baffles of my Thermarest. I was no longer fit for purpose as an adventurous duo. I no longer had someone to help define my worth. I was on my own and it felt like the end of the world. Little did I know it was to be the beginning of stepping into my own.

CHAPTER SIXTEEN

Moving On

Over the next few days I dragged ass, falling behind the crew on purpose to cry and not have anyone see me. I wasn't only sad and humiliated but also adrift. I was accepting the situation but also realising it had cut me loose, which as I walked and cried, I realised could be interpreted as both a good *and* a bad thing.

We passed plenty of people on the trail over these warm, summery days, sometimes the day hikers overwhelming us with the sweet smell of their washing powders and cologne. At New Jersey's highest point centre we got our free soda and hung about in good spirits, charging our devices inside and dodging disapproving looks from some staff. We chatted to some fun Nobos in the sunshine and petted their dog, admired their flamingo shirts and swapped intel on cool places to go and shelters to avoid. They were taking it slow; sun-dappled and laughing unhurriedly, talking about hiring a guide to summit Katahdin in winter so they didn't have to rush for the October deadline, and how they thought it would be more fun with ice axes than poles.

We were supposed to push all the way to the fire tower for the night, but my crying and overthinking had me exhausted, so when I got to the Mashipacong shelter and saw Wag and Maple chilling, we psyched each other out of hiking further and after some debate we decided to stay. Just then, Chimney and his girlfriend, Lauren, showed up too, making it clearly the right decision in the eyes of the Universe. So, in such good company, we laughed and capered about in the clearing and shared food.

A group of older men showed up and camped. They were *clearly* snorers, so I was damn delighted they didn't stay in the shelter. The had a 'Chicken of the Woods' mushroom that they had harvested, cooked and brought round for us to try, insisting it would all be fine. They looked so respectable, like they could be your dad, and *so* encouraging, so we all had a tiny piece and it *did* taste like chicken. I then remembered some horror film I'd once watched about drugging travellers and covertly googled symptoms of mushroom poisoning on my one-bar phone connection as the men cackled and told us they didn't know *what* it was they'd really given us and asked if we'd all started hallucinating yet. Such droll gents. Because I'm so suggestible, I was sure my lips were swelling and I was seeing things up until something else grabbed my attention. Luckily, just then, Maple asked me to test out his hammock and all mushroom-related worries were forgotten in an instant.

Things that can hurt you in a forest

Things you think will hurt you	Things more likely to hurt you
Mountain lions	Ticks
Bears	Hypothermia
Rattlesnakes	Getting lost
Crazy people	Falling down things
Poisonous berries and fungi	Post-trail depression

Later, amid deep, guttural snores from across the clearing, I tried to sleep. I was recognising that Buckshot had helped me more than I could have dreamed anyone would. He didn't have to. He'd taught me things, built my confidence and held space for me to unravel, and I paid for it all with a piece of my heart, and that was OK. He might have felt important to me, but he was maybe just the pebble that had rolled away from me, releasing the avalanche behind, and that's what I was facing through these days of deep grief. The woods, the silence, the loneliness. I was sitting alone in my head whilst all the rocks from my life tumbled about me as I walked. I could duck away from the rolling rocks and step off trail, distract myself with travel or people, beer or reasons to leave, but the rocks would always be there and I'd always be running. I needed to let them fall, and take the hits until the path finally cleared.

Without Buckshot I didn't have to be reliant on anyone. I was stronger, and now that he'd gone for good I was more aware of my progress, of all the things I'm *not* scared of that I had been, and had carried on being when he was there because I didn't have to face them. I now didn't need my tent next to anyone else's or to sleep right next to someone. I didn't feel like animals were going to come in the night. I didn't panic about going further or not as far as other people. I could be more autonomous and confident about having some control and making my own plans for the day. He always threatened to go, and that made me anxious. Now he'd gone, and through my sadness I felt some small measure of relief. I didn't have to *find* the courage to strike out alone now, because the decision had been made, and I could feel myself rising to the glorious challenge of experimenting with how I liked to do things on my own, rather than waiting for who I had thought was my partner to catch up.

PENNSYLVANIA

229.6 miles

CHAPTER SEVENTEEN

Between Rocks and Hard Places

We had left the Delaware Water Gap church hostel on the PA border and were having the greatest time. I'd been introduced to Lizzo by my beloved Maple and we were singing our hearts out on ridge lines and under the trees. It felt like Lizzo had been inserted into my life at *juuuust* the right time, with me especially loving belting 'Truth Hurts' out at the top of my lungs in my own personal broken-hearted revolt. Maple was sympathetic and supportive, a special man in every way, *but* he was also very interested in choreographing a Lizzo music video tribute of us all twerking on mountaintops. Practising for this was an excellent way to keep us all laughing, especially now we were in *Pennsylvania*, often referred to as 'Rocksylvania' through the gritted teeth of weary northbounders. Voted the fourteenth best state (of fourteen) on the whole trail by hikers everywhere, throughout time immemorial, it was the state we'd all been warned about since Katahdin, and it was now here. What could be so bad? It was relatively flat; so little elevation. The views were fine and the people were kind. But the rocks.

The rocks.

If you gathered 10,000 great white sharks, asked them to lie side by side for 150 miles of the PA trail and open their mouths so you could walk across their teeth, it might be less sharp and painful than the reality of the trail in Northern PA. We often ended our days in tears; feet pulverised and too tender to touch. It was relentless, and if the sharp, toothy stones weren't enough, then the edges of rocks would weigh in too, as if sharpened *on purpose*. Any mild grazing of a hip or thigh against a rock would bring a sharp bite and beads of blood. Hmm. I had thought Maine to be like the Hunger Games, but I now believed that *nothing* had such a *considered* amount of jeopardy as PA, as though our tenacity was being tested by a constant upgrading of risk the deeper we entered the state. Rocks! Snakes in between rocks! Rattlers you could hear but not see! Copperheads basking under edges and ledges you couldn't predict with the next footfall! It was, of course, nothing so sinister as pre-planned danger. Merely geological features and the nature that surrounded them; boulder fields and sharp ridge lines that made the trail the diverse and beautiful adventure we loved. In fact, the second half of the state was beautiful and a blissfully easy roll through after the rocks of the first half.

It was in PA that I got to hike with Dawson again. I hadn't known he was called that when I braced myself next to him on the Vermont bridge, or when I saw him defeatedly pack his bag and continue onwards, but now I did. A kind, quiet man who wrangled snakes and picked exotic teas in his real life in Florida, but who here on the trail was a mystery and enigma. Someone I was delighted to spend time with over the days that took us up to and over the precarious Lehigh Gap. Hikers divulge so much so quickly when you are in rhythm with them, and our friendship was formed in hours and days as we pushed through this stretch. I was sad to see him go ahead but knew we'd weave in and out with each other down the line. I needed a quick break, and so watched him hike on as I settled in to some Trail Magic at the base of the Gap. The Vortex had concertinaed back together at the roadside for a night of beer and wine, and then we duly stretched out again the next morning towards Duncannon and the famous Doyle Hotel.

We were 1,000 miles in. No mean feat! My daily mileage was increasing steadily again, even though the heat was punishing, and I was hoping to get to the fabled 30-miler in the coming days. Lots of us had already done 30 miles in a day. It wasn't as easy to reach it out here on the AT as it apparently is for other trails, such as the Pacific Crest Trail, which has longer, gentler ascents and descents. Here on the AT, the elevation and descent and rocky, muddy trails are prohibitive. Even so, I was determined to get my body to do it.

The day we hiked into Duncannon wasn't the day we were supposed to do it. We'd been a few days between towns and resupply and were all tired, fighting not just the heat but also the animals. Snakes were popping up between rocks and crevices everywhere and we needed to be on high alert for the rattling sound that would signal defensiveness and a potential strike. Also, the wasps. Wasps, hornets – who knew exactly what they were? But they made their nests on the flat ground of the trail with just a small hole for their entry and exit. A small hole perfect for the tip of a pole to go down when a hiker walked by above. If the first hiker agitated the wasps without realising, then the following hikers were the ones to walk through the angry swarms coming from the nest in protest, and it was never pleasant.

We were all victims in turn throughout these days, but this day was the worst. I was stung on the back of my calf and others were stung on their arms and face, and the wasps didn't let go, pinning themselves deeply into our flesh with fury beyond the initial injury. So it was, in the parching heat and pulling wasp barbs from our bodies in agony, we decided to push as hard as we could to get into Duncannon that night and not early the next morning. It was going to be almost 30 miles, across PA's rocks and running the gauntlet of flying beasts and tricksy snakes. I didn't know if I could actually make it.

By late afternoon I was done for. My calf had swelled large and deep red, my allergy to mosquito bites clearly not being exclusive. My feet hurt, my back hurt and I was dragging my right leg again imperceptibly. I would have been happy to stop and camp at the shelter 2 miles from town, but the team encouraged me to continue.

'Beer!' Cruise said, smiling. 'Beer and *pizza*!'

'Hot, delicious pizza and the church basement to sleep in, G! Town! Beer!' Wag knew just what to say. So, digging deep, I rallied and carried on.

Hustling down a steep, long descent in the dim light under tree cover, I made a misstep, an error that everyone and anyone makes. I stumbled in my tiredness, and the cadence of my stride, which was fierce and powerful in the fast downhill motion, twisted off to the side. And then I watched in horror as my back foot swung forwards with the full force of a 4-mile-per-hour descent – not forwards and onto the trail, but off trail at the angle my body had begun to stumble. Right into a huge rock on the side of the path. Plainly put – I kicked a goddamn boulder. Hard. With my soft trail runners.

'FUCK IT,' I yelled. The crew down ahead stopped and looked back up through the trees.

'Y'OK, G?' Anxious faces below; Cruise and TJ checking in.

'Yep, yep. Just kicked a damn rock!' I called back. *Damn* though, it really, really hurt. Well, no time to moan – so close to respite! I dug deep and hobbled on, knowing the burn in my foot would fade and keeping my mind off it by turning up my headphones.

*

After the road walk into Duncannon, we set up in the church basement and then hit town to drink beer and eat pizza. I was constantly in awe of the church community along the trail. Always trusting, open-hearted and kind, with very little in the way of *persuading* people about their faith. Just folks showing up for each other, being present and demonstrating such big hearts in the following of their principles. I was always very grateful. I lay on my mat amidst the other hikers on the linoleum floor of the basement. The day had been a success in the main, although at 29.4 miles I couldn't count it as my first thirty, which was very irritating considering how much my foot hurt.

The next morning we decided to explore. First the launderette, then the store, and after that Moose and Granola got picked up by a fabulous older couple who loved to host hikers and had been scouting the roads in their truck for people to treat. They called us up and arranged where we'd meet and we all dived into the back of their pickup, which would take us to their home. It was the best afternoon we could have wished for: a pool to swim in, fresh corn to shuck, and plate upon plate of homemade cooking and great conversation. As the sun dipped, the crew pulled themselves from their pool floaties and off loungers to be taken back into town. We piled out of the truck next to the legendary Doyle Hotel, originally built in the 1770s and where Charles Dickens was purported to have made a visit. Our thirst sated at the bar, it was another night's rest and then back to trail again. This time, Cruise and I were out first and heading up the crew.

Pennsylvania was to ease up on us after Duncannon. The rocks blunted a little, and the trails were gentle and flatter than previously. Perfect for my throbbing foot, which I was sure I'd badly bruised, and perfect for extended long days in succession. I debated with Cruise about why people don't manage to do long days and big miles, even if they want to. After discussing whether it was ultimately nutrition, physical health or strength, we came to the conclusion that it was probably mostly *mental*. That people's bodies can do most anything asked of them, but people's minds will try to trip them up: 'make a call, scroll Instagram, read that article, take a break', etc. The mind is so good at making you believe you can't, so you just have to rewire that can't to *can*. Easier said than done! Longer days were becoming the norm however, even with fun stops like the half-gallon ice cream challenge at Pine Grove Furnace. I don't know how anyone can eat half a gallon of ice cream against a timer and then hike out, but Maple certainly did, albeit slightly green around the gills.

The days blurred. I was happy in the company of Chimney, Cruise and Maple, the others slightly behind. Harpers Ferry over in West Virginia – the home of Appalachian Trail headquarters and all things officially *trail* – was only a little further and we were excited to get there. I'd pick up my packet of medication, sign the logbook and have my photo taken for posterity for the special folder containing Polaroids of all the hikers who make it through. Some of our team had hung back though, dipping into Washington, DC to see friends and the city, and were now revving up at the Mason–Dixon Line at the edge of PA and Maryland, the border that marked the start of the Four State Challenge: 42.9 miles in 24 hours.

Hikers would sleep at the Mason–Dixon Line, leave in the early hours and cross immediately from Pennsylvania into Maryland. Then 40.9 miles of Maryland would give over into West Virginia for only 6 miles, after which they'd step over the line into Virginia and collapse. It meant they missed the ATC in Harpers Ferry, but for some it was worth it. Not for me though; I was desperate for my codeine, having started steady withdrawal as my pills had run out in recent weeks. I'd noticed too late that this was having a detrimental effect on both my body and my mind. My legs twitched at night, my moods were erratic, my skin was itchy and I was becoming gradually aware of how long and how deeply I'd become embroiled in a relationship with the medication and what a grip it had on my life. I was determined to get off it completely, but on a trail in the middle of the most challenging experience of my life so far from home, it didn't feel like quite the right time to go cold turkey.

MARYLAND

40.9 miles

*

WEST VIRGINIA

6 miles

CHAPTER EIGHTEEN

Short but Sweet

Only 6 miles of trail, but West Virginia was a marker of note on the AT. It was not quite at the exact *physical* halfway point of the trail, but it represented the *psychological* halfway point. This was because the town of Harpers Ferry, through which the trail wove, housed the headquarters of the Appalachian Trail Conservancy. The ATC was the place where you had your photograph taken for their record books and received your hiker number, showing which number southbound hiker you were of those passing through this year. We hiked down into the town, excited to reach the central focus of the trail, and Harpers Ferry truly showed up for us. A beautiful town with the welcoming Appalachian Trail headquarters – holding parcels for me from my family, plenty of coffee and snacks, and Polaroids of us all for posterity.

I tore through parcels that had arrived with glee. There were some new shoes I'd sent forward to myself, as well as the parcel from home with a replenishment of my medicine. Thank goodness. Such a relief! Too much of a relief, I realised, just to know that I had the meds there in my pack, even if I was taking many less than before I started trail. It was clear that I had a deep dependency on codeine that I hadn't realised or accepted before this trip – both psychological and physical. I made a promise to myself right there to carry on weaning myself off of them, and that for the next hike I tried to attempt I wouldn't want to be taking them at all. Luckily, that was far off, because I had to finish this hike first, and knowing that I had a new stash of pills in case of a new pain surge was definitely reassuring.

One more parcel to open. I wasn't expecting anything else, so it was a nice surprise. Inside were two pairs of socks and three packets of THC gummies! They'd been sent to me by a northbound hiker called Ding Dong who I'd met the night I was deposited into the hostel at the bottom of Moosilauke after my panic attack. She and her father had been so kind to me, and she had said she'd send something to Harpers Ferry for when I got there because it was a lovely feeling to get parcels along trail. She had wanted to give me something to look forward to. I was in such shock that evening that I hadn't properly computed and had only met her for that one night, and now here was this wonderful parcel waiting for me. The socks were perfect; the THC gummies were less so for me because I wasn't ever very good with smoking weed or feeling stoned, so I passed them out amongst those in the gang that wanted them and saved a few for myself to experiment with when the time felt right.

After the excitement of the parcels I sat back nestled deeply in a comfy sofa. It was here that I pulled out a few of the letters I had been carrying from the start of the trail. I hadn't thought about them much beyond feeling the warm hug of the knowledge that they were there in my pack, nestled in double ziplock bags in a pouch between the frame and the pack itself. Letters I had asked for.

As I was preparing to leave the UK for this journey I knew there would be lows. Sometimes so low that I'd want to give up. It was for those times that I asked my loved ones to write to me, imagining a me with a grimy, tear-streaked face having a meltdown and wanting to go, to run away from the challenge and give in. I asked them to write to that Gail and to give her their best words of advice and encouragement for whatever it was I decided to do. And they had. I was carrying almost twenty letters in my pack that I had barely touched, never feeling that it was *bad* enough to warrant opening a letter. But now I wanted to see at least one or two to refuel my heart-tanks and to see who these people believed I could be, now that I was almost halfway and had been through so much. Perhaps I could put some of them in my sock and the love in them would heal my poor, throbbing foot? I focused, wondered which ones to read; deciding I needed to know the message from he who said the least, I plucked my father's letter from the pile.

It was printed from the computer rather than handwritten, perhaps so that I could discern every word without the ups and downs of his handwriting, or perhaps because he found it easier to write more when he could type. It didn't take more than reading a few words for me to understand that this was a departure from his usual way of speaking to me. This was raw and honest, sharing times in his youth when he felt lost and alone: his first trips away at sea, far from home and all he knew in the creeks and on the beaches of the Helford. He spoke to me of the pride he had for me, and his belief in my tenacity and strength.

I held the paper tightly, rereading words together in twos and threes so as not to get to the end of sentences; not yet. I wanted to savour every moment of this expression of love that was harder for him to show me face to face when the cacophony of our ups and downs would stand with us. I yearned to make him proud, and although I knew I always had, this letter was the tangible proof of it I could hold forever.

I hadn't realised I had been missing the love and acceptance of my family so much until I read the letter, letting it wash through and warm me like a stiff drink. Then I carefully placed it back into the envelope and plastic shields of the ziplock bags. It couldn't get damaged. It was too special. They all were. I could see the one from Mama in there. I wasn't ready for the emotion of that on top of Dad's right now. And my amazing sister had written me more than one. She had written one for me to open as I arrived, one for the end and an extra one, which was for if I decided to come home anyway, even after reading everyone else's pep talks. This was called 'You're Coming Home – And It's OK'.

Juiced up on love, encouragement and a new packet of pain medication, it was time to think about moving on again. It was here in Harpers Ferry that our trail family in its current shape fragmented, and not before time in many respects. Moose and Granola had been distant and aloof with me in the past weeks, and they left the ATC for Washington, DC with their trail friend Shakespeare, who was completing a section hike. TJ and Wag had bonded hard and beautifully and were behind us now after their trip to DC – determined to do the Four State Challenge together. So my 'tramily' was now deliciously made up of Maple, Cruise, Chimney and a new addition – K2 – who had to finish the trail in time to make it to his wedding, a deadline that he seemed very relaxed about, repeatedly giving us anxiety for him and simultaneously making us hoot at the lunacy of it.

West Virginia came and went without further fanfare, and then we were in Virginia – the longest state on the trail by far, and one that takes more hikers off the path than any other. The Virginia Blues were a well-known thing for northbound hikers, who hit the steady monotony of hiking throughout this long stretch in one state. Southbound hikers didn't hit that state at the same point in the thru as the northbounders, but we still experienced the same feelings when the exhaustion began to compound. Was it time for the Virginia Blues for me too?

VIRGINIA

550.3 miles

CHAPTER NINETEEN

The Virginia Blues

Early in my Virginia days I knew that my foot was hurt more severely than I'd realised. I really didn't want to tell anyone but mentioned to Maple at varying turns that I was in a lot of pain. This was familiar territory to me though. Pain. I had many coping methods: breathing in a particular way, disassociation, grit and pushing through – and also, of course, the new stock of painkillers I'd picked up in the mail at Harpers Ferry. As much as I knew they weren't my friends, the meds were definitely making the day easier. Maple was, as ever, a supreme buddy and offered to carry my pack as well as his own on the elevation where my full pack caused my foot to shoot pains up my leg and me to gasp out loud.

We had dipped into Front Royal to get supplies for our coming days in the Shenandoah National Park, through which about 100 miles of trail meanders. I was so excited for the park and all the views it would afford but had been told that the AT was routed through tree cover most of the way; if we wanted *views*, we'd need to hop on and off 'Skyline Drive', a route with the very best vistas that had been built for people to drive along, not walk. So be it. I was no purist but I knew that for some amongst us it was going to be hard to equate their purism with also missing some of the greatest views on this part of the trail.

I couldn't have loved the Shennys more. There were regular 'waysides' throughout the park, ranging from expensive bars and restaurants to more humble campgrounds with great basic facilities. We were able to resupply regularly and our days together were filled with some of the greatest joy I experienced all through the trail. I had hiked long enough to know what I was capable of. I wasn't carrying so much *stuff* anymore – the 'packing of my fears' had much abated as I'd learned and grown. The men I was with were like my brothers, and I felt such love and peace in their company: Maple, Chimney and now Moon, a younger guy who'd stepped onto trail from nowhere and joined forces with us after taking a few weeks away from trail on his earlier attempt; Cruise had been with us in the beginning, and I loved him still, but as we meandered through local apple butter festivals and dined at waysides at the request of kind and interested strangers, he felt the urge to move faster, and one morning had departed early and gone far, too far for us to catch him for now. And so the rest of us wallowed in our time together. My foot was given some breathing space at this slower pace, and we were all kinder to ourselves. We lay around campfires under the stars, slept outside together eschewing canvas, and shared our deepest fears and hopes in the cover of darkness and in the arms of the trees. I had never been so content as I was with these beloved men.

Days later, for all the fun I was having and for the rest it had got, my foot wasn't showing any sign of stopping shouting for my attention once I revved up the miles. So it was, with a heavy heart, that I called for a ride to get into the next town, Waynesboro, jumping a few final miles of the park. I was beginning to fear that my foot was getting worse and not better. I'd strapped it up with tape but didn't know if the pain was worse because I was tired and run-down or if it just needed more stability in my light trail runners. The black bruising was fading though, which could only be a good thing. My pack was lighter after 5 days in Shenandoah, so the weight through my feet was better. I knew that another zero was needed, and Waynesboro was the place to get it. As I waggled my phone in the air to get service alongside a road, I was passed by three hikers I didn't recognise but whose names I'd heard on the grapevine. We chatted briefly, and in the course of the conversation I heard words that stopped me in my tracks.

'Oh, yeah,' said a pretty girl with a small pack and fast-looking legs, whom I would later know to be 'Yallah', 'and whatever mileage we're doing is nowhere near as full-on as that guy Buckshot. He was crushing it last night when he went through. He only stopped for a quick meal and then into the night he went!'

What?

Buckshot?

The last I had heard he was many miles behind with Captain and his gang. Drinking, smoking and carousing their way slowly down trail. But what was this? He'd struck out alone. Oh my God. Would I see him? I was gripped with a panic that he'd gone past me already. I had been long waiting for the moment when he'd come up behind me on trail and have to go past, to have my moment to speak to him calmly, to thank him for how he'd spurred me on but also give him a solid piece of my mind about his shitty treatment of women. Oh, but who was I kidding? It wouldn't just be that.

'Oh!' I said as casually as I could muster. 'Buckshot! I didn't realise he was so close. We were buddies back earlier on the trail. I haven't seen him for an age now.' I tried to keep my voice light.

'Well he's somewhere round here for sure, taking roads through and not just trail. I'm sure you won't miss him!' And just then my phone pinged to tell me it had found signal.

'OK. Thanks, guys! Well, happy hiking and see you down trail. I have to make a quick call.' And so they smiled and took their leave and I called for a shuttle from the hostel in Waynesboro to come and collect me, now dizzied and my heart beating in my mouth as well as thumping in my foot.

Buckshot. I was going to get to say goodbye.

*

I texted him as I got into town. It had been a while and I was nervous to make contact, but this might be my last chance.

He replied almost immediately, and with one thing leading to another he arrived at my motel door a few hours later. He jumped into the shower and we sat drinking cider on the balcony, chatting and laughing as if the down times had been a figment of my imagination. Minutes of anxious tension turned into hours of companionable catching up and then dinner, more beers and a night that transported me back to our earlier and most connected times together. I was under no illusion, however, that this was a divided man, in more than one direction, and I was a scarlet woman.

I didn't ask if he had finally ended his long-distance relationship, because I knew he'd either lie or get cross that I'd asked. I hoped he had but I knew the real answer. As much as I felt terrible spending this kind of time with another woman's boyfriend, I also couldn't quite compute that he really was 'taken'. I knew she existed across oceans somewhere, but since I hadn't known she existed for so much of our time together, it seemed permissible for me to continue with this man who had meant so much to me, and that me saying this final goodbye was somehow OK. If it *was* the final goodbye, of course.

Buckshot would not be drawn on specifics – only that '*Of course* we'd be hiking together in the coming days', as well as many words of admiration and kindness about my hiking achievements, strength and courage to this point. He made me feel capable, and had done since the start, but I was aware this time around that I didn't *need* his words to feel the strength I had inside. I had become aware of it all on my own.

After our night spent together, we resupplied at the store the next morning and I felt the familiar lurch of sadness as he packed in the motel room to leave. His transient nature was built so as to never get too attached. He'd already explained that he'd become so attached to me in the beginning that it had distracted him from all he was trying to achieve on trail this time around: speed and solo time. I would have liked to remind him that booze and weed had also contributed a fair amount to his distraction, but it wasn't the time or place and I waved him off to the trailhead with some sadness but also deep relief that the moment had come and gone, and now he was no longer behind me waiting to catch up, but ahead and pulling away. To that end I hiked to the town's hostel, where the boys had arrived, and checked in, and we took a second zero all together, feasting on an 'all-you-can-eat' Chinese buffet and watching movies. Perfection.

Our little bubble swelled at the hostel with the addition of Baby Milkshakes, who had slowed to hike some days with his mother and had ended up with us at the same place. After our time with feet up, enjoying the hot showers and indoor sleeping, we were fit to leave.

I strapped my foot up as much as I could, looking at it in dismay that morning: the puffiness creeping up my ankle and the bruising appearing at the base of my calf muscle. What was going on? I had researched online about deep bruising taking a while to appear, so that must be it, but it was disconcerting and extremely frustrating not to see healing happening. As I hobbled around, I was giving myself blisters and hitching my bad hip to compensate. It was not what my body needed or deserved, so I resolved to keep my gait balanced, bite down harder against the shooting pains, and ignore the snapping and grinding I could feel whenever I put too much weight on it. I would *not* be left behind.

*

My bravado and positive thinking got me a fair way, still pulling long days with stiff mileage and enjoying myself. Hiking up The Priest was a slog as we just weren't *used* to such one-note elevation anymore after many hundreds of miles of more undulation than ascent. The climb was worth it though as the shelter atop The Priest was unlike any other, containing as it did a *confessional* logbook. Hikers had taken it upon themselves to reveal all to The Priest mountain and we spent a long time laughing our heads off at all the misdemeanours listed, from unclean hands on other people's food to coveting sleeping pads and peeing where they shouldn't.

Many said that Virginia was long and dull, without the variation that one might feel when jumping from one state to another across state lines, but I was loving my time here. The terrain changed repeatedly, the history and sights were plentiful, and sometimes the landmarks were out of this world, like the sunset we saw at Lion Rock before spending the night there and making our way down into the next town. For me though, Virginia was tough going despite the beauty and wonder, and it was on the stretch down into the next town that I fell so far behind that I knew I needed to take action. I couldn't pretend that my foot was OK anymore. I called the closest hostel I could and explained my situation, to which they were very sympathetic, arranging a ride to the local hospital (local being 35 miles away) and sending the car to the trailhead for me. I limped there slowly, feeling deep fear that I was about to be told to step off trail and heal. Words I was not prepared to accept.

*

The hospital was efficient and friendly and I didn't have to wait long before I was shown to a little cubicle. A nurse came to chat, and I found myself dissolving into sobs as I told her about my foot, my friends, my hopes of continuing and how the pain had ground me into exhaustion. She listened and comforted me, explaining that they'd send a mobile X-ray machine to my bed and then we'd see what was what. She asked if I'd eaten and I replied, 'No,' amazed that I had actually hiked 17 miles without eating since breakfast, so focused was I on pushing through on the pain. So, whilst I waited, a kindly security guard brought me two sandwich snack boxes from the staffroom with a wink and a smile, while another nurse came toting some homemade soup she'd brought for her own lunch, and yet another with some herbal teas. I was being very well looked after.

A quick zap from a fancy machine was next, and then 45 minutes later I was in conversation with the nurse practitioner who was parsing the X-ray results for me. 'No break visible… Nothing out of the ordinary… Don't worry.'

THANK GOD.

I was advised to rest a little, perhaps to jump a couple of days ahead of my friends to rest the foot whilst they caught up. Indeed, if it was a choice between going home or missing some miles to carry on with my friends, then skipping the miles it was! A stiff $1,200 later and I was out, back at the hostel in town and celebrating with the boys over the phone. They'd pitched up in the park down the road and were settling in for the night. We decided I'd catch a ride ahead of them and meet in Daleville, where we'd all catch up after I'd rested and take in the trail highlights of McAfee Knob and then Dragon's Tooth after that. I was so relieved to have a plan that the flood of joy and the course of heavy anti-inflammatories the hospital had given me for the next 10 days helped the foot feel better already. Tendinitis was the diagnosis! Just an irritated tendon. Rest would be great, and then I could gingerly carry on whilst keeping the injury in check. Crisis averted, I tucked into a huge bag of Lay's and set about making friends with my new hostel mates in front of the TV, foot hoisted in the hospital bandages and my worries behind me.

I got a ride from the hostel to Daleville with a member of the hostel staff, who was kind and thoughtful but couldn't stop talking. He took the wrong road because he was busy recounting one tale after another about how he'd had to get off trail in a previous year and ended up here working at the hostel – and so the trip which should have been 45 minutes became 2 hours or more. Eventually I got dropped off where I needed to be and booked myself into the hotel across the way from where the AT picked up again. I was sad to miss miles but happy to wait for a day and a half and rest the sore foot sprain until Cruise and the gang hiked through to get me. I checked in and looked out of the window. Who should I see, tired and dirty, walking across the lot to the check-in desk, but Buckshot. *Shit.*

Of course. He was ahead and was probably taking time out here for a night. I hadn't even considered that he might be here – I was too busy worrying about my foot and the potential of getting pushed off trail with injury – but I didn't expect him to believe me when he saw me. When we eventually bumped into each other in the hall, we reverted to the inevitable chatting, laughing and flirting that always rose up when we were together, especially when others weren't around. The chemical connection was undeniable, but I was trying to extricate myself from its hold over me because I knew now what he was capable of and I needed to be free from thinking about him, and especially about thinking of him hiking on and leaving me again, despite the inevitability of it.

We were both booked in for two nights, but we kept our separate rooms and didn't sleep in each other's spaces. The dance was still present between us – he backed off and I stepped forwards; I stepped away and he moved to me – but it was hollow for me and perhaps meaningless for him. I didn't know what we'd become now, but it made me sad that it was a far cry from our excitable closeness in the early months. However, I was now focused less on him and more on my foot. It had to improve. It had to.

*

My trail family emerged from the woods earlier than I had expected. They had taken a shortcut and also really pushed the miles to arrive before lunchtime on the day before I expected them. So, with a little time to spare, they booked a room and gathered me up. We went to the Mexican next to the hotel all together and proceeded to drink huge margaritas and eat tacos and burritos until we were bursting. It was a lovely mix of folks, including old friends Cruise and Baby Milkshakes, and new ones in the form of Pineapple and Yallah. Tipsy and happy, we piled into the hotel rooms together, filling the tub and soaping up both Cruise's airbed and my own to try to find and patch the tiny holes we both had that left us on the dirt in the mornings after slowly deflating under us all night. More beer, more fun and then all crashing out in exhausted sleep – ready to strike out again the next day… A full day earlier than my foot and I had planned.

Before hitting the trail the next morning, I took an Uber down the highway to the post office and sent another parcel to Captain's parents' house. Such kind people, they had accepted packages from me of things I realised I didn't need to carry all along the trail. This was possible because they lived in Georgia, and I could collect all the parcels at the end of the AT before I flew home. I'd initially sent one box of things back to the UK, thinking it would work fine, but the customs duty my mama had to pay to accept it was triple the value of the junk inside, so I was forever grateful to Captain's lovely folks.

After that was posted, I picked up a new pair of more sturdy shoes from the outfitter to help protect my tendinitis and ran into Maple at Bojangles. We hugged – delighted to be reunited after the past few days. Then Buckshot appeared on his way to buy biscuits and liquor and chatted but kept his remove as was usual. He wanted what he wanted and to give nothing in return.

Off we went. My bag was heavy and my new shoes weren't helping as much as I thought they would, but it was only 16 miles until we got to the stunning McAfee Knob for a sleep and to take the famous photo at dawn.

Maple and Moon caught up with us the next morning, having left Tinker Cliffs at 4 a.m. to reach McAfee. After the iconic shots had been taken for all of us on the jutting outcrop, we moseyed on down in staggered groups. We knew there was a very famous all-you-can-eat Southern food restaurant near our next stop for the night – the Four Pines Hostel – and we were desperate to get there.

Four Pines was rustic and great. The owner was another huge character who didn't suffer fools gladly but was full of kindness and generosity to those he considered good folks. We drove to the store and filled up on snacks and cider, then made our way en masse to the restaurant everyone had been raving about (Buckshot included, as he'd turned up just before we left and climbed in with us). I had my first experience of grits, biscuits, fried chicken and collard greens, stuffing myself until I could barely breathe – no food tastes as good as food after walking miles and miles every day. This never changed, and food never got old.

That night, drunk, full and happy after all of us playing Cornhole in the yard and singing our lungs out to music under warm, starlight skies, Buckshot and I were as predictably drawn together as ever, moving away from the small group and firelight up to the back fields where we set up our camp. This time though, our coming together was for more than physical touch. We held each other closely and there was a sadness and sombreness to him as he explained that he hadn't known how to deal with how he'd been feeling – so frustrated that he couldn't stay away from me, yet consumed with guilt and still in love with his girlfriend. I knew he was torn, and I knew we'd had something very special, but the best of us was a long time past. His drinking, rudeness and dismissal of me since he returned from his vacation had hurt, and even though I knew why he was so conflicted and lashing out, I had moved a long way beyond caring what happened next and from needing him in the way that I had before. I had never really envisaged a world off trail with him as the trail forces you to only live in the moment. We had existed in a far different and unrealistic dimension than real life, but my heart was still heavy at the finality that I felt in this night. We shared the contents of our hearts lying under a tree in a grassy field surrounded by the wild woods that had brought us together, and, although we would weave in and out of each other's pathways over the following 2 days, we chose this to be our final goodbye – in the best way we knew how.

CHAPTER TWENTY

Leaving the Trail

I was last again. Trailing behind Maple and stopping often to rest my weight on my heel. When that didn't offer enough respite, I found myself leaning heavily on one pole and lifting my foot in the air slightly, as though I could detach it from any weight at all. It pulsed, the purply red creeping up my ankle. The many weeks of walking on something so painful had migrated the pain upwards and now my shin ached with a cold dullness that made me repeatedly and absently touch it with my palm whenever I was sitting. I guessed my shin was crying out to me because the voice of the foot had not been enough. How could I have ignored it this long? My stubborn bull-headed desperation to be 'normal' and to not slide backwards, not slip. No two steps forwards, one step backwards anymore. Enough. I was strong now. I was a *hiker*. This was my new life. I was a person that didn't need to make an excuse, didn't need to take a seat, tell a lie, not join in or meet people 'afterwards', never admitting my agony. I was supposed to be *fixed*. And now I was here again, and it was too much to bear.

I barked out a sob. Silence. The trees held me as I slid down, hands slipping down my poles, onto my knees then further, head in hands. Floored. My pain has always dived inwards – a swallow, a grimace and it's gone from view, but here in the forest I knew there was little need to pretend. The woods knew all my secrets by now, and the grief I felt was theirs too, for they recognise a broken bough. I cried for a long time, unmoved by the time of day or where my friends were. I wondered if I could just stay here and suspend time until I healed.

Wiping tears from my dirty face with dirtier hands, I pulled my phone from my breast pocket and dialled the only person who knew the contours of my journey to this moment as though they were her own.

'Mum?'

There are no ends to the intonation of this simple word, and no end to my wonderment of how she translates them correctly every time.

'Are you OK? What's happened?'

'Oh, Mum.' I choked up. Her voice was her cool hand on my hot brow, her wisdom the only possible lifebuoy to this bobbing, drowning moment. I scrabbled to sound OK because I didn't want her to worry so far away and with so little she could do, but I just couldn't do it. I was broken.

'Mum, ummm. You know my foot?' The question ended in a high-pitched wobble. My voice was wavering and I paused, desperate to control myself. 'Well…' I drew the words out. 'I think… I think it's really bad, Mum.'

A little beat of silence. Her thinking. Weighing the response.

'It's OK, sweetheart,' she soothed, slowly and calmly. 'It's OK.' There was some quiet whilst she waited for my breathing to slow. 'Gail. There is no shame in this.'

I bowed my head, but she couldn't see me. The Shame. I bowed my head and squeezed my eyes shut so hard I could see stars, sinking further against the tree. 'I. Can't. Give. In. Mum.' Words between the waves of grief. 'I can't. It's not fair. I can't stop. Why am I broken? Why can't I be good at this? I try so hard. I have tried for so long. I am a good person. Why can't I not be like this?' Tears poured from me, and my chest hurt so badly I found it hard to breathe. This unspeakable and incredulous unfairness.

'I am old, Mum. I haven't been able to be young like this, to move like this. I want it so much. I can't tell people I didn't make it. I can't *not* do this. I can't. I can't fail. *I CAN'T FAIL!* I am so ashamed.' I was wailing, and she was holding the space for me to let it out until it was time to pull my shit back together.

'Gail, I want you to breathe for me. Gail, listen. Please listen. I want you to breathe with me please. In and out, slow and steady. Breathe. I can't help you if I can't understand you. I'm here. It's going to be OK.'

I breathed with her through the phone, my sleeves pasted with snot and my eyelids already swelling into my own periphery.

'What shall I do?' My voice so small.

'You know your body, Gail, and you know your limits. Your father and I could not be prouder of you – we are always so very proud of you, and I've every belief that you know in your gut when it's time to rest. Listen, you can't argue with your foot, you can't walk it better. It's been long enough that you've been pushing through with this. It could be worse than you think and if you don't rest it now then you'll be off it for longer and perhaps *any* future trail will be off the cards.' She paused to check I was there. Listening and gauging my emotional state from my breath, and from whatever rich alchemy has always existed between us. 'There is still time for you to rest it now before you go back. And you can always go back.'

She was right. I wouldn't have called her unless I knew this was what I was ready to hear. In all honesty I had known for a while now that my days were numbered on this go-round. I had been growing increasingly exhausted, pretending it wasn't as bad as it was. The pain was keeping me awake all night, leaving me emotional and fragile walking 20 miles a day. It wasn't feasible to go on. I just needed some permission.

'I'm coming home.'

'It's the right thing, sweetheart. You know it's the right thing. We're here, and we'll get you back there.'

'OK, Mum. I have to go now. I have to figure out what to do next. I have to get to Pearisburg and see my friends. I have to try to see Buckshot. I can't believe I might not see him again now.' This was heartbreaking for me. The ways my heart had broken for this man and all he represented to me in this emotional odyssey I had taken on trail were endless. He was a saviour, cheerleader, charlatan and grifter, but he had helped propel me this far.

I hung up the call and placed it back by my breast. Breathed. Knew and acknowledged that I'd felt these things before – this grief, this loss – and I'd lived through those times to this moment, so I could live through this too.

As I lifted my head, I registered a less colourful woods. I had been on the phone for longer than I realised and the sun was saying fond farewells to corners of boughs and undersides of rocks. It was fitting, the dimmed light. An acknowledgement from the place that had saved me.

Heaving myself up onto my foot, I made another quick call to the hostel in Pearisburg and was proud of how I kept my voice steadied. The hostel owner was coming to get me at the closest trailhead and I had to get there before dusk. The force of pain as I took a step took my breath away – sharper and sick-making. I retched once then stopped. Clearly, my determination and bull-headed forceful approach to finishing the trail and keeping up had given me some buffer between my brain and the injury, and now I'd accepted my fate, all was revealed. I had been cruel to my body in order to heal my soul, but perhaps it was OK because my body knew that my soul was due some time in the light. Now I knew I needed to get home and take stock.

As I bundled myself into Doc's car at the roadside pull-off, she smiled and made some hiker small talk. I felt like a fraud. I wasn't a hiker anymore; I was a quitter and I was heading home. I couldn't eat all-you-can-eat buffets and feel good; in fact, fuck it, food would probably never be guilt-free again. Urgh. I held my poles between my knees and looked at my filthy battered shoes as the truck swayed back and forth over rough road and turned onto highway. I liked this woman and her passion for helping hikers. She got me to open up and I explained the situation I was in.

'Girl, I'm a chiropractor *and* I'm studying acupuncture! If that's just tendinitis, then let's see what I can do for you! And your friends are back there in the bunkhouse, talking all on what they're gonna get for food tonight – the Chinese buffet is a favourite or there's the Mexican where y'all can get a margarita.' She shot me a sidelong grin. 'Yup, you're gonna be OK.'

I asked her about why she had set up her hostel, lulled into a semi-fugue listening space by her kind voice and tales. I was simultaneously anxious about getting to the hostel and desperate to arrive. My people were there – my tribe, my family. Would they still feel the same about me when I told them that I had to go? Would it be like when you resign from a job but have notice to work and all your colleagues become distant, polite acquaintances. The slow reversal of the arrival process back in to the land of the stranger? I hoped not. This little group of people had finally got me feeling accepted. The last few weeks with them had felt fun and safe and had given me room to grow. Sure, it had been emotional. Yes, there had been some meltdowns, but I loved them and I didn't want to lose them. And then I was stirred from my fears of arrival into the jolt of arrival itself and slid out of the high truck seat onto my good foot. I registered in the hut, chose a sleep spot (bunkhouse) and grabbed my things, limping towards the single-storey building that would hold my friends.

I elbowed the door open and was met with the usual miasma of damp, warm rot. Yes, the bunk room stank, but it was so incredibly comforting. I liked this muggy, loamy air, this cocooning of folks whilst they fed and rested in order to head back out into the wild, like bears in a den. The air might have seemed crowded, but currently only Cruise was inside.

'Hey!' He looked up at me, his sharp and thoughtful face taking me in. 'You made it. Good. Not the greatest day then, I guess.' He glanced back down to fish his wallet out of the brain of his pack. Clipped with most people at the best of times, he was thinking carefully of what to say as he and I had passed clipped a long time ago. He fussed with some clothes hanging round his bunk and then turned to sit on it, facing me with his elbows on his knees. 'Gail, you have to do what you have to do. It is what it is. You're struggling, you're slow. We can wait for you at the end of our days, but you'll get tireder and fall further behind, and one day it'll be too far and too long and we won't wait. That's not fun for you.'

I had shuffled towards a bottom bunk as he was speaking, listening to him with my back turned and dumping my belongings on the shiny blue waterproof mattress without a cover. I faced him and sat heavily.

'What are your options, Gail?' He turned to look directly at me. 'You can push through and keep up but you'll be in agony and damage yourself further – it's not going to improve whilst you're doing 25 miles a day. Then you'll be off trail somewhere more remote. We might not be all together at the time and you'll be left trying to figure it all out on your own. No goodbyes, no help.' He was right. 'You could cut your mileage to 10 miles a day and take it easy, but then you're on your own anyway, with people hiking past you every day – that's going to make you feel awful and your foot's still not gonna heal. Neither one will leave you in a fit state to hike or get back here soon.' Now he paused and took a breath. 'Or your last option, the one you don't want to consider. You end it right here and you go home. You rest, then you get back here and you make new friends in the winter.' Cruise was a cut-to-the-chaser. 'Whichever way,' he said sombrely, 'we'll be gone.'

He was right, but I was struggling, my phone call to Mum faint and far away. I might have already resigned myself to the fact my foot was done, but after the ride back and on seeing all their kit in the bunkhouse, I wasn't any closer to believing I had to leave these people. Who would I be without them?

'Think about it and remember this. You used to have *chronic* pain. You could do nothing. You thought it was over. Now, you've come this far and you're called out again… but with a *regular person injury*! Celebrate it! It could be me, Maple or any one of us. It's a trail injury, not a "*you*" disease. It's not the same. Take that in the best possible spirit and, in the meantime, let's get some food.'

We walked, me hobbling on my heel, to the store. Cruise had been adamant that he needed to resupply because he was going to head out in the morning. Efficient and clear. I had begged him not to, to instead take a zero at Angel's Rest so that we could all be together for one more day. We were overdue a zero, the heat and drought making us extremely tired and weaker than we should be. I knew that Maple was keen to zero the next day, as were Chimney and Milkshakes, but if one person went on, often the group would do a slow turn into going with them. I desperately needed them all to stay. A little buffer of suspended animation between the forest and the real world.

In the supermarket I felt like shit. There they all were – my people – filling baskets with Pop-Tarts and Mexican rice for the days ahead. My lack of shopping was a pretty clear indicator that I was going nowhere, and I didn't like it.

The next morning Maple was extremely excited to grab me outside the bathrooms to tell me, 'We're zeroing! We're all zeroing. Cruise too. I can't bear the thought of leaving you here alone this morning.' He pulled me into a hard, long hug, his hand on the back of my head. I loved this man, this bright spark of emotion and consideration in human form.

With the impetus to be up and ready to say my goodbyes postponed for a day, I felt myself relax. I mooched over to the large, static caravan with a ramp which served as the communal kitchen and poured myself a coffee, even going so far as to poke through the hiker food box to see what'd been left. The kitchen slowly filled with people: Chimney, Milkshakes, Earnhart and Maple, among others. Cruise and I decided to cook a huge breakfast for everyone, so off I hobbled to the mart again, this time with a homemade poultice on my foot. Soon we were making massive stacks of pancakes, bacon and syrup, handing them down the line to hungry hikers like in a Depression soup kitchen.

The sun beat down and the dry leaves crackled in the yard as we stretched the day out as long as we could. It was no mean feat for me to simultaneously research my best route home on my phone and at the same time studiously be repelled by this planning and therefore not engage with it at all. Somehow a vague plan of extraction materialised, involving a long private shuttle to Virginia Tech university, a bus to Washington, an Airbnb overnight, then another bus to New York and *then* a plane home. Over 24 hours of travel for a 7-hour flight to the UK, and then 10 hours of travel to get home to Cornwall on the other side. Crushing.

By mid-afternoon we were squashed together on the sofa and across the floor of the static under blankets, eating snacks and watching *Lord of the Rings*, followed by countless episodes of the American *Office*. Clothes had been laundered, resupplies had been stripped of their boxes and packed, hiker boxes had been pillaged, and the crew knew they were set to leave as soon as the light came in the morning. Soon, those who were hiking early made moves for bed and I went along with them; a family set to divide.

The morning was sombre and short. I was collected by a quiet man in a black truck, and with only Maple awake, it was a brief hug, some tears and then I pulled away. The seams that stitched me into place in the woods were tearing and the rip was loud and painful. I was not ready to go. Later, on the coach to DC, I watched the road skip by beneath me. The ignominy of it, taking me back up the East Coast in mere hours alongside the route that my feet took me weeks to achieve. Rest stops were loud and bustling, the catapult into real life scalding my senses. The trail had changed me. It had dissembled me and given me back the pieces without a manual for rebuild, as if I should innately know how to put myself back together. I wasn't sure. I was a different human, standing blinking in the city sunlight, and I wasn't sure going home to rest was going to change me back.

PART FOUR

Home

CHAPTER TWENTY-ONE

Back on Trail

166 miles left in Virginia

A series of planes, trains and automobiles delivered me back to the spot I had left one month before: the check-in booth at the Pearisburg hostel. Same but different. Colder, frost on the ground under my feet. A new trail but the same one. I was so nervous. Prepared to do the next month alone but so hoping not to.

The bunk room smelled the same, and on the shelves to my right as I entered, I could see items I'd left a month before that no one had yet needed: a gas canister I couldn't take on the plane and some toiletries. I raised my head – there were people in here, talking about some other people I didn't know.

'So, I dunno if he's gonna want to zero, Bopit. I think he'll just want to keep going tomorrow.'

'Sure. Well OK, but it's super cold now and I'm going to hang out here whatever y'all do. I'll catch you, Spud. It'll be cool.'

Two women. One young and one around my age, wearing jumpers and talking across the back corner bottom bunks. I slipped in and put my pack on an empty bed, a stranger in a familiar place.

'Hi!' one of them called. 'How're you doin'? Just got here?'

I explained that I was just *back* and it felt great but weird. They came over and we sat to talk awhile. The thing with hikers is that they'll mostly welcome you wherever you meet them – always welcoming, all one family. So we got acquainted and went to the trailer where I'd spent my last zero with the boys. New boys were in there: Acid Jesus, Bunkhouse, Space Cake – the hiker treadmill showing me that everyone's special moment in special places was replicated daily by new trail families in the same spot. I was so glad to see friendly folks, and they pulled me into their gang with conversation like I'd never been away but had just been hiking a little slower or faster and was only now in sync with them. It helped that I'd heard of Bopit in my early trail time. We had been so close to meeting in Maine and New Hampshire, but she'd fallen into a vortex in Gorham with Rock Naps, spending weeks meandering off trail exploring rivers, smoking weed and taking stock. Rock Naps never turned up and was now a more fabled mythical hiker who would appear occasionally on Facebook feeds in random photos far behind, hanging out with various trail locals and characters. Wherever he'd got to, he was doing the trail slowly, steadily and probably still stoned. Bopit made it along though and was here now; all caught up, lean and fit-looking as hell. So we all ate and drank, and I was mightily relieved to feel at home in a full bunkhouse with the murmurs and snores of my new tribe.

But the next day I set out early and alone, my new friends deciding to zero, which I couldn't afford to do so early in the game and with a flight booked home on the 9th December. It was so *very* cold, but as I hiked I was comforted by thoughts of my old trail family trudging up these very tracks a month before me. A different time back then: heat, drought and the fear of no water. Today it was frosty and as I neared the tops of climbs, the cold wind stung my cheeks. *How was I still doing this?* I stopped to pull on my thin gloves and put my buff around my neck much sooner than I'd anticipated. It definitely felt like home, coming back to these pathways and trees, but it was changed beyond recognition from the trail I'd left.

It had been hard to return to rest in the UK. I had thought returning to trail might be even harder, but my body and mind had yearned for it. What was I if not walking in the woods now? What was my *purpose*? The need to get back and finish had been consuming me.

My foot had improved slightly in the time that I'd rested it, but it was still sharply painful as I moved up and through the elevation with weight on my back. Maybe it was one of those sprains that meant *really* resting it, for months. Hmm, no chance – I was going to hike these last 500 miles if I had to drag the leg behind me like a corpse.

I'd missed the beauty of the leaves turning, and now most of the colourful fluttering scraps of leaf were underfoot, turning into a carpet of multi-hued mulch. I felt less *adventurous* because I'd stepped off and reunited with family and friends so recently. It had softened me and taken the hungry bite out of my steps, broken the awe-spell of being lost outdoors. It would return, but at the moment I felt like a *day* hiker and too close to the home comforts of my loved ones to feel as brave as I knew I'd need to feel. The cold was doing a good job of hardening me up though, and the wind would quickly follow suit. Cosy thoughts of tea by the fire with the dog and homemade dinner were soon to fade and give way to the brutality of snow sleeping and iced nostrils.

Today's goal was Wood's Hole Hostel, run by Neville. I figured I had a while to get there, so started the day slowly, allowing my foot to figure out how it was going to feel – but too late I realised that the evening had drawn in and night was coming, and with it the cold deepened. I sped up, feeling a knot in my tummy that was different to my earlier fear on trail. This time I was more resigned to being alone but had a different kind of loneliness in knowing no one was behind me or in front. The hikers had thinned out; no one was coming. There'd be no one rolling in after me this evening with a high five and a smelly hug to talk about their day – I needed to be faster and smarter this time around.

The hostel sat deep and quiet in the thick woods, a wooden lodge-style building set back on its own track with views over the wide valley below in the dusk. Candles and dim lights on the veranda. No one answered the door, giving me pause. Cars in the lot, but no sounds anywhere save the cracking twigs in the woods on either side that came with night-time and the beasts out here. Then she came, solidifying behind the glass from the dim space behind, like surfacing from a lake.

'Hello,' she said softly, opening the door a foot. 'We were meditating.' She slowly breathed in then out. 'Please come in. We will be a little while. Take your shoes off here and leave your pack. You're welcome to look around downstairs, and I'll be back in a while to show you to your room. You're the only one here tonight.' And with this she turned and floated away to a door marked 'private', giving me a glimpse of candles and a hushed explanation to whomever was within. The door closed. I looked around, feeling off balance and uneasy, and walked into the warm old kitchen to sit at the round wooden table that filled most of the homely space. I felt strange sitting there, so walked back out the way I'd come and outside.

Later that evening we sat around the kitchen table with her farmhands and meditation guests. Out host was called Neville and was very welcoming, chatting about Buddhism, her past husband and her new love in India as she dished our delicious homemade and hearty food to the table. I was the only hiker and she was adamant it was too cold for me to stay alone in the bunkhouse across the yard, so she put me up in one of the semi-private rooms upstairs for the same price. She was so kind. Vulnerable but with stoic strength that I hoped would see her through this first winter alone in this generational family home built by her grandparents in their youth. I cleared some plates, made my excuses and retired to bed, tired from my first day back. In the morning the purplish sunrise brought me almost to tears with its beauty. I washed, ate and walked out into another day alone in the leaf-strewn autumn woods.

That night I was welcomed at Weary Feet Hostel, an oasis of Southern hospitality, kindness and charm. It was as akin to being pulled into a family home like a long-lost relative as any experience I'd had on trail. I slackpacked from here out the next day, but it was far too cold to hike far, my throat hurting from breathing icy air and not wearing nearly enough layers. I hadn't anticipated the cold spell would become more intense in the daytime, expecting the sun to warm me through. At a road crossing I called it quits for the day and called Weary Feet, who came to collect me.

It seemed the universe had plans in store, because back at the hostel were Spud and Bunkhouse from Angel's Rest 2 days before.

They had tried to hike an extremely long day, passing the hostel earlier and throwing the towel in just before me. The kind Weary Feet folk had done a number of out and backs to pull in freezing hikers today. Now I had some hiking buddies after all. We stayed the night and the hunters came, filling the space with loud laughter and kind gestures, cooking bear meat and eating plate after plate of food.

I'd been warned that the hostel might fill with these big men in their camouflaged finery. It was why my hat was orange for this stretch of winter hiking – it was hunting season and if you were going into the woods then it was highly recommended you wore orange to not get shot by the hunters who were secluded in hides or up trees. Great, I had thought, another thing to overthink when peeing or digging a cathole off trail where you think you had some privacy. I had taken to peeing and waving at the same time to make the hunters I thought could be watching know I knew they were there, even though they probably weren't there and I was just overthinking. Still, I didn't like the idea of being watched by men with guns hidden deep in the woods as I hiked along like a doe for the capture.

In reality though, and far from my fevered mind, the only hunters I encountered on trail were courteous and made efforts to be as unthreatening as possible, lowering their guns, nodding and tugging their caps at me with 'Good morning, ma'am' and deferential queries about how I was. Occasionally I'd be passed by pickups with large burly men sat in the rear, only the deer's bloody, lolling head and huge antlers visible to me, propped over their legs and under their victorious faces as they whooped and drove on by. Once, a man with a crossbow stepped out from behind a boulder, making me scream short and high, but he was very nice and I ended up feeling like I'd met a chivalrous Daryl Dixon in the woods.

Virginia continued to be long and welcoming but exhausting and cold. In Atkins I took the advice of Wag, who had messaged to exhort me to contact an older lady called Murray who loved Cornwall and would provide Trail Magic for me as she had for them when they went through. I called Murray and set it up, arranging to meet her at a gas station with myself, Spud and Fitbit – a girl we'd met on the way when she was dropped back off at a trailhead after a week with family. Murray was a warm, older woman with a huge heart, driving us 30 minutes to her home for showers, waffles, pancakes and any other manner of food and wine we desired. Her late husband had hiked the trail and she had loved supporting him do it and seeing his enjoyment. They'd remained Trail Angels in the years since, and she continued to do so after his passing, telling all whom she hosted about her husband and having us sign her logbooks. We were dropped back the next morning, happy and full, and to my total joy I met up with Milkshakes, who had seen where I was on social media and let me know he could stop by the gas station on his long drive moving cross-country to Denver. We hugged like the long-lost trail buddies we were, even though it had hardly been a month, and then he handed me his bag of supplies for my new fam and bid us farewell.

I plugged my headphones in and listened to the rest of *The Handmaid's Tale* on my 11 miles to Partnership Shelter. I felt out of step and out of sync, feeling that at some point I'd have to skip miles and yellow blaze, even though I really didn't want to. I didn't see how I could keep up 22–25 miles a day with my foot pain building again and the nights drawing in so early. With my flight an immovable date in December, something was going to have to give.

That night at the shelter our high mood was crushed. The park service had turned the spigots off with no warning so there was no water to be had. We had drained our bottles to almost empty in anticipation of good, clean tap water and now we were desperately thirsty with only half a litre each to cook with and drink before we found a source the next morning. We debated hiking on in the dark to the next shelter, but it was starting to snow and we were all cold and tired. Instead we found a pizza menu tucked in the back corner and called for takeout to be delivered. It was very bizarre – they would drive out with pizza but refused to bring or pick up any water on the way, no matter what incentives we offered, financial or otherwise. So, unwisely, we stuffed ourselves with hot, salty pizza, played cards and, laughing, swigged some whiskey we had. We then all lay back in the soft, snowy dark, our mouths dry and prickly, wryly regretting our very fun life choices.

Early the next morning we heard cars pull up to the park's visitor centre, which had been shuttered and dark the night before. We'd done the rounds, pulling on door handles and trying outside faucets, but to no avail. In the same moment, Fitbit walked up to the shelter with blue hands and red cheeks to ask for help. Her hammock rain fly had frozen so hard in the night she didn't know how to warm it to be able to fold it down. She yanked at ice in her hair, grinning and cold.

Just for a moment, looking at her I felt out of my depth – we were hikers not mountain climbers! We had shorts and trail shoes, not boots and thermal trousers. Maybe it was foolish to press on today. I could hear Spud groaning as she did every morning at the biting air touching her soft skin as she changed from sleep clothes to day clothes in her quilt, letting out the cocoon of warmth from the night and letting in the spiky fingers of Jack Frost. Perhaps we needed to stop and check the weather. But then I remembered how damn thirsty I was and directed my attention back to the lingering echo of a car engine switched off in the still morning.

The air was bitingly cold on my cheeks as I stepped down out of the wooden walls and skidded over through the inches of fresh snow, with the others not far behind me. I saw a shadowy shape through the glass door and before long had attracted the attention of a portly ranger, who was initially unsure about my entreaties for water – but after a few moments of British accent and my best dry-mouthed charm, he ushered us into the warm to chat. We got water and once I'd downed a litre and rallied, I attempted to go all in.

I smiled. 'Do you perhaps have a cup of instant coffee that I could buy?' This was unfair on the poor chap really, as he had already shown a shuffling anxiousness at letting us in before hours. But sadly for him I already knew that he was too kind to *sell* me a cup of coffee, *and* that if he would be open to giving coffee away, then his nice nature would dictate that he would want to do a little better than what I'd asked for. I mean, he'd already let me in the door and I was sleep-addled and messy.

So, of course, not long afterwards I was back in the staff room brewing up a pot of some other guy's (who wasn't in that day but probably wouldn't mind) coffee for everyone, including the nice man who let us in. All was well for ten idyllic minutes until the boss lady, who had clearly let herself in from the back lot, came through to the office and glared at us all, especially at our portly saviour. Not long afterwards, and after defending said saviour from her cold direct questioning of why four smelly, dirty hikers were in her office staff room, we were out and back on the trail; full of Yogied coffee and ready for the day. Well, we thought so. Little did we know that the snow was coming in hard and the temperature, in a freak cold snap akin to an apocalypse film, was going to go through the floor – along with our ability to hike.

*

I couldn't see the ground, my vision blurred by the snowflakes landing on my lashes and the disconcerting lack of depth in my field of vision caused by all the 'white'. I kept up with the others for a while, then dropped back out of sight as was customary for me. The sight of others ahead made me feel like I was last: demoralised. But once they were gone from view, I could reframe it: alone, brave, in the lead.

I peed, and the snow hit my naked, pink backside making me jump and start peeing on my shoe. Not a day goes by that one of us doesn't pee on our shoes, but in winter there was much less getting away with it, and secret wees were a thing of the past, with hikers leaving yellow patches like someone had walked their dogs through trail. I didn't like it so made sure to always kick fresh snow over to cover my tracks. Because I also didn't like being too far behind, I hustled up over some peaks to ensure I could still see the others in the distance. I shoved my hand in my coat and grabbed my 'Hot Pocket' with relief. The temperature was dropping considerably and I was glad I'd shared them around. I had Hot Pockets in each glove and one stuffed in the front of my knickers. There was sometimes one in my sports bra too. So fucking cold. I needed these warm spots to remind my body to heat the hell up.

High on the unavoidable ridge line, the wind blew ice crystals at me horizontally, stinging my face and brutally blinding me. I could see Fitbit close ahead. She usually runs hot but had stopped, desperately pushing her solitary Hot Pocket from hand to hand. I fished out one of my extras and gave it to her as I passed, trying to also give her my spare gloves, but she demurred.

Fourteen miles later and feeling crushed by the cold, we congregated at a road crossing. No one needed to suggest we call it quits for the day – everyone was broken. We strung out down the road, trying to hitch a ride, a few metres between us. Cars passed in small sets, spraying us with dirty slush and leaving us behind. I figured it was really mean to be left near a hiking trail in this weather by the passing cars so called each of them assholes after they'd gone by. The wind was howling up the road in the bottom of this valley, and snow swirled as the dark crept up, billowing jackets and burrowing down the back of necks. Some men pulled in for a short hour's hike before dark and told us that this cold weather storm even had a name because it was so rare and scary in November, set to break records across the USA.

A large pickup slowed and pulled in. A big man leaned out of the window, warmth and light spilling out around him onto our chapped faces. He asked if we had an emergency and the others said, 'No, no. Just looking for a ride,' probably wondering why he would have thought so, but then they hadn't seen me at the end of the line behind their hitching thumbs, making praying signs, waving with both arms and mouthing 'PLEASE' at the passing cars because I was so fucking cold. Success!

'We would so appreciate a ride to Troutdale,' Bunkhouse said through numb, cracked lips.

'I'm not sure, guys. I just don't think I have room in here, and you'll freeze to death in the back.' He swivelled his neck to look through the back window. That chink of possibility was all we needed. We perked up and gleefully assured him, 'We can fit in!' And then, with his permission, we made it happen. I'd normally take the truck bed but I was blue, so I squeezed in the cab, making small talk and discovering this man surfed all his summers, and his best friend lived in Newquay, a mere 30-minute drive from my house in Cornwall.

Our new friend dropped us in a barren, desolate-looking village. In fact, it wasn't a village, as this seems a uniquely British term, but I wouldn't have ordinarily called it a town – just a slick, snowy road forking ahead, left and right, with some crumbling industrial buildings, a shuttered and decaying old-time, saloon-style inn and a small post office being the only signs of life. We turned as one and looked up over a snowy rise: a church, then set further back the tops of some other buildings. We walked, frozen, up a curved icy path past one building with signs and arrows, directing us to another with more arrows pointing in different directions. One to a shower, and the other saying 'Portacabin

Bunkhouses'. We slogged and slid silently upwards through the flat light of the early evening.

Two units. Two separate cubicle portacabin rooms. We peered through the frosted window to check it was the right place, happily seeing a worktop and two bunk beds. Praying they were open, we stepped up onto the unmarked snow of the porch and tried the door. It gave inwards and our shoulders sagged with relief. We piled in after taking our shoes off and leaving them outside, but still we tracked in snow and ice onto the plastic-filmed laminate floor. I bent to crank on the heating bar. It took hours to heat that damn room. Bunkhouse hung up his thermometer and we kept checking it, intermittently jumping off our bunks onto the burning cold, uninsulated floor. We'd all pulled out our quilts and couldn't speak much until we felt less ill from the low temperature and exertion.

I leaned back and looked at the bottom of the bunk above me, wincing as Fitbit moved next to me, her wet, puffy jacket huffing out a belch of warm hiker stink. We sat in twos on the bottom bunks, shivering, staring at the walls and reading the graffitied wood of the old units, too cold to move for quite some time. We started with snacks, then cooked food, all in relative silence, bar the rustles of blankets, quilts and bags. We were all desperate for the loo but too scared to go outside in the ice storm.

It was too cold and extremely stultifying in the cabin. Adventuring into the neighbouring unit provided nothing more. The hiker box was minimal and discarded, with few people coming into Troutdale and fewer still to this bunkhouse. After some searching on the walls, we saw a B&B advertised for hikers. Spud looked it up on her downloaded Guthook app. The reviews were poor; it was overpriced and the reviews hinted at something distinctly 'odd', but I called them with the tiny bit of service I had.

They weren't pleasant. Not to me or to any of us who called. The B&B team were a stern, mean woman and a man shouting dissent and annoyance in the background. We had only really called to arrange a slackpack the next day, so we could get up and over Roan Mountain, but they scoffed at our 'foolishness' and refused to drive us in such cold weather.

When, on the second time, I said I was a journalist – a fib, but I didn't care – she warmed up, keen for us to stay at their place, and wheedled for us to pay for her B&B for two nights and then she'd help us. She stressed that the portacabin was dangerously cold with no one else around. I explained that some of us couldn't afford to pay, so that's why we were in this church shelter.

'How many can't afford it?' she pressed. 'One could work for staying and help me in the kitchen with food prep and cleaning.'

It was strange. They were strange, and I didn't enjoy talking over her inflated rates through her vacillating mood swings. We cut a deal that we were going to remain where we were and call her at 7 a.m., thinking that they'd probably capitulate and drive us to the trailhead. We just wanted to keep going.

For the rest of the evening we tried to get warm. We ate, chatted and got ready for bed. Spud and Bunkhouse played cards, as they often did. Bunkhouse struggled to sit still so went through the hiker box with a fine-toothed comb, announcing all the items out loud to us, making coffee and running water errands to the pavilion. I lay back on my bunk as conversation faltered, and we tried to sleep with the snowy wind howling through cracks like the devil denied. I touched my nose and mouth and cheeks – all cracked and dry from the terrible cold. One big breath in to ease the tension in my chest was also one inhalation of the stinking miasma of my friend Fitbit's jacket, and that was enough to wipe me out. I rolled over to the single-pane glass by my head and shoved a discarded buff into the crack, rolled back and sank into a sleep like the dead.

*

Our plan didn't fly. The Troutdale equivalent of The Twits deliberately refused to take us to the trailhead, knowing that we wouldn't last another day in the portacabin as they gloated down the phone about their huge log burner and the warm home we could stay in. We gave in and he came to pick us up – a huge, serious man swathed in ceremonial robes – and took us on a 3-minute drive (for which we were charged a shuttle fee) to their house. It was a strange bungalow oozing normalcy but with a dystopian undertone we couldn't quite explain.

After listening to an introduction monologue from his wife about how she was suing his family for the estate of his dead mother, and him chipping in that they're all money-grabbing whores, she informed us of their strict faith and the holy standards of their home. No drinking, no entry to here, here and here, no long showers, no extra blankets, nothing for free – everything above a bed was billable. No entry to the kitchen, no exit from the rear. The whole place was really a pile of nope. I was grossed out by them and their home – she obsequious and hand-rubbing, and he a sinister, authoritarian presence in the background. We wanted to leave as soon as we arrived, but we were trapped by an ice storm, the location and a lack of taxis, having already exhausted every other shuttle number for the area.

It wasn't until later that one of us realised why our accommodation felt so strange, and that moment made us feel a little sick. Our single beds in a series of small rooms with lino floors. The counters on one wall, with kitchen-style cupboards below and space for a rolling chair, wipe-clean surfaces and a sink placed mid-worktop. The perfunctory doors and handles. The strange reception hatch, where the wife sat to bark questions, locking the door behind her to sit and glare at us through sliding glass when there were only four of us here. Bunkhouse spotted it first.

'Guys,' he said quietly, even though we could see the large hostile couple were moving to leave for their own house next door. 'Guys, don't freak out, but I think this place was a doctor's surgery.'

All of us took a split second to consider, and then our faces contorted. Light dimming, tree shadows moving in the wind across the floor where we sat by a fire. Dear Lord. Controlling hosts in a disused surgery, miles from anywhere in a dilapidated industrial town. We had walked into a horror film.

Later, padding across the cold lino by my bed with bare feet and barricading the door with my pack, I imagined who had lain in this space before they had wheeled a flimsy, cheap bed in here; how many tears, scrapes, results revealed I lay on. Christ. I couldn't wait to get out.

*

Finally the weather lifted and we were able to leave. We paid through the nose to escape and started our ascent to the Grayson Highlands, a top spot for hikers with its wild ponies and breathtaking views. Alongside these, in mid-November, we also faced storms of ice crystals, snow drifts and exposed balds where the wind cut us near in half, but the ponies were warm and welcoming.

After ice and snow at elevation, we hot-footed it to Damascus, the trail town loved for its annual 'Trail Days' festival and a veritable constant welcome party for hikers. Trail Magic raised its head again in the guise of Chris from the Vermont Magic booking me a room ahead of time at Crazy Larry's Hostel. Larry, a slightly eccentric character with a heart of gold and a chequered past, was a delight. He was a Hemingway-esque writer, with tales of running to the AT on the lam from the cops and jail-cell revelations with the Lord shared over grits and bacon at his breakfast table. We enjoyed his hospitality, rode bicycles for a day to give our walking legs a break and lolled around watching TV and drinking beer. Then we took our leave under the famous Damascus arch and crossed over into Tennessee.

TENNESSEE

287.9 miles

*

NORTH CAROLINA

95.5 miles

CHAPTER TWENTY-TWO

Giving Thanks

The trail through Tennessee and North Carolina wove in and out of each other's borders like stitching a muddy quilt together, often leaving us not knowing where on earth we were. One way of knowing was that the Tennessee shelters often didn't have privies at shelters at *all* – quite a shock after becoming used to having them every now and then. We managed though, following the LNT principles and respecting the trail despite the bone-chilling cold.

These weeks were further blurs of ice and snow. There was silence through the woods as the layers of autumn were pressed down upon by the heavy foot of winter. We passed through Pisgah and Cherokee, picking up random and delicious Trail Magic from walkers and day-visitors to parks and viewpoints who were keen to find someone to gift things to. Hikers were hard to find out here in late November, and just as Trail Angels couldn't find us to nurture, we couldn't find the Angels we needed. Luckily though, there were still some homemade cakes and cans of beer to be found in hollows, car parks and the trunks of trucks that stopped to holler hello to us at trailheads.

When we got to Erwin, the little trail family I was with asked if I wanted to join them on a side trip into the city of Asheville. Bunkhouse had a room booked with two double beds, and a car rented to go there to meet his parents. We were all invited. I ummed and ahhed for a while as, although the offer was tempting, I was worried it would eat into the short time I had left to get myself to the terminus at Springer Mountain and catch my flight. But with the other three all going and Fitbit assuring me we could fit it all in, I threw caution to the wind and jumped in with them.

I was so glad I did. A couple of days in a cool city wasn't such a shock to me after having been home to the UK recently, and it was really interesting to see what life was like for people *off trail* in this part of the USA. We explored antiques stores, drank in micro-breweries and bought homemade spicy jerky and hot sauces for our packs.

After our city adventure, we drove down past the AT to the town of Hot Springs. Spud and Bunkhouse had cooked up an interesting plan. You see, it was soon to be Thanksgiving, and although I had my doubts about celebrating, it was truly a time that families in the USA liked to get together, cook together and open their homes. The hiker families were no different, and every year a kind Trail Angel would gather together all the hikers that were still on trail within an 80+-mile radius and put on a huge Hiker Thanksgiving for them all. She'd source volunteers from all around the community to cook trays of delicious food and donate beers and spirits for everyone, and it was something that had been talked about on trail and social media for weeks.

We had a plan to hike in and enjoy the fun too, but this year the location of Hiker Thanksgiving was different from in years past, and if we continued as we were, we would hike *past* it about 5 days before it happened. It was to be set in Erwin, and our clever plan was to drive down trail to the famously welcoming Laughing

Heart Hostel, check in for a night and stash our gear, and then hike *northbound* back up the trail to Erwin to enjoy Thanksgiving. From there, our lovely hosts at Laughing Heart – Tie and Solo, who would drive up to join in the Thanksgiving – would drive us back down to their hostel for a night's rest and to collect gear before we set out southbound again from their place.

It was a bold plan but it worked a charm. Fitbit and I had fairly similar paces, hers being faster than mine with my damaged foot but not fast enough to break past me into the next day. We also enjoyed hiking together, so we buddied up to hike the 70-ish miles back into Erwin. Spud and Bunkhouse were very fast, so they lingered a little longer and set off later with a slackpack organised and much heftier mileage.

It took a few days, but we made it to Erwin in good time for the festivities. We met some nice folk coming southbound on the trail as we headed north and it was interesting to meet people who would be otherwise hiking too far ahead of us to have met naturally. Hiking north initially felt like cheating on southbound, but we settled into it and were just glad to be ticking off miles. We took turns waiting for each other as the evenings were drawing in more quickly, and neither of us loved hiking in the dark alone. We had our reasons, and they were occasionally amplified.

One man I passed late one dusky afternoon asked to photograph me and snapped pictures as I went by, but other than that creepy interlude (after which I hiked knife-in-hand for a few miles) I was safe and happy. Fitbit fetched water for me at camp when my foot was too painful for extra mileage, and I shared food and other kindnesses with her. We generally settled into a supportive cadence of each other's sporadic company through the day and campmates at night. She'd string her hammock across the front of the shelter that I'd sleep in and we'd keep each other safely company in the dank, early-dark evenings. I was damn glad to have her as my hiking partner and friend.

We arrived in time to drink a late morning beer and get into the swing of festivities. Hiker Thanksgiving was a busy feast down by the river, with heavily laden tables that we were positively drooling to get our hands on. Both the outdoor and indoor spaces were full of hikers from up and down trail that we had heard of but not yet met, and after eating piles of delicious food we began to play games and chat. There were folk of all ages and nationalities, drawn as if by a magnet towards this hospitality from within a cold and wintery 200-mile radius. We had been brought together for a few hours like long-lost family.

I spoke to many hikers I didn't know and caught up with those I'd only met briefly before at springs and shelters. Chatter was as high as the vibes, and laughter filled the air along the banks of the Nolichucky River – firm friendships being formed around the huge fire, with some strong drinks to boot, before it was time to go home. I marvelled at the fact I'd come so far and felt so at home here with these athletic, driven, outdoorsy folk. This wasn't the *me* that started this trail, just the *me* in my mind I had always wanted to become.

I realised standing in that moment that obstacles don't stop coming, no matter what we achieve. We never entirely *arrive* if we keep pushing ourselves, because there are always new boundaries to push. This is no bad thing. Every time I had met my own limits, I had managed to step through them into something new, something unprecedented. It was reassuring to know that we will always find a new way to cope with adversity; we just need to be willing to fall forwards into trusting our own resilience and power. I always knew that beyond my chronic illness was a different life, and that the force of my will to recover and thrive would take me there. And now I knew that I had room to grow so much further beyond those limits too. I truly realised, standing with a cider in hand and the sun on my face, discussing the next long trail I'd hike, that there are no limits except those we place on ourselves.

And then, just like that, the sun was dipping, and the day was drawing to a close. We piled into the back of Tie and Solo's camper, tipsy and smiling: Bunkhouse, Spud, Bopit, Kid, Fitbit and myself. Happiness-tanks full. Ready for the final stretch.

CHAPTER TWENTY-THREE

Into the Smokies

Fitbit and I were on our own now and it was getting cold as hell. The incomparable free spirits and big hearts Tie and Solo had dropped us to the trailhead from their hostel with full packs, full bellies and the warm glow of having been in a place that ran on love and kindness. Laughing Heart Hostel had soothed us all, especially me with my battered, agonising feet. Compensation, away from the pain of tendinitis, had allowed deep blisters to form across the sides and balls of my feet, and now socks pulled away thick layers of flesh with bright pink open wounds beneath. Walking was a punishment until the cold and painkillers disassociated me from my lower legs over the course of a morning's hobbling.

We nattered for a while and then Fitbit's longer legs took her off into the leaves and branches, pulling ahead until I couldn't see her. Drizzle came through, so my brolly went up, cleverly propped under my front strap and held firm against my chest. I figured I'd be an outlier with the umbrella, and I was, but instead of giggles the most common reaction was 'aw shucks' envy and asking where I'd got it from, as people straggled past soaked and miserable. Today though, there wasn't anyone around to comment one way or another, the pathways ghostly and still.

Every now and then I caught sight of Fitbit ahead, always stopping to photograph any set of steps with over four rises for her postgrad project, for which she'd received funding for the trail. She had stopped and photographed every set of stairs on the whole trail, counted the rises for each, and noted stone, wood, etc... and was *still* faster than me. Ha! Here towards the end of the journey I cared so much less about it – where I was, how far behind. My limits were my limits, and I was working with them to grow rather than railing against them and pushing. Plus, my foot was deeply painful, the cold making the bone-deep throbbing a near-constant now. So slower was OK. Except close to dark, of course. Still can't shake that primal fear – will I ever?

White blazes loomed on stakes across hilltops through the mist, feeling alien and other. But soon the path turned sharply downwards, moving from muddy slope to cut mud steps then wooden risers to concrete stairs and a metal railing. We were hitting a highway. It was always unsettling to descend and hit civilisation – that didn't change – but it was especially so when the high mountains were so wild and the street level so mundane. Highway signs, cars whizzing past giving eyebrow raises and uncertain glances. What were we to them in their warm cocoons heading from one indoors to the next? Perhaps vagrants, perhaps hippies. Once you venture more than a few miles from the trail in any direction, your cachet decreases and your move from 'Hiker, let's help them out' to 'Crazy person, stay away from them' is swift.

Over the next few days we kept our mileage as high as we could, with darkness descending early and dawn taking its time to come. It was early December and snow was coming. I could feel it, and the weather forecast told me so. The tickle of worry in my tummy that wouldn't fade was all about that weather and its trajectory towards our next target: the Smokies, our final fierce mountain range before the end. I had few days left and none to spare, and I couldn't afford a weather day. My trail buddy had more time, so she could wait out a storm, but she didn't really want to hike alone either – not now in the dead of winter when so few people were around and conditions were so much more dangerous. She was also a purist, so even if I wanted to jump a day to fill it in when I could come back in spring, she wouldn't. It was a tricky juggling act and it was clear I was going to have to sacrifice something somewhere if I wanted to finish this journey at the AT's finish point for Sobos – Springer – before Christmas.

Through Waynesville, through Cosby and at Green Corner Road near Hartford we crossed the road up into the Smokies, posting our permit notifications into the box near the parking lot. It had started to snow and the afternoon light was already dim. We debated – should we go up? It was still nearly 5 miles of elevation up to Cosby Knob shelter and the snow was coming down thickly now. Five miles, all up steps and slippery, narrow paths that gripped sheer walls and dropped into rhododendron-covered abysses. I was so happy to be doing this with Fitbit. We started out.

Hiker clothing is light and quick-dry. Hikers also don't carry more than they need to. Except me. I always carry more than I need to and *none* of it is useful beyond the one singular occasion when I might need that one specific thing. Which never happens. Even so, there weren't many layers to pull on to deal with this snow, and every layer that did get pulled on was soaked through either from the inside out from sweat, or the outside in from snow. My Altras, shoes that I loved fiercely despite their innate ability to fall apart, were mesh-topped and my feet were now snowy over the ankles. The heat of my toes melted any flakes that landed, and my ankles were treated to near-constant tiny avalanches into my socks. It wasn't fun.

Really, I knew that I was looking for any reason to stop, but there isn't any ad hoc stopping in the Smokies. The rules are strict and you have to sleep only in shelters. You can't even hammock or tent. Everyone in, together. I was imagining a claustrophobic space, filled with hikers even at this time of year, nowhere for them to disperse. I also contemplated yelling to Fitbit for us to put our tents up here, anywhere; no one would stop us, and hiking on in the snow as we increased our elevation in the growing darkness was not a solid plan. The words were in my mouth, but I couldn't say them because I knew I didn't have time to stop. Pressing onwards was the only option.

A side trail to the beautiful Mt Cammerer emerged ahead in pristine white blankets of soft drifts. Fitbit stood waiting.

'I really want to go see it. Will you come? Thought you might want to too. I don't know how clear it's gonna be, but... Come. It's worth it.' She smiled and gestured into a drift of snow. Fuck. I really wanted to. I'd seen photos of friends who'd been there for sunsets, and the sun was indeed setting now. But it was also dim, cold and my foot was brutalising me. On the other hand though, how could I let her go alone? It wouldn't be wise to split up at this time of the evening, no? Or was that my fear talking? I couldn't really tell anymore and had kind of given up trying to work it out.

'Mate, you go. But I'll get to the shelter now and get things set up for you. Gather some wood if I can find anything dry, and get a fire going. *Go*, enjoy. Take some photos for me.'

'Are you sure? I understand though. Your foot and all. Y'know.' I appreciated her giving me an out and not highlighting my slow pace, age and general knackeredness.

'Yep. All good. See you up there. Have fun!' I threw the words over my shoulder as I turned and headed up, up, up some more. Too cold for me. The kind of cold that your brain tells you suddenly you should be worried about. I think that's at least better than the kind that tells you it's all OK though, when you're too far gone and blue.

It wasn't a fun walk. I had my buff pulled up and over my mouth, meeting the top of my hood pulled low. My eyesight was obstructed in order to keep warm, but my knees and shins paid the price, scraping rock edges hidden in soft snowy disguises. The dusk was upon me and my heart rate rose in harmony with it. I started singing to myself out loud to ward off the fear and the tingly heat in my hands. Snow dropping off thick leaves to my left and right gave my heart extra beats and a fierce pump of adrenaline. Not long to the shelter. Not far to the shelter. Not far.

Slow. I was so much slower than usual. I stopped to fuss with my bag and yank out the head torch I knew I was going to need soon. So hard to understand exactly when was right. Too soon and you lost all vision apart from that directly in front, but too late and you risked a trip or a fall. I wrested the torch's thick band over my hat and tucked it down into my neck. Ready to switch it on. Ready for anything!

Not ready for a stream that had crept its watery fingers across the narrow ledge and frozen solid. My favoured foot skated out to the left. I was airborne. The Altras aren't as grippy as I'd like. I watched myself in the moment, slowed down and limbs moving in different directions, like a series of frames from *Inception*. I wondered idly whether I'd go over the edge, giving in to the fall. No. I didn't. One knee hard down on raised bobbles of black ice, one face scraped on tree roots that stretched from the wall and one leg immersed to the knee in mulch and freezing mud over the edge. Not bad – better than dead and enough to give me relief.

I stayed there for a moment to gather myself. Sometimes you need to do that, don't you – catch your breath, appreciate the moment? I rolled over and sat down, caring not a bit that my ass was now in snow and everything was wet. I was bathed in the heated flush of post-fear that warmed me.

Shocked, I moved to my usual comfort reflex – pulling my phone out of my pocket on automatic pilot. Did I have service? No. None. My wet glove idly poked the photo app and I looked at the last few photos I'd taken, scrolling back further and further to get away from this moment in the cold and dark. I looked at a picture of a warm wood burner and my cosy bed at Laughing Heart. Finally I felt the wet coldness on my butt cheeks and got up. Looking up from the phone screen, it was clear I'd idled away the last minutes of good light.

'Fuck. Fuckity fuck.' I was literally my own worst enemy. Don't like being last? OK, let's idle away precious minutes of hiking and break my consistency with phone scrolling. Need to catch up with people? Ohh, yes, let's chat to strangers on trail instead. Always standing squarely in my own way on the daily, and then wildly flailing for ways to improve my life and situation.

My brain: 'Erm, 'scuse me, ma'am – couldn't you just step to the side with your bad habits?'

Regardless, it was now dark and the fresh pain of my throbbing knee had recruited the bastard foot into a duet. I pulled up the head torch ready to valiantly make it to the shelter and make a damn fire for my friend, pressed the button, strapped it on tighter and looked up. Jesus, it was so dim. Like waggling a glow-worm's bum around. I used it to get over the slippery ice ribs, then stopped in the snowy swamp around the bend, under some branches to save fresh snowfall getting on to what I was about to do.

Pack swung heavily off my shoulder and on the ground, I ferreted around inside and then emerged triumphant with fresh batteries. *Yes*! Ha-haaa! It *was* worth me carrying all this crap. This was a moment of validation for the non-ultra-lite hiker. I had batteries on *lock*.

Then the multi-job tango began of holding my iPhone between my teeth for light, removing old batteries with one hand and having the new ones ready to go in. There was a moment between the two where dropping my phone would be super bad, as it was now dark-dark. My cold fingers worked, proud I wasn't too ham-fisted or accidentally flicking the fading batteries out into snow. Neatly I popped them inside the maw of my fanny pack and then flipped the new ones in, a little bit of dribble spooling down the side of my phone as I looked down to focus with the back of it between my teeth. *They were in*! Good job and thank *God* – the battery on my phone was a precious commodity. My Anker packs were amazing but weren't holding charge like they used to after 6 months of constant use, and we were now 3 days from the next supply spot in this weather.

Still using the phone, I packed all my shit away and slung my pack up on my back, feeling the cold wetness like a fresh winter's kiss. I put the head torch in place again. Phone off. Finger up to depress the button. *Press*. Ready for high-wattage joy and… nothing.

Nada.

Zero light.

Fucking HELL.

I gave it a little jiggle, then a shake. Maybe I put the batteries in the wrong way around? No. I double-checked for sure. But maybe I didn't? I was so tired lately. OK. Let's have a look. But now it was totally dark. OK. iPhone again.

I opened the head-torch case but everything looked fine. Perhaps these weren't good batteries anymore? Oh, for Christ's *sake*, I had carried SHIT DEAD BATTERIES all this way. I was indeed the lamest hiker in God's green land. Nothing for it but to swap the glow-worm batteries back in.

Down went the pack again, off with the outer gloves, off with the inner gloves, tucked under armpits and dropped on the snow. Into the fanny pack the new batteries went, trying to crane over my chest to see down into it in the dark with my phone. Digging for the old ones. Grabbed them! Well, them and all the other paraphernalia that comes tumbling out of a fanny pack in the dark when you're fishing around for small, heavy things that have fallen to the bottom. I was beginning to lose my rag but shoved the old batteries in. I used my phone light to scrape up all the detritus from the ground and then stood up to toggle the head-torch switch again.

Still nothing.

This couldn't be right. I poked it hard, thumbed it and then dropped it in fury. Threw my head back with my eyes closed, clenched my fists by my side and bellowed, 'FOOORRRRR FUCCCCKKK'SSS SAAAKEEEEEEEE,' around my little evergreen snow ledge and out into the ether.

Much later, in total darkness after half-feeling my way along the pathway and sporadically using my phone light, I arrived at the shelter – a stone building which was much like an old grain barn with one wall blown off and now covered by a loose flapping tarp with bottom edges tucked in by snow. I ducked in the gap, knowing from the darkness and silence that no kindly souls were here to greet me with a fire and a hearty hello. I had a job to do though, and I was going to bloody do it. The snow was relentless and Fitbit was coming. She had to be. Some damn good human had left a small pile of twigs inside away from the elements, with some larger logs stacked next to them. I started trying to light the fire and sat back to see if it sank or swam whilst imagining where she might be and how she might find the route now under snow, a good 2 hours later.

Happily, she arrived to the crackling orange glow of conviviality, the only light I really had. No warmth though, as the gap between tarp and wall sucked out any heat, but the colour of the flames helped us imagine warmth. The lookout was worth it – she showed me photos. We made our nests, put on all of our clothes after peeling off the wet, cold ones to freeze overnight (her) or to put in my sleeping bag with me so they were at least *warm* and damp in the morning. I'd also somewhere lost my spoon, so food was tricky. No head torch, no spoon, little warmth and very little phone battery, with four more days ahead in the snowstorm that was being forecast. It wasn't boding well, so I tucked myself deeply in my triple layers up on the top wooden platform and watched Fitbit climb into the hammock she'd slung between beams over my legs, and tried to dream of warmth, respite from pain and a clear pathway for the morrow.

We woke early and to pin-drop silence. Every head movement brought an unsealing of the nest-like warmth in my bag and started me a little more awake each time. A full look up and out was going be like dipping my head in a bucket of ice water, but I needed to know what it looked like through the gap to the outdoors. The cold shock opened my eyes wider, but I wasn't ready to speak yet, let alone yelp. I inched myself to the edge of the platform under Fitbit's hammock and looked down and out. Her eyes peeped over the lip of fabric. 'Can you see that down there? Look!'

She gestured to the floor. A tiny white creature darting back and forth on the ground, then jumping high and swooping back down, an arc of slick white liquid. It had heard me move above but wasn't too perturbed, watching me momentarily before waterfalling itself across the floor and out into the snow drift, which I now noticed was knee-height against the gap between tarp and wall.

'Weasel!' she said, and it was. Such a joy out here to not only see nature but to be as another animal rather than a spectator of it. The danger of being back in a food chain in our position, before guns and dominance, was far outweighed on this journey by the pleasure of being accepted by creatures and seen as just another beast.

Getting out of our sleeping bags hurt like hell.

'It's like being born every morning,' I wailed, doing the fast switch from peeling back the bag, taking sleep clothing off and exposing bare skin to the frigid air for as short a time as possible before the day layers went on. God help you if you had forgotten to put them in the bottom of your sleeping bag the night before, because you'd be unfolding frozen layers of fabric down on yourself and using precious body heat to thaw them before the clothes eventually capitulated and started to warm *you* up instead.

'What do you think?' Fitbit had come out behind me and was rounding the back wall again after a morning pee, our yellow patches melting pee tunnels to the earth like lightning strikes in a child's cartoon.

'I don't know. Can we get service?' We bounced around with phones aloft, sliding down snow into unseen gaps between unseen logs, our legs burning then numb through light leggings and shorts. I sent a weather request on my inReach® and that eventually pinged through at the same time Fitbit managed to get a ranger report. It didn't look good. Snow was set to start again in a few hours and lay down a few feet on top of the drifts we were already facing. On the top ridge lines where we were heading (and had many miles to cover), rangers were warning of blizzards and danger. *Don't venture out* was the plea. *Don't risk our lives and yours by getting stuck in the Smokies!* The starker message was that they might not even be able to come and provide rescue. 'What about the others? Spud, Bunkhouse? What will they do?'

She thought for a moment. 'Last I heard they were about one shelter ahead of us. I bet they've stayed hunkered down there. They're high up, they won't be able to move backwards or forwards. It'll be all day for them and another night in that shelter. I hope they have fuel, light and wood.'

'They will,' I said, nodding. 'They knew this might be coming in. It'll be too dangerous to try to get down to Gatlinburg today. But listen, I don't know if I can take a couple days sitting in shelters. My deadline's so tight, I don't have light, I don't have batteries, no spoon, phone dying. I think, I just think it might be best to go down.'

Fitbit looked so sad. She was keen to go on but it just wasn't an option, and staying for 24 hours in this frozen shelter, when there was a hostel 5 miles back the way we had come, seemed masochistic. It meant going *backwards* and no one wanted to hike back down the way they'd already come – especially considering what a massive uphill slog it had been to get here. But return we did, passing one lone hiker who said he was prepared for the worst and had heavy winter weather gear, appraising our light hiking clothes with some measure of shock.

It was a miserable and frozen duo who walked into the yard of a bizarre hostel, set miles from anywhere up a narrow road. Gunfire deafened our approach, and when we finally found a wild-looking man – after poking around the wooden outhouses for a moment, yelling that we'd arrived – he explained, mumbling, 'Goddamn fuckin' morons, tole 'em not to shoot the damn coyotes, but they won't listen to shit,' my eyes went wide as dinner plates. Seven months in this country and I still wasn't used to guns. I was now accustomed to passing hunters with them on trail, but hearing them being fired, especially in such close proximity, was a whole other thing.

Fitbit and I checked out the bunkhouse and saw evidence of another hiker we'd been being polite to but avoiding where we could. A nice enough guy but too eager to befriend and offer booze or weed, with little understanding of no or the need for personal space, and plenty to say about how much he liked us. He'd been making progress through the trail but had seemed to stall out over the last few hundred miles, limping from place to place and overstaying his welcome, offering to help out for his room and board, and drinking too much. We asked the wild-looking man, Jim, who was renting the bunk, just to be sure.

'Goddamn that guy. He's a nice enough asshole but we've been trying to get rid of him. He's been here *days*. He's so annoying.'

He looked quickly over to check we weren't friends about to defend the man. We weren't.

'How can someone be so annoying even when they're sober?' he wondered aloud, scratching his beard. 'Anyway, he'll be out back drinking whiskey and shooting them guns with the morons out there. Kinda think he's got a moonshine vibe about him…' And Jim trailed off as he walked ahead. Lost in thought.

'So where could we stay if not there?' I asked him.

'Oh we got a cabin free. Got a stream that goes under it. Kinda pretty. Cold though, but so is everything.'

We jumped at it and settled in for the night. Various bearded men in multi-layers and fur hats came to the door through the grey and snowy day, bringing plates of homemade turkey soup, freshly baked rolls and Pabst Blue Ribbons, setting them by the fire and sharing snippets of the action outside.

'They're looking for the dogs now!' exclaimed Feather on one visit. 'Shooting those damn coyotes meant the little dogs done run away. Small little things, they ran off together.' He looked sad. 'They only small.'

'Oh no!'

'Yup. They often run away, but now with this ice and snow they won't figure out how to get back. We're going out looking.' And he withdrew. Poking his head back in to say briefly, 'You girls want a beef burger? Can make you up a triple each? Just found some old meat in the freezer out back. Can put some special mustard on it?' We shook our heads and smiled nicely at him. No. Fucking. Way. And he was gone.

Later, as the dark crept in fully and we'd organised a ride, he returned with some more beers and propane for the fire. 'Dogs are probably dead,' he said, placing the tins on the wooden floor above the sound of the rushing river and turning, leaving without another word.

I dreamed of coyotes with new pack members, huddling together for warmth, and two small dogs who had just started the adventure of their lives.

*

We'd picked up a ride with Fitbit's friend Elk, who had just completed her flip-flop thru hike and was heading home, keen to deliver Trail Magic on her way back. She scooped us up the next day and drove us along the length of the impenetrable Smokies. We were sad, feeling the loss as the fast car made mockery of our efforts. In order to have a shot at making my flight, we needed to be taken as far as the Nantahala Outdoor Centre, a good few miles past the exit of the Smokies proper, and I knew without doubt that I'd be back to fill them in as soon as the winter snows thawed in a few months' time.

And so, rested, we began again. Over snowy hills and trails into Georgia, closing in on the final miles, feeling a sense of unreality. Me nursing the agony of my tendinitis and Fitbit, the purist, aghast at her mile-skipping.

GEORGIA

76.4 miles

CHAPTER TWENTY-FOUR

Where We Have Become One

Only 76 miles: a surreal concept. I didn't feel like I knew any other life now, and even though my month off trail recovering had taken me back into the bustle of real life, since my return I had felt I was back where I should be. Where it felt like coming home. The 3 days of slackpacking through the state that would take us to the top of Springer Mountain were a slow ascent from the depths. An inverted suffocation, as though it was only when I burst through the surface to the end of the trail that I would be unable to breathe anymore. I breathed with the trees now.

We had found a sweet couple that ran a B&B off trail and were happy to slackpack us. We were a week into December and too cold and exhausted to go fast or far with full packs. My foot pain had reached Virginian levels and I was contorting my body to move forwards with breathless gasps when my toes caught on rocks or twigs. My foot was strapped, with multi moleskins and bandages over the broken skin. I had lost both big toenails now, and so my poor feet pulsed with pain inside and out. Not far. We could make it.

Down past Chunky Gal Trail, through Blairsville and Neels Gap, where the shoes dangled in their hundreds from a large tree by the road. It was here that northbound hikers in the early stages of their thru had come far enough to know they needed to stop, and so they flung their shoes into the tree: a statement of defeat or, couched differently, a proud announcement of knowing one's limits. Either way, in the frosted fog of a rainy dawn in December, it was bleak to see.

But we smiled, Fitbit and I, because we were heading up Blood Mountain and we were close. Close to rest, to ending, to achieving what we'd set out to do. Only the stain of the Smokies sat upon us, but we weren't arrogant enough to fight nature, so it was OK.

Atop Blood Mountain we were socked in completely with thick fog, the rocks slick and slippery with frost and rain. And then, as night came early, it was time for our last sleep together, here under the trees. Anti-climatic, peaceful and not before time, we huddled our squeaking sleep pads next to each other and layered up for a final night against the elements. There wasn't much to say but there was lots to laugh about, and now in place of mile mapping and resupply planning we were just enjoying. Laughter pealing through the naked boughs all around our final shelter. We had done it, and our friendship, though shorter than others on trail, was deep and true. We'd seen the core of each other in recent weeks, stripped back to the bones by the elements and effort.

*

The next morning – the final morning – Fitbit pulled ahead as I struggled to tape and bandage my foot. Now so swollen as to not fit inside my shoe, it made me feel unwell to look at it. I didn't know it then, but my foot was never suffering just from tendinitis. It was broken. In two places, with one fracture displaced. This was not to be discovered until I returned home to our glorious

343

NHS and the X-rays that would show the damage, leaving the radiographer open-mouthed at what I'd managed to achieve with the injury. But here and now I was still working with what I'd been told was an irritation to the tendon, one that I felt my pain threshold and tenacity should be well able to cope with. And so, just like every day, I found a way to push past the limit of the obstacle and forge forwards.

Today my foot had become so distended that my laces needed to be left wide open – the elephantine-like flesh and bulbous ankle enough to hold the shoe in place. And so, nurse work done, I struck out for home. Each footstep a little death, yet also a little victory. A little voice: I will not be stopped.

And I didn't stop. Not until I was 3 miles from the summit – that incongruous summit of Springer; neither majestic nor awe-inspiring by sight, only by a sense of achievement wrought through arriving. I had been listening to podcasts and audiobooks through the freezing rain and mists of the last weeks, desperate to remove myself from the immediate reality of the heavy hours of movement. At this point, 3 miles out, I turned them off and stopped to take stock under the tip-tap of rain on my umbrella. What was I feeling? What had it all been for? It didn't feel like the final ticker-tape line-breaking achievement that I had imagined.

Originally about a *start* point and an *end* point, the messy middle was always going to be a morass of the unknown. Challenge, adversity and the potential catastrophe that the wild outdoors can bring. Joy, terror and learning. Relationships, disappointments and heartbreak. *That's* what it had all really been about; everything except the beginning and the end.

I wasn't ever alone in the unknown. The others on this trail had been learning too, from hikers to angels, rangers to trail towns. The path brings us together and pinballs us into each other on different trajectories of learning and fear and hope, but we're all on one path – The Dirt Ribbon. Barrelling around on this tiny, singular strip, trying to elevate ourselves beyond what we are told our life is *supposed* to be.

But I didn't feel a lot in this moment. Is that strange? My arrival at this place felt like an inevitability. Inevitable that with my grit and determined spirit I would have got here eventually, even if I had to drag myself a mile a day. So it wasn't a surprise to *arrive*, but it was a surprise to arrive so humbled. So opposite to the usual fist-pumping swagger of a challenge accomplished. I hadn't 'beaten my chronic conditions' to finish hiking the trail. I had instead walked with my many broken, damaged parts until each of the pieces of me had reconciled with the others. Until I accepted them all as being *me*.

I wasn't fixed, mended and repaired. I wasn't born-again freshly with no scars or gifted with a winner's medal. I was simply… forgiven. By the forests, the people, and by the trail that had absorbed my tears of joy and sorrow for over 2,000 miles. By myself. James had been right all those months ago on that busy London street. I was always walking home, but the place was inside me all along. I had walked an unimaginable distance to reach my own front door and see myself as if for the first time – with love.

And so now, regardless of endings or beginnings, I was arriving at this place with great reverence. Quietly whole. To sit at the foot of the great trail and give my thanks. The trail had never seemed more like wisdom made material – into earth and trees, birdsong and ermine, rushing rivers and cleansing rain. The trail had given me the gift of acceptance, and I had never been so grateful for anything in my life.

My final steps were slow and laboured, riven with steady determination. Up, up, up to the top, leaning heavily on my poles, but I made it – to the flat stone place where the plaques rested. Plaques set into ancient stones, the recipients of countless thousands of fingertips and prayers. This was it. The end. The beginning.

In the wind and freezing rain I peeled off my glove and stretched out my chilled hand to the sign. Flattening my palm on the bitterly cold letters, I closed my eyes, bowed my head and gave thanks.

The lesson had ended, and now the living would begin.

A LETTER FROM GAIL

I'm so grateful that you're here! I'm delighted that you chose to pick up my book and read it, and have now taken this monumental journey along with me.

If you have enjoyed the book, then it would mean the world to me if you were to leave a review to show others why they might like it too.

It has meant so much to me to tell my story and share my adventure with you, as well as bring you along for the adventures that are coming up. If you enjoyed it and want to discover more inspiring memoirs, just sign up at the following link. Your email address will never be shared, and you can unsubscribe at any time.

www.thread-books.com/sign-up

I wanted my book to be the story I was looking for when I was lost and needed hope, a tale of tenacity, of grit against the odds and of gambles that paid off. When I was unwell, I read voraciously, devouring tales that were *almost* right, but I couldn't find the one I needed. So when I couldn't find it, I went out to live it instead.

I wrote this book with you in mind, so I could feel as though I was beside you, urging you on and letting you know that whatever obstacle you face, you *can* do it. You who feel invisible, who suffer silently, with fear taking up space within your bodies, minds and spirit… This book is for you. It is for the people who are brave but who haven't quite realised it yet. For people who don't fit a traditional category, who are stuck in a rut, who feel misunderstood and have so much to give but don't quite know how to or when.

I wrote my story to be your fuel, or the match that sets your own fuel alight. And the fuel itself is hope. At the bottom of the darkest pit, in the deepest hole, it's the candle that will show you that what looks like a shadow is actually the doorway out. There is always a way out.

If you enjoyed this adventure then come and join me for more. I'm always hiking, exploring and living life to the full, hoping you'll do the same with me. You can find me at:

@thegailmuller

thegailmuller

www.gailmuller.com

And sign up to join me for adventures of your own at
www.unlostoutdoors.com

Then come and join my welcoming, inclusive outdoor
community 'Unlost outdoors'
www.facebook.com/groups/unlostoutdoors

ACKNOWLEDGEMENTS

My mama, Linda, for loving me unconditionally and supporting me in every dream I ever had. You inspired me from the very start with your expansive view of the world, your kindness, your compassion and your love of literature, Leonard Cohen and life. You held both my hand and my pain for me through the darkest times, and you will always be my rudder.

My dad, for loving me unconditionally and inspiring me to be honest, decent and brave, just like him. You showed me what hard work, generosity and courage are, Dad, and your love of the outdoors, the elements and the wonders of nature have translated into my own life and helped to heal me. Thank you for being such a good man.

My sister, Nicky, who is my best friend, coach, inspiration and rock. No one makes me laugh like you do and no one gets me more. Your bravery, patience and creativity have taught me so much and I am always thankful for how you show support and share your wisdom. Thanks for talking me off so many ledges and making me pee in my pants with laughter.

The whole of my extended family on both sides: the Mullers and the Cormacks. A family unit full of love, support and kindness.

Richard Carr-Hyde and Fabio Disconsi – the men who saved my life by working tirelessly on my body and mind in Northern Italy – for the treatment that put me on the road to wellness and gave me my body back. Thanks, guys, for your generosity, your time, your expertise and your friendship.

The many therapists, practitioners and specialists who kept my creaky bones going. They have been legion and I am grateful to you all. But special thanks go to Helen Jones, artist and chiropractor, for your gentle understanding and being patient with my grief and depression whilst helping to heal me, and to Lizzie Bird, osteopath and movement specialist, who taught me to see my body in a new and revolutionary way, taking my healing forwards in leaps and bounds.

Fitness Wild, an outdoors training company in Falmouth, who with humour and in all weathers helped me to build strength in my body whilst also having the great patience to do so when bits of me were too injured to use and I swore my head off at great volume.

Stu Slater at The Movement Project, who advised me on movement patterns and now trains me to be a better hiker so I can complete more long adventures with less physical pain.

My friends. My wonderful friends without whom I couldn't have survived this far. I am so lucky to have people in my life who have lifted me, listened to me and supported me to keep going. I am so grateful for your friendship.

Kinsey (Andrew Morris), a dear friend whom I lost a number of years ago, but who stays with me in my heart and comes on every adventure in spirit. He loved getting outdoors, and I felt his presence often on the AT.

My boyfriend Kris and his three wonderful children – Ruan, Ellery and Effie – who have been in my life throughout the writing of this book and who encouraged me, fed me and kept reassuring me I could do it, even when the last thing I felt I could do was write.

Everyone involved in making this book a reality. Particularly my wonderful agent Hannah Ferguson, who believed in my story and guided me with such masterful skill through the process of getting it to readers. Also my very talented editor Claire Bord, who understood me, my writing and the story I wanted to tell from the moment she cast eyes on it. If this book is good, it's because these brilliant women helped to coax it from me onto the page.

The Trail Angels, who are all up and down the great hiking trails, making the dreams of so many of us possible. Thank you for your tireless generosity, kindness, good nature and nurturing. These trails exist in the wonderful way they do because of you.

And Kate. For showing up for me when I was let down. For forging friendship with me after we'd been through so much. For jumping into the unknown on the trail and being far braver than me, more stoic than me, and for possessing a preternatural level of logic and accuracy that I still can't fathom. You're a real one with a big heart. Thanks for sticking with me through it all.